P9-DHA-467

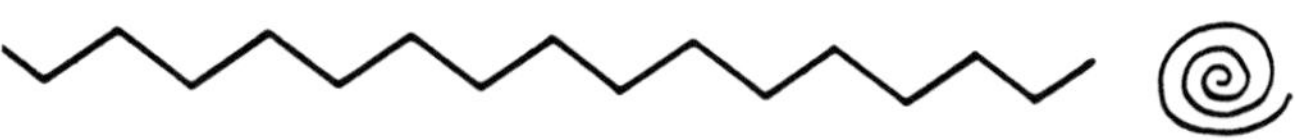

ALSO BY SPIKE LEE

Spike Lee's Gotta Have It: Inside Guerrilla Filmmaking

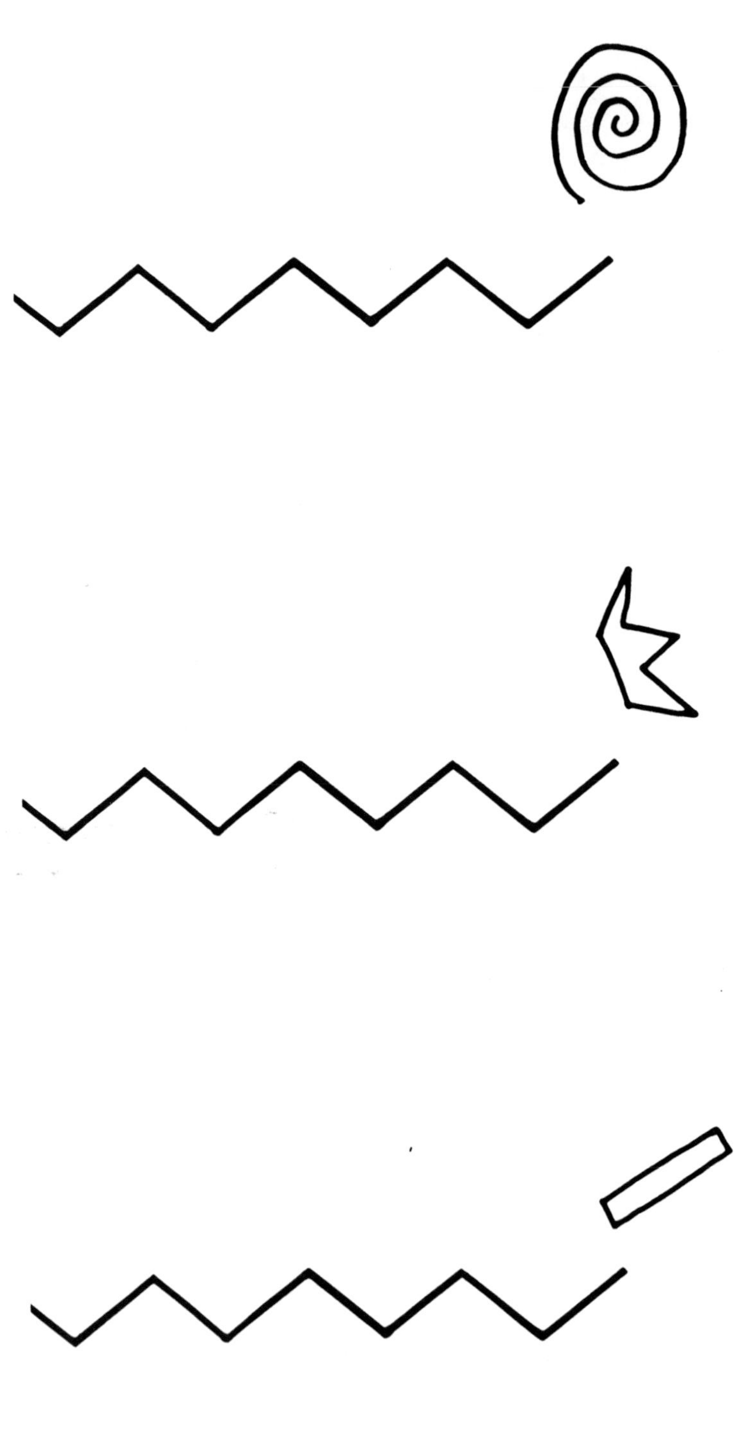

UPLIFT THE RACE

THE CONSTRUCTION OF SCHOOL DAZE

SPIKE LEE

WITH

LISA JONES

A FIRESIDE BOOK

PUBLISHED BY SIMON & SCHUSTER INC.

NEW YORK ▲ LONDON ▲ TORONTO ▲ SYDNEY ▲ TOKYO

A FIRESIDE BOOK
Published by Simon and Schuster Inc.
Simon & Schuster Building
Rockefeller Center
1230 Avenue of the Americas
New York, New York 10020

Designed by **SNAP•HAUS GRAPHICS**
Manufactured in the United States of America

10 9 8 7 6 5 4 3 2 1

Library of Congress Cataloging in Publication Data

Lee, Spike.
Uplift the race.

"A Fireside book."
1. School daze (Motion picture) 2. Afro-Americans in motion pictures. 3. Afro-Americans—Drama. I. Jones, Lisa. II. School daze (Motion picture) III. Title.
PN1997.S31353L4 1988 791.43′72 87-36599
ISBN 0-671-64418-1

DEDICATION

This book is in memory of

Anna Lois Russ Jones

Harold Vick

Dr. Wendel P. Whalum

Willi Smith

and

Kwame Olatunji

The Jesse Jackson speech.

ACKNOWLEDGMENTS, THANKS, AND BLESSINGS

The following list is just a small portion of the hundreds who have helped me along the path:

Malaika Adero, Tracey Willard, Cynthia Simmons, Grace Blake, Pamm Jackson, Loretha Jones, David Picker, David Puttnam, Dennis Greene, Katherine Moore and Columbia Pictures, Earl Smith, Branford Marsalis, Wynton Marsalis, Stevie Wonder, Raymond Jones, Marcus Miller, Aunt Consuela, Amy Olatunji, Toni Morrison, Ossie Davis, Ruby Dee, Larry Fishburne, Gerry Griffith and Manhattan Records, Barry Alexander Brown, Zimmie Shelton, Alberta G. Lee, the cast and crew of *School Daze,* Ernest Dickerson for the images, my father Bill Lee for the music, my brothers and sisters—Chris, David, Cinque, Arnold, and Joie, the entire Lee family, my main man, Monty Ross, and Lisa Jones for staying on my butt about this book when I was doing eight million other things.

CONTENTS

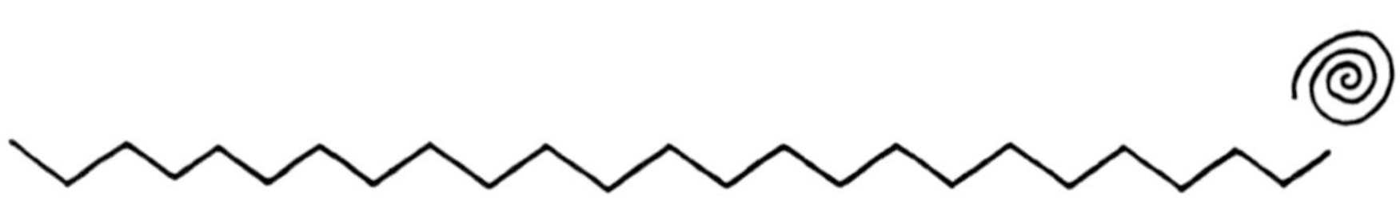

FOREWORD

OSSIE DAVIS

I was honored—even flattered a little—that Spike Lee should ask me to do a "cameo" in *School Daze*. I was most anxious to do it, but I know the business, and directors are not always able to keep the promises they make. I was performing in *I'm Not Rappaport* on Broadway and had only one day to give to Spike's production. A million things can go wrong—besides bad weather—in spite of the best of intentions. Things can happen that leave the schedule in a shambles, with nobody knowing exactly what the hell is going on. I had to be back in New York for Tuesday night's performance come hell or high water. So when Grace Blake—executive producer for the film, and friend—met me at the Atlanta airport and said all was going well with the shooting, I felt better.

I also felt proud. Hollywood and the rest of the industry were watching Spike. His first film, *She's Gotta Have It,* had caught fire at the box office and had taken the film industry by surprise. Spike, with no visible means of support, as Hollywood sees it, had done the impossible. The question now was: Had Spike's first film been a fluke? Was it a lucky break, a flash in the pan, pure dumb luck—that even happens to Black folk once in a while? Or was he really a filmmaker? Could this young writer-producer-director—some even

The day we shot the Wake Up scene. It was the last time we were all together. To be quite frank, I was happy a lot of the actors were going home. (I betcha they felt the same.) They had worn me out. If I had to, I was gonna pack their bags and drive them to the airport my goddamn self and I don't even drive. A lot of the people were working for the first time and still didn't appreciate what the film was about. A lot of them should have taken notes, kept quiet, and listened to the elders: Ossie Davis, Joe Seneca, Art Evans, and Ellen Holly. They have survived this cutthroat industry.

Ellen Holly and Joe Seneca. All the veteran actors—Holly, Seneca, Evans, and Ossie Davis—were advised by their agents against working on *School Daze* because of the small amount of money. Thank God they didn't listen. Maybe this one time they saw that it wasn't about the money.

whispered, genius—this young Black boy who came out of nowhere, borrowing money from his friends and relatives to make his film, put another winner in the can?

Spike himself is independent, both in thought and action. He doesn't give much of a damn for Hollywood's opinion of himself or of his works. But he is perfectly willing to use Hollywood money—why not? Spike is first and foremost a damn good businessman, tough as nails! But that's about as close as he will allow Hollywood to come. Leave me the check, go home, and wait till I send for you. That's Spike's attitude, reminding me of Malcolm X a little.

If Spike was indeed just a fluke, if he couldn't perform up to professional standards, if he wasted time and money, if he went down to Atlanta and fell on his ass, this would be held not only against him, but against the rest of us as well. That's what racism means. So when I heard Grace say, "Spike is ahead of schedule," I breathed a deep sigh of relief. Time is money in filmmaking, and if Spike had time under his control, that was half the battle.

Monday, I went to the location on the campus of Morehouse College to join the other actors, most of them young men dressed in football uniforms. The crew was integrated, there was no nonsense, and I felt a sense of discipline and purpose over all. Spike came to the truck where I was getting into costume and makeup to welcome me, then went back to the locker room to finish setting up the scene. He was all business—quiet and proficient. There was a minimum of hassle, and no confusion that I could discern. It was obvious to me that this director knew exactly what he was doing, and was doing it well. On the set, he thanked me again for doing the part, and introduced me to the rest of the cast and crew. Then he talked to me about Coach Odom, what he wanted from the scene, and how the scene fitted in with the rest of the story. He brought me back to camera, and after a rehearsal or two, we shot the scene. Then we did close-ups, reverse angles, cutaways, etc.—all the things that constitute the grammar of filmmaking. I was still aware—and thankful—that I was in the hands of a professional. He gave me few specifics in the way of directions, leaving Coach Odom's passionate plea to his team of inveterate losers up to me. But Coach Odom was no stranger. I played him out of my own Black college student background, out of my background as a practicing Baptist, and out of my own experience with *Purlie Victorious:* the open voice, the flashing eye, the rolling cadences, the fire and brimstone—anything to get my team heated up and ready for battle. I haven't seen any of this, and have no idea whether the scene is still in the film or was left behind on the cutting floor. One thing I do know: I had a ball.

That night, after some other shots at the stadium, I was taken to the airport in plenty of time to catch my plane. I reflected on my one-day experience with *School Daze* and Spike Lee. This is a crazy business. I don't know what the upshot will be. *School Daze* may be a hit or a flop, or just do so-so, at the box office. But I flew from Atlanta knowing deep in my heart that whatever the case, win, lose, or draw, this was a Spike Lee Production, and nobody else will have done exactly what *he* set out to do! And most important, he will have done it blackly. That was enough to make the whole trip south worthwhile . . . to remind me just a little—one more time—of Malcolm X.

September 1987

PREFACE

SPIKE LEE

Last night an earthquake rolled my butt out of bed, and now, as I write this, I'm "getting the hell out of Dodge" back to Brooklyn, New York, where I belong. I likes L.A. but . . .

This is *Uplift the Race: The Construction of* School Daze, and Lisa Jones and I have tried to make this book different from *Spike Lee's Gotta Have It,* which was strictly in my own voice. Getting *She's Gotta Have It* made was a one-man war—aside from the help of Monty Ross and Pamm Jackson.

School Daze, the film, is light-years away from *SGHI* in scope, size, everything. Consequently, we felt it was important to include the voices of others who worked on the film. We included some of the film artists—cinematographer Ernest Dickerson, production designer Wynn Thomas, and others—tell how they contributed to the making of *School Daze*. For better or for worse, *School Daze* is much more of a collaboration than *SGHI*. I've been fortunate enough to have the opportunity to make movies, but getting a chance isn't enough. It's beyond that. I have to produce. Being a Black filmmaker isn't a novelty anymore. It's about the work, 'cuz all that other shit won't matter. People aren't gonna shell out six bananas to see any Black film. The question is: IS THE WORK GOOD OR NOT? It's that simple.

Château Marmont
Hollywood, California
October 4, 1987

My role in film, for the most part, is as an instigator, starting up shit.

1

TO THE BRIDGE

ISLAND GIVES US THE BOOT

SPIKE ▸ I was in the bed fast asleep, jet-lagged, worn-out, beat, and tired. It was a Monday, January 19, right before midnight. I went to bed happy. Earlier that afternoon Louis Orr threw in a lucky shot at the buzzer as the New York Knicks beat the hated Boston Celtics. *School Daze* was in preproduction. Things were good. Then the phone awakened me from my peaceful slumber. On the other end of that late-night long-distance call was Laura Parker, VP at Island Pictures. What could she want at this hour? I thought. I had just returned from a week in L.A., with Robi Reed, casting for the film. "Spike, are you up?" I said, "I'm up." "Spike, they decided not to do the picture." They being the head honchos at Island, Chris Blackwell, Russell Schwartz, Mel Klein, and Jessie Beaton. I couldn't believe it. I'm awake, I thought, I'm not dreaming. This can't be happening. Laura explained that she tried to talk to the group but it didn't work. I thanked her, hung up the phone, turned over, and went to sleep, good night.

In the morning I called my attorney, Loretha Jones, who in turn hooked me up with her boss, Arthur Klein, who just happens to be

David Picker's lawyer of some years. Picker had just recently taken over head of production at Columbia Pictures and was in New York. Picker called and said he wanted to talk to me directly but he was leaving for L.A. later that day. I jumped onto the subway with script in hand to meet him. David is a fellow Knicks fan. He has season tickets and soon as I walked into his office he asked if I wanted any of his seats for upcoming games. I remember thinking, Damn, he knows my weaknesses, I gotta watch it. We had a polite twenty-minute conversation, I gave him the script, and he said he would read it on the plane and let me know something tomorrow. Twenty-four hours later *School Daze* was at Columbia—with a negative pickup deal—bye-bye Island Pictures.

Picker told me later that he knew that afternoon when I came by that he wanted the film. As soon as he got back to L.A., he walked into David Puttnam's office (then he was the big cheese at Columbia) and said, "I read Spike's movie. It's available. If we don't move fast, it's gone. Nobody else had a chance." Actually, we could have done the film at Touchstone (Disney) too. Jeffrey Katzenberg at Disney and I still talk. But instinct told me Columbia was the right move. I had an internship at its Burbank studio the summer between Morehouse and NYU. Also, the past October I had had a nice meeting with Puttnam. We didn't discuss the possibility of Columbia's involvement in *School Daze* then; we did talk about the possibility of us doing something together in the future. But I had a premonition.

My relationship with Island Pictures had been rocky for at least two months before its decision to pull out of *School Daze.* Island executives had expressed reservations about the content of the film, about the production team, and about my ability to handle the project; but when all was said and done, it was da money, moolah, cash dollar bills they didn't have. Island's financial straits made it impossible for the honchos to exceed the $4 million ceiling they put on the film. When it became apparent that *School Daze* couldn't be made for the amount they gave us, Russell Schwartz suggested scaling everything down, even cutting musical numbers, and I wasn't having it. Given how well *SGHI* did for Island, it was a slap in the face that the president of the company, Russell Schwartz, didn't even have the heart to tell me himself. Why put Laura Parker up to do the dirty work? Often people ask me why it happened the way it did with Island. What has to be understood, first and foremost, when one is an athlete or entertainer, the team owners, the record companies, the movie studios, are not in love with you. Don't ever believe it, no matter what they tell you. They're in love with the money you are making for them. That's it. That's it only! The minute you stop producing, stop selling records, stop selling movie tickets you'll be singing "Where Did Our Love Go?" when you shoulda been singing "For the Love of Money" instead.

The transition to Columbia was smooth; we pushed back the start date only one week. I flew out to L.A. to meet everyone at Columbia, then went with Branford Marsalis to see the Giants win the Super Bowl. We were with a big studio, in the big leagues, and we were fired up.

JESSE JACKSON'S BLESSING TO *SCHOOL DAYS* CAST AND CREW

In some sense our challenge is to make a difference beyond opportunity. We fought—from the back of the bus, for access to public accommodations, for the right to vote, for open housing. Basically, to open up the doors of opportunity. Many of you have seen, if not most of you, the film clips of Dr. King giving his speech in Washington in 1963. Please read the speech, don't just watch the clips. Because the clips always omit the pointed climax of "I Have a Dream." The substance of the speech is not about dreaming. It's about coming to get your share at the bank of justice. . . .

One of the striking challenges that your age has to face is the fact that freedom without equality is not enough. Freedom didn't cost very much. Equality does. Because in freedom, you simply have the option to push from out to in and from in to out. But with equality, it's about moving up. It's about equity and parity, as opposed to welfare and charity. It's fundamentally different. It's about moving up. It's about parity. About reciprocity as opposed to generosity. It's a fundamental shift in relationships. You are of the equality generation. You are of the equity generation. At least you have the opportunity to be about that. . . .

When team X and team Y hit the basketball court, five players each and one basketball, they have equal opportunity. But that's not even exciting anymore. Opportunity is not worth paying for.

People will not come to see your opportunity to do a film, because it's not really exciting. Well, it was at one time, but it isn't anymore. We've kinda gotten used to that. What they will pay for is to see the team who's going to win. So beyond opportunity is the whole question of effort and character and results.

When the score is zero–zero, you have equal opportunity. But at the end of the game, a red light goes off in one of the dressing rooms and that's the one that seized opportunity. And with a combination of effort, and character, and discipline achieved the victory. So the fact that *School Daze* is opening production, that's a small item of news. Perhaps it means something to your relatives. They're the only people interested in it other than you. But if at the end of eight weeks, through your effort, and your character, and your motivation, you have achieved success, it is because you have kept your eyes on the prize. Then, the whole world wants to celebrate. Let me say this, I am sure it will happen. I am overwhelmed by this opportunity and with Spike's ingenuity, his professional integrity, and his youth. Because he represents a live alternative to misopportunity. . . .

It's just a tremendous statement if you just make sure that Dr. King and Medgar Evers did not die in vain. And every time an opportunity is missed, it's like they died for naught. So I kinda beg you, implore, appeal to you, to do your best against the odds. And then be strong on the inside. Because sometimes you think you should have had it, and you didn't get it. But your strength is not measured by how fast you run, but how fast you get up when you've been knocked down. Because when it's all said and done, it's not the talented that survive. There's so much talent in this nation. If you think you can sing, go to the next church. There ain't no shortage of talent, but there becomes a shortage of character. Those who hold out, sustain themselves, will be seen through. . . .

So, opportunity is not enough. We have to go from the opportunity to do a movie, to doing it, and doing it well. And doing it so well, not only so our mothers and fathers feel good—because they saw their sons and daughters—but so our enemies can say, it's the best they ever saw.

Jesse Jackson
March 8, 1987

ERNEST DICKERSON (DIRECTOR OF PHOTOGRAPHY) ▸ I've always thought that a Black college homecoming would make a lively cinematic experience. It's an idea that Spike has had on the back burner for a long time. Just to cover the energy that surrounds a homecoming, and the music. What I remember most about the homecomings from my undergraduate days at Howard University was the fabulous music.

To create *School Daze,* Spike went back to *Homecoming,* a script he wrote shortly after film school. I am glad he wove a political context into the revised script. In *Homecoming,* the basic conflict is whether Mission, a small Black college, will be absorbed into a large, predominantly white state university system. In *School Daze,* the conflict centers on how Mission College's investments in South Africa divide the student body. The South Africa angle definitely made *School Daze* more contemporary.

In the summer of '86 we began talking about how to approach *School Daze.* We both agreed about the energy we had to bring to the screen. We wanted to keep the camera moving. The camera was going to whiz all over the place. We felt that this was a way of really capturing the energy. I don't think we did it as much as we wanted to because of time constraints, but that was the initial goal—lots of camera angles and movement.

We also knew that *School Daze* would have a huge Black cast, more Black people than have been seen on screen in a long time. We were determined to make a film which would allow Black folks to see themselves up on the screen and really feel proud; proud about who they are and how they look. And since the film is about beauty—how there are different types of beauty, not just the Western standard—we knew that we had to make all the Black folks in the film look good.

The debate over Black beauty that you see in the film is a political statement unto itself. The Wannabees have straightened hair and they wear blue contact lenses. They are pursuing a Eurocentric form of beauty to the point that they deny all that is Afrocentric. Even though both forms of beauty are valid, the film says don't turn your back on what's really you. You notice that the Gamma Rays (the ultimate Wannabees) look slightly ridiculous with their blue contact lenses and exaggerated hair styles. They're beautiful women, but there's something about them that's just not right.

Even more than their eye color, it has to do with their values and aspirations.

ROBI REED (CASTING DIRECTOR) ▸ Spike and I started throwing around casting ideas as early as July 1986. All summer we talked through the different roles: the president, the coach, and the various cast groups—the Fellas, the Gammas, the Gammites, the Gamma Rays, and the Jigs.

The week before Christmas I released the breakdown of available roles to agents in L.A. I spent the first two weeks of January prescreening people in L.A. Spike came out the week after. We spent that week holding callbacks and dance auditions. During the first two weeks of auditions, I averaged about sixty people a day. I met people on Saturdays. I saw just about everyone. If I didn't see them, then they were working or out of town. There aren't too many people who can say they didn't get to audition for *School Daze,* either for me or for Spike.

I lost all my privacy during our audition process. I had people wait for me outside the office, and come to my house unannounced to drop off eight-by-ten photos. Since a project like this has never been done before—a film with so many roles for young Black actors—everyone felt as if it was his or her chance. And although we had a large cast to fill, we saw more talented people than we had roles for.

Darryl Bell ("Big Brother X-Ray Vision") gave the best audition out of the hundreds we saw. And he never had any acting experience; it was all natural ability. Darryl did a monologue he wrote himself about a guy getting dressed to go out. He stripped down to red Calvin Klein underwear (he tried to wear the same in the finale, but we wouldn't let him) and got dressed again. All the while he talked about this woman he was on his way to see, how she has bad breath, how he wants to kiss her but isn't sure how to tell her her breath is bad. Darryl had a tape recorder with him. At the end of his monologue, the tape recorder piped in, "Hey, man, you forgot your bag." Darryl did this double take, like Wait a minute. Who was I talking to?

Spike was very excited about our decision to cast Tisha Campbell as our female lead, "Jane." I had never heard of Tisha before her picture made its way to my office. In fact, I didn't see Tisha's film

Dialogue from a scene that was cut:

BIG BROTHER DR. FEELGOOD

You know what, you're a tall motherfucker.

SLIM DADDY

I'm a tall motherfucker.

BIG BROTHER DR. FEELGOOD

You're a big motherfucker.

SLIM DADDY

I'm a big motherfucker.

BIG BROTHER DR. FEELGOOD AND
BIG BROTHER LANCE

And you're a Black motherfucker.

SLIM DADDY

I'm a tall, big, Black motherfucker.

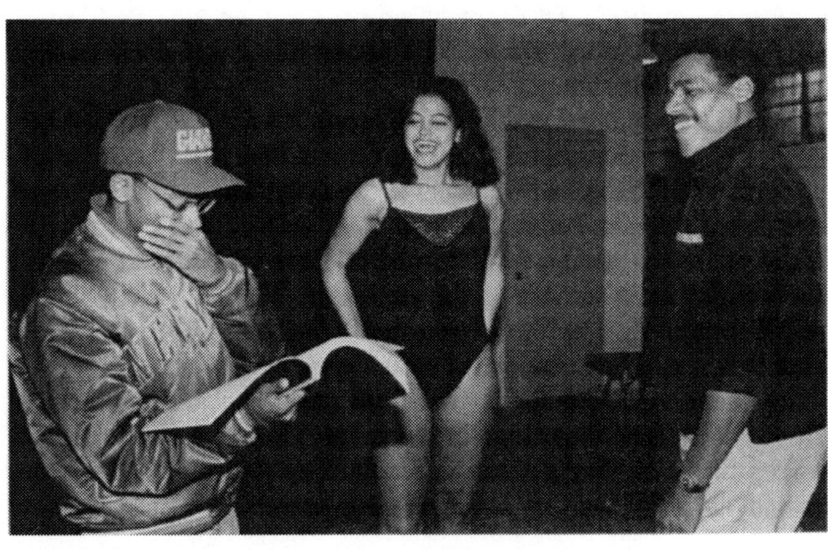

Once I arrived in Atlanta, Robi Reed and I immediately put the word out that we were looking for the biggest, tallest girl on campus. Everybody said, "You mean Kelly Woolfolk." She heard it on the grapevine and appeared, all 6'2½" of her. We were lucky. She was "Vicky." "Just as I pictured it, skyscrapers and everythang."

debut, *Little Shop of Horrors,* until after Tisha's dance audition for *School Daze.*

When Tisha came in for a first audition, her acting was fine, but I don't remember anything remarkable. Then she sang "God Bless the Child" and blew me through the window. I called Spike immediately after she left. I told him how excited I was about this girl named Tisha Campbell and that I couldn't wait for him to meet her. Vanessa Williams was still a possibility for "Jane" at the time. Even if Spike still wanted Vanessa as "Jane," I was sure that I could sell him on Tisha in the role of "Dina," the Number Two Gamma Ray.

Spike came to L.A. shortly after Tisha's first audition, met her, and was just as excited as I was about her talent. When she left the office, Spike was shaking his fist up in the air and running around as he does when something's just right. Tisha became a possible "Jane," but Vanessa Williams was still in the running in Spike's mind. I was convinced that Tisha was the right choice. I was hoping that Tisha's dancing was as good as her singing and acting. It wasn't until after Tisha's dance audition that we definitely decided to go with Tisha as "Jane."

Tisha thought that she had blown her first audition. When she got the callback to audition for Spike, she was surprised. When we called Tisha back a third time for a dance audition she freaked out and insisted she wasn't a dancer. The day of her dance audition my sister was helping my assistant in the office because we had so much to do. Tisha called to cancel and it was my sister who convinced her to go to the audition. Of course, Tisha did a great job. It's hard to tell she isn't a trained dancer. She moves like Janet Jackson and has the fire in her eyes.

Tisha is such a sweet and humble person. It's a cliché, but put her in front of the camera and she comes alive. She transforms into a "performer." If Tisha had not come to the dance audition, she would have blown the role. I'm sure, though, that we wouldn't have let her off the hook that easily. As it turned out, she was a great "Jane." She brought an innocence to the character. When "Julian" (Giancarlo Esposito) dumps "Jane" you really feel sorry for her. I don't think this would have happened with Vanessa Williams.

The dance auditions for *School Daze* were brutal. Many people disappointed us at that stage in the game. They told us they could dance and when they got to the studio they flaked out. But then again, Otis Sallid is a very tough choreographer to audition for. You could cut the tension with a knife at the New York auditions. They were definitely more competitive than the L.A. auditions. All the trained dancers are in New York City.

I was pleased overall with the cast we decided on. Retrospectively, there are always things that you wish you had done differently. It's bound to happen when you hire people who have not worked on film before. You go on your instincts, their résumé, their audition, and what you get from them personally during the ten minutes you meet with them. There are a couple, in my opinion, who just didn't come through as much as we counted on. There were roles that I would have cast differently. Not many, just a couple, and I think that's pretty good out of sixty-five.

Many of the actors who auditioned well for *School Daze* but didn't get parts have their agents to blame. Agents undermined their chances by asking for ludicrous amounts of money. We didn't spend time bargaining with these folks. There were so many other actors who were just as capable. Agents are there to help actors, but sometimes they end up crippling them.

The perfect example of how an agent can backfire is the case of ensemble Jig Eartha Robinson. We originally cast Eartha as "Tasha," the darkest Gamma Ray. Eartha was signed with a TV show called *Dancing with the Hits* for a five-year period. She had five more months to complete on this contract when she was cast for *School Daze*. Eartha's agent wanted the School Daze Picture Company to buy her out of her contract. The amount in question was $5,000. We went back and forth, and finally the agent told us that unless we bought Eartha out of the contract she wasn't going to do *School Daze*.

We moved on immediately. We had to. Casting the picture was our first priority. We went with Tyra Ferrell, our second choice for "Tasha." Well, Eartha called me a day or so after her agent's ultimatum to say that she had the money to buy out her contract, and by the next day she would know if the TV people would let her out of it. Eartha really wanted the role and she had planned all the time to buy herself out of the contract. By this time it was too late. We had already promised the role to Tyra. Shortly afterward, Eartha's agent called me up in tears; she felt horrible. But there was nothing I could do. If only more agents had a better sense of when to be an agent and when not to be one.

Another classic actor-agent problem we had involved actress

Erica Gimpel. We cast Erica as one of the Gamma Rays. When we called to let her know, Erica responded that since she wasn't cast in a leading role she wasn't sure whether she wanted to do the film at all. She hemmed and hawed a little too long. While Erica was debating, her agent continued to ask us for more money. We made it clear from the start, both to Erica and her agent, that this was a scale film, and everyone, with few exceptions, was getting paid the same.

Eventually Spike began to have doubts about Erica's commitment. He told her it wasn't going to work out. So we cast Cheryl Burr (the dancer in *She's Gotta Have It*) in Erica's place. It's interesting how that particular role was turned around again. Cheryl broke a bone in her foot the second day of rehearsals and couldn't perform the role. And Frances Morgan, the assistant choreographer, replaced Cheryl.

In contrast to the actors who made unreasonable requests for money, there were the veteran actors—Ossie Davis, Joe Seneca, Ellen Holly, and Art Evans—who saw the project as more than a paycheck and went out of their way to support Spike. Joe was always willing to play the role of President McPherson for the amount of money we could afford to pay him, though his agent did try to get a hundred times more money for him. She took it down to the last possible day, the day he was to travel to Atlanta. Joe's agent seemed more than willing to blow the deal for him. He wouldn't have starved, but we would have been up the creek with no paddle.

Joe called us the day before he was scheduled to fly (we were into our second week of shooting at the time) to assure Spike he had no plans to jerk him, that he would be on that plane come hell or high water. His belief in Spike and the project was the important thing. Joe made that clear time and time again.

The film was important to most who worked on it because, to us, it represented a world that we too want to bring to the screen. Spike is doing what so many people have dreams of doing. He's taking that chance. And he believes in himself and in other people enough to make it happen. Everybody wants to be a part of something positive. We see Spike as someone engaged in uplifting the race, you could say. I got calls from folks in all professions who wanted to fly in, pay their own way, just so they could be anywhere near the shoot and be a part of it. Just to say they were on the set of *School Daze*.

MONTY ROSS (CO-PRODUCER) ▸ Winter 1986. Spike's attorney, Loretha Jones, was handling the negotiations with Island. Nothing official concerning the production of *School Daze* had happened between Island Pictures and Forty Acres and a Mule. Everyone was still basking in the glory of *She's Gotta Have It.* Spike was saying in interviews that *School Daze* would be shot in early '87 with Island funding to the tune of $3 million. It was true, but it wasn't a deal carved in stone. It was incumbent upon both parties to get some type of agreement signed to confirm that the project was indeed going to take place.

On December 2, Spike, Loretha, and I met with Russell Schwartz and Laura Parker. Chris Blackwell, the president of Island, was supposed to show but he didn't make it. Everything was in a state of flux with Island Pictures. We opened the meeting with a discussion of *She's Gotta Have It* to break the ice. Then we got down to the issues at hand, the script of *School Daze* and Island's investment.

The Island people had concerns about the script which ranged from political—they felt the issue of divestment in South Africa would "date" the film—to the treatment of women—they felt the scene where "Big Brother Almighty" dumps "Jane" was too "harsh" and needed to be reworked. Spike got upset and told them that he had never written by committee and he wasn't going to start now. The atmosphere became very tense. Laura Parker suggested that we table questions about the script for the time being and talk about the budget. Russell Schwartz said we needed to talk more about the script because ultimately it's the script that determines the budget.

Eventually we moved on to the budget. Without beating around the bush Russell Schwartz told us that Island Pictures didn't have the money to finance the film. He said it would take some time for them to commit themselves and raise the kind of money we were requesting. Our preproduction start date, January 5—thirty-five days away—would have to be pushed back. And furthermore, Schwartz said, if the project was going to happen at all, we should consider remaining at the $3 million mark. We didn't reach any sort of agreement at that meeting.

The next morning at work I gave Spike my thoughts on the subject. I felt that Island had no right to tell him the project should be pushed back. I told Spike that his next meeting with Island should be a man-to-man with Russell Schwartz. He should remind Schwartz that *She's Gotta Have It* made money for Island and there was no reason on earth why we should not be in preproduction on January 5.

I reminded Spike that the ball was in Island's court now. We had started our work already: the script was ready, budget reports were complete, actors were lined up, and the press was fired up. There was too much going on for the operation to come to a stop. Spike Lee should not develop a reputation for beginning projects and then not be able to produce them because of money. We did that with an earlier film called *Messenger*. There is no way we would let that happen with *School Daze*. Too much was at stake.

After my speech Spike called Russell and they had a sit-down. Island sent us a letter shortly thereafter committing to a $3.4 million budget, subject to a few stipulations. My position as coproducer was in jeopardy. They felt that I should have an executive producer over my shoulder. And they wanted to oversee the hiring of a production manager and some other key positions. We agreed. Preproduction would start on schedule. Paperwork was exchanged. The money was to be wired in increments on an as-needed basis, and every week we had to send Island a budget report. Even after we signed the agreement with Island, though, they continued to harass Spike into trimming the budget down to $3 million. Before I left for Atlanta, Spike and I were at his house every night trying to tailor the budget to fit Island Pictures' pocketbook. The more we tried, the more I'd shake my head. It just wasn't going to work. Our first advance of $50,000 didn't clear right away, so Spike had to initially put his own money up.

I flew down to Atlanta on January 3, 1987, to set up our production office. The second week of preproduction Spike called me late one night to say be strong and that Island Pictures wasn't going to do the film. We had already begun to audition people. Our production office was working around the clock. We had hotels set up, vendors contacted. Cast and crew in New York and L.A. were packing their bags to head for Atlanta. The phone was ringing off the hook. The publicity was out. It would have been helpful if Island had told us earlier that even a $3 million budget was over its head. We could have gone with another company earlier and saved ourselves the bother of dead-end negotiations with Island.

Nothing was jeopardized by the break with Island. In fact, only a few people knew about it before it was announced that we had signed with Columbia—the lawyers, the director of photography, production designer, the office staffs in Brooklyn and Atlanta, and a few people close to Spike. About ten people at most. But everybody who knew was upset and shocked. The next day, David Picker saved the show.

Signing on with Columbia was very simple. Other than moving production back one week, nothing was altered by the new arrangement. David Picker and David Puttnam gave us a warm welcome. They had been out on the frontline themselves producing films. They sympathized with filmmakers and didn't have suit-and-tie attitudes. It is still surprising to me that Columbia's involvement during production was so minimal. David Picker came down once during the shoot (he was in town visiting another Columbia production) and took a quick look at our operation. I made sure the grass was cut and the office was neat. I think the Columbia people were impressed because we had everything under one roof: a rehearsal space, wardrobe, and our office.

Overall we really felt good about the Columbia deal. Here we were, an independent film company, working with one of the major studios so quickly. There was a mutual respect between us. We respected the people who were assigned to the film at Columbia. And they respected us as a company that would challenge Hollywood and would continue to be successful despite the odds.

DOWN FROM WAY BACK

MONTY ROSS ▸ Spike always put me in a leadership position on the projects we worked on in college. I guess he liked my way of working with people. I have a loud voice. As soft-spoken as Spike is, he often used my vocal cords to his advantage.

When Spike took off to NYU film school it was a sentimental event for me. We had grown close that senior year. The day Spike left, his grandmother fixed breakfast for us. His father had driven down to pick him up, and after breakfast we loaded up his stuff into Mr. Lee's car. We didn't know what the future held. But all that we talked about, in terms of making films, we pledged to make happen. During Spike's first year at NYU, I worked in Atlanta theaters doing any jobs I could find. I had gotten married while I was still in college, so I was supporting a family as well. And we all know how hard it is to be in the arts and support a family.

Spike shot a 16-mm short called *The Answer* his first year in school and brought it down to Atlanta the following summer. The film really blew me away. Even though it was a student work, it had a certain quality that hit you on the head. I remember jumping up, feeling elated, yelling out loud, "This brother's bad!" Compared to other Black films I had seen, this work was in its own category. This is what I'd been waiting a long time for. And I'm not saying this because I'm the guy's friend. The quality was just there.

Spike brought his second film down the following summer. It was a syrupy piece called *Sarah*. It was a nice family drama that he did for his grandmother. Even so, you could see that he was capturing a slice of Black life that wasn't a stereotype or a coon show. Spike also brought down the script for his thesis film. I read it and was so excited I asked him if I could act in it.

In October of 1981, I went up to New York to do what I had to do, leaving my wife and kid at home. I went to stay with Spike in his uncle's basement. I didn't have a cent. I was a struggling writer/poet/actor at the time. I sold my poetry books and just about everything else to the crew, which consisted of Ernest Dickerson primarily. I couldn't wait for lunchtime on the set because it was literally my only meal. Sometimes we would stop at night and get a bean pie or a cheesesteak hero. I'd get a beer and Spike would have his quart of Tropicana orange juice. That was our dinner and we'd go straight to bed.

We'd wake up each day at dawn, lug all the film equipment out of the basement, load up the van, and shoot our scenes for the day. Spike was supposed to have other film students out there helping him, but I can remember only two folks showing up. They'd stay ten minutes or so and cut out. Ernest would say, "Hey, Monty, could you hold this light? Could you move that prop?" It was all part of my job as driver, set PA, and lead actor.

Joe's was shot in one month. The only time we could use the barbershop we shot in was on Sundays. Our van broke down three times. On the last day of the shoot, we were on our way to the location and as we pulled up to a red light, Spike said, "What's that sound?" We looked down and a tire was flat. I had just fixed one of the tires that morning and now I had to do it again. We had to stop and fix the tire. It was only by sheer luck that we were able to. Spike spotted a friend of his across the street. The guy had been out partying all night, but we recruited him to help us fix the flat. We got to the set just in the nick of time.

Spike was so tired when he finished shooting, he went straight to bed. I was headed back to Atlanta that night. He was supposed to go with me to the train station, but he was dead to the world. I left a note on Spike's table saying that everything would be all right. God would take care of it. The next thing I heard was that the film had won the best student film of the year award from the Academy of Motion Picture Arts and Sciences.

I did a drastic thing that year. I joined the Army Reserves (because of the pressures of being married, to be very truthful about it). I didn't want to work a nine-to-five job. I just wanted to get away. I was in the Army for almost two years. Spike wrote me the entire time, cursing me out, asking me what the hell was wrong with me. Having a family had not been the easiest thing for me. You want to do well by your home, but you can't deny the need to be an artist.

When I came back from the Reserves, I met Spike at his grandmother's house in Atlanta. He cussed me out royally. Then he told me about his next project, *Messenger*. I gave my wife my last check from the Army, loaded up, hopped on the plane, and came up to New York to shoot another film with Spike. I had no money again. It was just me and Spike trying to make this film. It turned out to be a traumatic experience. We were in preproduction for eight weeks. The money was delayed. We had to push our start date back a number of times. People on the crew began to doubt Spike. He had been a filmmaker with a chance. Now they were looking at him like, Who does he think he is? Spike isn't exactly an extrovert to begin with, but he was even more quiet during this period.

I was second assistant director on the project. It marked the transition for me from actor to businessman. I never had told Spike this, but it was a tough transition. I had always wanted to act, but I was needed more in the other area. I didn't like the way people involved with *Messenger* were coming down on Spike. I told him that he didn't have to take their disrespect. That was all Spike needed to fuel his fire and go on to his next project. He knew he had a solid backing with me around. So that's how I became production supervisor on *She's Gotta Have It*.

After *Messenger* flopped, I put down two bottles of Jack Daniels and went back to Atlanta. My bags were waiting outside my house and my wife was telling me that I was no longer welcome unless I intended to provide more income. I was a substitute teacher during the day and delivered *The Wall Street Journal* at night—anything to avoid a nine-to-five gig. The experiences I had with Spike in New York City had led me to believe that our time was on the way. All we had to do was put out the right project and the only way to do it was, again, by ourselves.

Spike sent me the script of *She's Gotta Have It* around December of 1984. I read it front to back in one sitting. It was a great story. I kept thinking, The sex, how the hell is he going to shoot that? But that turned out to be the least of our worries.

Spike called me in June and said to pack for New York. My ex looked at me and said, "You're going to do this film, aren't you?" I quit my jobs, all three of them, and Spike came down to Atlanta with money to fix the brakes on my Toyota. I did my paper route that morning, Spike came over, and we hit the road. Spike stayed up the entire drive with me, feeding me his grandmother's chicken and blueberry muffins. We stopped once in D.C. to pick up Pamm Jackson.

The morning we got in we went to the New York State Council on the Arts to get Spike's grant check. His old friend Earl Smith came over the next day with his entire life savings of $5,000. We set up preproduction in Spike's tiny apartment. It was just a closet really. We kept the film under Spike's bed and all the paperwork on the kitchen table. That was the production office. I did the budget and Spike did the shooting schedule. We did everything.

One night I was over on Myrtle Avenue in Brooklyn and I found a cot in the street. I brought it to Spike's, threw on a sheet, blanket, and pillow, and that was my bed until we finished the shooting. I was sandwiched between Spike's bed and all his stereo gear. Spike would say, "Monty, hit the radio." I'd turn the radio off. Click. "Hit the video, Monty." Click. And day in and day out, we'd work on the film.

We finished the twelve-day shoot on schedule. Spike was able to raise more money to meet postproduction costs. He turned the film over to John Pierson, our producer rep, who suggested that Spike take it to the San Francisco Film Festival in March. Three distributors saw it there. Island signed a deal with Spike; *She's Gotta Have*

It went to the 1986 Cannes Film Festival and won the Prix de Jeunesse. The rest is history.

I was in Atlanta when *She's Gotta Have It* went to Cannes. I had made a five-year commitment, or so I thought, to settle down and to be more of a family man. That summer, I was fabricating leg braces for the handicapped. It was dirty work—you breathe all these toxins and they pay you slave wages. But I never gave up hoping that when the film took off I could work with Spike and Forty Acres and a Mule and collect a paycheck!

Two weeks after *She's Gotta Have It* opened in New York (August 1986), I came under contract with Spike as Forty Acres' vice president of production. I didn't move to Brooklyn right away. Spike was coming down to Atlanta in November for Morehouse's homecoming with some people who were going to be involved in the next production. He wanted to shoot a little footage at the homecoming football game. So I stayed in Atlanta and worked on all those plans.

My wife and I had reached the point of no return. Shortly after the homecoming trip, I left Atlanta, moved to New York, and got a divorce. Spike brings it up a lot. I think he feels that I chose work over family. Perhaps I did. As Black people we just don't get the opportunities that our counterparts do, especially in film. So if we have a shot, we'd better jump on it. That's why I was so gung ho, so dead set about sticking with Spike. Not because I wanted to be famous or any of that shit. It was just a great opportunity to make a difference. Challenge the big system and kick it in the butt. It was going to be hard. It wasn't supposed to be easy. And nobody was going to give us anything. But we were going to do it.

Spike got pissed at me once, right around the time *She's Gotta Have It* opened in Los Angeles and we were gearing up for *School Daze*. I said something to the effect of maybe I should go to graduate school and get a degree. I had said to him, "I'm not sure if I'm up to working as a producer on this new project." Spike said, "Goddamn it, Monty. You can't be insecure about what you do. You do a good job. It's good enough for me and look where it's got me."

2

BY ANY MEANS NECESSARY

MATIA KARRELL (PRODUCTION MANAGER) ▸ In the fall of 1986, Island Pictures called me in to do two weeks of pickups for a film called *Street Wise* that was coming into L.A. from Paris. I was coming in as an assistant director, but they needed a production manager so I did both the jobs. Basically I was communicating with these people in Paris through a fax machine, trying to find locations in L.A. that they wanted, without a director or a producer around to advise me. But they were really happy with my work. Russell Schwartz brought me in to talk about Spike's next picture. They were a bit concerned about how this director, who had just finished a small project, was gonna deal with a much larger project: a big crew, a bonds company, SAG rules, and all this stuff. Basically they wanted to know how someone like that was to be "handled," to put it delicately. They were afraid. They weren't sure what this Spike Lee entity was. You hear horror stories about first-time directors who on the second project like lose it. They have no control over the project. I have worked with a number of first-time directors on non-union pictures and the issue usually is how do you support them and inform them of things at the same time. Because they don't know. They don't know the structure. They don't know how it works. They don't know that you only get a half hour for lunch break, and everything else.

I had this sort of conversation with Laura Parker (VP of production, Island Pictures) and Russell Schwartz. Laura liked something I had said about filmmaking. With my background—working on smaller films—you can tell when people believe in the process and what it's all about. When they know that it takes a group of people together to make something work. But the Hollywood system doesn't allow for this. Hollywood projects are here to make money only. They don't come from anybody's gut, soul, or heart. So Laura set up an interview with Spike and me.

I hadn't seen *She's Gotta Have It.* I was out of town on John Sayles' film *Matewan.* So before the interview I went to see it. I didn't know who or what to expect from Spike after seeing the film. He showed up for our meeting just like off the movie screen, with hi-top sneakers and a hat. It was a very strange kind of interview. Basically he sat there with his head in his hands looking up at me through his glasses. And I thought, This man doesn't want to see me. Island was bringing me in as a production manager. But it seemed to me that this tension was manufactured, a technique to divide us, me and Spike. It looked as if I was Island's person as opposed to being a part of Spike's film, and I didn't want that to happen. I had to recognize the fact that he saw me as someone Island was bringing to introduce him to. My first impression was that this guy was looking at me and thinking, Here's this white woman, what do I want this woman for?

I don't know why Spike even hired me. I guess it was partly my work on the John Sayles film. Spike has a lot of respect for John Sayles and his work, and I think that helped me get the job.

I was supposed to hear from Laura Parker later about the meeting, but she didn't call. I called her and she said Island turned the picture down. What I had heard was that Island got themselves into a financial problem and wanted to limit the money for *School Daze.* Spike was right in what he thought this film was gonna cost. It was a big film, big cast, big production. I figured that after my interview with Spike I didn't have a job. No one had called me. Were you going to call me and let me know, Laura? She didn't understand that I'm free-lance. I'm not like her; she has a job to go to every day.

I thought I had lost the picture, and then a couple of days later Spike called and said, "Matia." I said, "Yeah?" And he said, "Matia," and I said, "Yeah?" and he said, "Matia," and I said, "Oh, is this you?" I was surprised to hear from him and we met again for another interview.

At our first meeting, Spike had given me the script to read. At the second meeting, he asked me how I felt about it. I was real impressed. As someone who works in film, in Hollywood, in Los Angeles, you notice the lack of anything that's worthwhile as far as the films that are made. A little less so now maybe because of *Platoon* and *River's Edge,* and what Island and Alive have done with distributing small films. But most films that come out of L.A. are bunk.

I thought the script of *School Daze* was very rich in ideas, experiences, and circumstances. It dealt with people; it dealt with stuff I had never been aware of. I mean, certainly I was never aware of the conflicts between light-skinned and dark-skinned Blacks. Reading the script was like stepping into a culture that you realize has been around you but you've never ever known it. Also it was not totally specific to the culture of Black people. It commented in a wider sense. Spike was questioning, for instance, relationships between males and females, and that was intriguing to me. It was the sort of script and an experience outside of myself that I found valuable, and I thought nothing like this has ever been done on such a scale. It's gonna be worthwhile and certainly important. Needless to say, I was excited about the project.

We began principal photography March 9 and we started rehearsals two weeks before that. We had our Greek Show contest on February 27 . . . to audition the fraternities and sororities. We didn't have much time for preproduction. Basically, five weeks, and we had a lot to do. It was rough coming into, but it always is when you're from out of state. It is difficult trying to set it up, a production company in a city you don't know. A week before we started shooting we didn't have any of the locations for the first week. We didn't have Kentucky Fried Chicken, at that point, or the president's home. Grace and I come from a formalized, structured way of filming. Spike's and Monty's experiences were less formal. And we had to make both jell. That was probably the hardest thing. When you get used to doing something a certain way, it's hard to go back to something less formal. It takes a while to relax with that.

. . . The outstanding costs required in making a film call for you to be specific and exacting with your plan. You have to commit to being that way. You can't just say, "Well, let's do something else," just to throw it out; as well. I mean, sometimes you can make it work.

I think sometimes I go to extremes in my work style. I know Spike said this. And I know I had to deal with people thinking I was too nervous or too hyper about things. You shouldn't go overboard in it, but there's a sense of urgency you have to feel to get things done at the exact moment; so that they will happen.

Sometimes experienced people resent having to pull the slack for the inexperienced. But that's what filmmaking is about. Certainly, though, it can be learned by doing. I didn't go to film school. I acquired all my electrical experience by working for no money. But those with experience have to understand that their resentment, or their attitude in general, can affect the rest of the crew. Sometimes it depends on how much money people are getting paid on a film. If they receive the full rates, for instance, they might be more willing to accept having to train people. If they are not getting paid what they're worth and are still being asked to do more, it tends to cause resentment and hostility. You have to respect each other.

Inexperience creates a situation where a crew takes two and a half hours over its meal break. With a union project everyone would automatically get paid for the time and nobody would worry about it. But on a nonunion shoot, it's another story. In that situation two and a half hours is unheard of.

I had to come to the *School Daze* set and deal with a crew that wouldn't go back to work after lunch until the meal-penalty business was settled.

Spike said he would honor a crew meal penalty, but nobody told me, no one came to the office and said, "Okay Matia, you have to be aware that Spike agreed to this," and so you have to pay them. Now if I don't get to know about it, then I don't follow through on it, and the accountant doesn't know. The system of communication started to break down, and that can cost you a lot of money. I believe that in film you can bring people who you want to work with, and be with, and train. We were very lucky in the people we brought in. The reason Spike could have a first AD who was less experienced was that he was willing to work hard himself to get the day done.

Now for another director, who couldn't keep up with the pace, it would have posed a problem.

Our costume people had never done a feature film. But the women who were working under them had, and were paid a lot less, and that kind of situation creates conflict. So what I hear from these two assistants is how much they had to support the production designer, the costume designer and her assistant. There's no way for them to understand it. It's okay for me to be a production manager and take up slack for people under me. That's a key position; I should be doing that. But it's not okay for an assistant to be supporting someone in a key position.

A lot of people had been quoted salaries even before the final budget was finished. The list of PAs we chose from came from Spike. We had to deal with a lot of people who were supposedly told that they were on the film but were indeed not. Then there were the people who were willing to work as locals at first, but when we talked to them later said, "No, no, no. Where's my money? Where's my per diem?" Everybody knew Spike, so they would run back to him and say, "Spike said this." I think Spike develops very personal relationships with the people he works with. I know he felt bad that he had to hire another assistant director. But ultimately, it's only the picture that's worth worrying about, the end product. So when we got there, Grace and I had to go to the people who had been made promises and say, "We can't pay you that 'cause the budget is this" and "Everybody is getting this, and can you accept that?"

I talked with Spike during preproduction about what happens when you hire people whom you trust, but didn't have the right experience. I don't remember how I said it. But I was warning him that it might cost him. Another concern I had was how all these people, with no experience, were going to learn if they have only one person to learn from. If everybody is brand-new, who's learning from whom? And Spike said to me, "Matia, they told me I couldn't direct a film. They told me that I didn't have enough experience, that I didn't know. I showed them." And I said, "Spike, you did it but you did it on a $175,000 film. Your first film wasn't $6,000,000." It's a very different thing. I said, "I will do my best to work with these people if you will be open to the fact that if they don't work out, if it starts hurting the film, we have leave to fire them." He agreed to that.

What I appreciated most about Spike was that he didn't let his inexperience as a director work against him. He was always willing to respect my opinion and the opinions of his keys. I think it was a really good and rare quality. Spike had never shot on a soundstage, but had to make a decision about one. We had two different choices. We went over what both had to offer. Ultimately, when making this kind of decision there are always unknown factors like not knowing how bad the noise is going to be at certain times of the day. So as we reviewed the considerations, it was nice for Spike to turn and say, "What do you think?" Spike worked within the schedule throughout the film. When he wanted more days to shoot a certain thing, he was willing to hear another opinion. And sometimes directors are not. You can take an additional day to shoot something here, but you'll lose something there. He was very willing to do that. You have to do the work within a finite number of days.

A six-day week is a standard location schedule. You have to pay SAG actors for Saturday and Sunday. So why not work them on Saturday? Who wants to have two days off anyway? On location, you want to get the film done and get out of there. You can save a week if you add up all the Saturdays. When I first met Spike, he said, "We're gonna shoot for five days a week." Now you have to understand that that's unheard of. Later, when I had my second interview with him, he said, "Well, we're shooting six days a week." And a big smile went across my face that said, I know you know what I mean. So he said something like, "You knew that, didn't you?"

With the dressing rooms. We should have really had dressing rooms in the back, set up with fabric or plastic or something, to save money. Otherwise we would have been renting motor homes and that would have been expensive. Plus, we had no place to park them, anyway. But what we thought before was that we would get places in the school. That's what we were depending on. That we would get additional buildings and rooms, and that we would be able to sort of filter them out in other buildings. And, of course, we lost all the campuses, so that just sort of shot that idea.

We had to cheat a lot on the accommodations for actors. But it was hard. There were thirty-four to fifty-six actors. 'Cause even if we were at AU we couldn't go to Clark or Morehouse. But then we came up with the idea of like just changing them all in the warehouse. On the John Sayles film we had big days, a lot of extras. We would just take them directly to where they would change, and then just bring them to the set. And that would help us. But then we still should have really provided some type of dressing rooms.

The difference was that the actors never complained about anything. James Earl Jones had this little room with a chair, you know, and a little light. This man just like took care of himself, you know. But some of the kids on *School Daze* were getting their first big break and wanted more to work with. You work with someone like James Earl Jones and these other people on the Sayles film—and we had no stand-ins. We didn't have stand-ins here either. But no one ever, ever complained about anything on the Sayles film. I mean, once in a while they said, "If you don't really need us can we step out of the light." And that's all they were concerned about.

There seemed to be a lot of competition between the actors on *School Daze*. I mean, there always is with actors. These actors had less history, though. I mean, this film means more to them than maybe James Earl doing John Sayles' film. For a lot of them it's their first time or their second time doing a film. I think it made them a little more nervous. I felt as if they were out for themselves, you know. I know that there were divisions within the film, you know—the Wannabees and the Jigaboos. And I know that even in the case of John Sayles' film, you had the bad guys and the good guys.

But again I think if they were more experienced they could rise above it. They could leave that on the set or wherever they had to leave it. Then come back to regroup again. And I felt that that didn't really happen.

GRACE BLAKE (EXECUTIVE PRODUCER) ▸ By the time I got to Atlanta, Monty and Tracey Willard (production secretary) were already operating out of the production office. Before I arrived and before things were finalized with Island, Tracey called me to ask what she should buy for the office. I said, "I have no idea. I'm not on this picture yet." I hadn't even read the script. I said, "If I were you, I would buy two of everything: pencils, pens, and paper, because you don't know where it's going and why put out a whole bunch of money for something that may not happen. Buy enough to cruise along until something concrete happens. If the film doesn't happen, it's going to come out of Forty Acres and a Mule."

Matia Karrell was coming in as a production manager, so I called her before I left. She said that she was in as much of a fog as I was. So I got down to Atlanta and tried to understand what Monty was doing. We did not have an auditor. So I tried to take over and to structure what he had so that when the auditor came in at least I could give him as much as I knew. I had never worked as an auditor, but I had worked closely with auditors on productions. So I knew what he would be expecting. I tried to get Monty to do petty-cash slips and so on and so forth and just the whole situation was a mess.

The money that was being used at first was some money that Spike had put up and apparently some money that they had gotten from Island. I kept telling Monty that regardless of who put it up, they have to get it back and we still have to account for it. The budget was in a mess and I was working twenty-four hours a day. Matia and I used to work until three o'clock in the morning. We had the budget redone. And I wasn't sure even then what my function was. I didn't feel that I could come in and say, "Well, I am the producer and I demand this and I demand that." I came in there with the intention, or the idea, that we've got to get this thing together and we've got to get it together right, because, ultimately, if it's not right, the powers that be are going to say, "See, we gave some Black people money to do a picture and they couldn't do it."

That's what was on my mind. I read the budget that was made up for Island Pictures, and to me it was a disaster. So I did ask Spike to let us have the budget remade. This way we would know what we were working with, not some budget created by somebody Island Pictures had hired from California. So a lot of time was spent getting this budget together and trying to find an auditor. It took me a long time to find the right auditor. I felt it was important to have somebody from the New York area.

This production needed somebody who knew what he was doing, whom I could depend on, and who was calm. And I think Graig Hutchinson was just such a fantastic find.

I was real excited that I was going to be working on a movie with Spike, Wynn, Ernest, and all. I would be at production meetings where for the first time in my life the people making the decisions would be Black. That was the most exciting part for me about coming aboard *School Daze*. At one point at an early production meeting, I looked up and it dawned on me, Wow, all of us are Black and there's one white. And I said, "Matia, paint your face!"

Many times I did things on this project that producers don't usually do. But it didn't matter. What did matter was getting the picture done and done on schedule and done so that the money people would at least see that we *can* do it. I feel that some people who were on the production still need a lot of training, and I think it was unfair to a lot of people to be hired in positions that they had absolutely no experience in. You cannot hire a weak first assistant director. You cannot hire a weak locations person. That locations person is going into somebody's place, to somebody's house, bringing in a whole crew. He has to know how to talk to people. He has to know how to pull back and when. He also has to know when to go for the blast.

ROBI REED ▸ Casting *School Daze* was more than just a job to me. It was a part of me and it was my biggest project to date. I wanted to stay until the end. Normally casting directors don't stay till the end. We cast the actors and we're gone. When my deal was made, I opted to stay on and do the extra casting.

I ended up doing things that weren't part of my contract. But whatever it took to get things done and in on time, I did.

I had never done extra casting before. I didn't think there would be a problem at first because of our access to the Atlanta University Center. I felt that even if we weren't paying extras, the enthusiasm would continue. And it probably would have if we hadn't run into the problems with the school administrations. We had to continue to be as creative as we could to capture the students' interests, which kind of wore thin after a while. If we had money, we would have been guaranteed extras and we wouldn't have had to run into some of the dry spots we had. I called potential extras daily. Because of all the changes in the shooting schedule, we never knew when we'd need people. I would try to get them to confirm for as many days as possible even though we never knew until the day of.

We started casting extras a couple of weeks before the shoot began. I kept a card file of all the people I had met when we were in Atlanta auditioning. I kept all those names, addresses, and phone numbers on file. I referred to that a lot. While I was still in New York, Hillary, my assistant, who lives in Atlanta, had started work on the extras then. She circulated information around the colleges, and let folks know when we were set to begin and when our first big day was: the football game.

Clark is Hillary's alma mater. So she knew many people at the Atlanta University Center already, which saved us a lot of time.

The football game turned out to be great. We didn't get the thousands Spike requested, but the feeling was right. The people who did show gave us their undivided attention and support. There were some who kept coming back to work as extras. They were real special to me. I called them my personal extras and they were there whenever we needed them. Graves and Thurman Hall are two dorms at Morehouse and the students there were really supportive.

They spread the word about the shoot around the campus. They let folks know that it wasn't just a movie we were making, but history, even if they had to stand outside till three o'clock in the morning in the rain for no money.

My most memorable experience with extra casting was the day when hardly any extras showed up. We were at the Fox Theater shooting the coronation. It was the worst day of my life, and I cried my eyes out. I did. Nobody knew it then. Our location was moved too far away from the school. Even with the free transportation to the theater and everything, we got maybe twenty folks max and we wanted two hundred. There were things going on on campus that day that I was not aware of. Mainly, the *Cosby Show,* which was paying its extras $50 a day. They took most of my people, even the most devoted. I will never forget that. We ended up putting crew people in the shot (which we did often). We had enough to get by. But during the time when no one was there, and not one extra in that huge auditorium, I was in pain. In my opinion, the only proof that I'm doing my job is when people show up. So when they didn't, it seemed as if I wasn't. But I was; it was just that no one wants to work for free. I didn't know what to do. I wanted to go jump off a cliff somewhere.

We wanted two hundred people ideally, two hundred, and we may have had forty—half of whom were crew.

Shooting the fraternity's Death March was a rough period for all of us. We worked well into the nights. There were two extras who had eight-o'clock classes and they stayed. It wasn't too tough getting people to watch the Gammite pledge line go over, but it was hard just getting them to stay around, trying to explain to them that once they're established in the scene they can't leave. The scene wouldn't make sense anymore if they did. That was a little difficult.

Looking back, among the things that I would do differently would be to insist on a budget for extras and I'd let them know at all times what's going on so that they feel a part of the film. They can't just feel like atmosphere. You have to explain to them what scene is taking place, or that it may be an hour before we need them again, because we're setting up our next shot.

The script was written so loosely it was a perfect vehicle for an actor, you know. It was up to the individual to create his or her own character. And I don't think enough of them took advantage of that. They just went with what was written. If you compare those performances to a performance like that of Leonard Thomas, who played "Big Brother General George Patton," you see how he just became this person that people who see this movie are going to remember.

Pete, the generator operator, at first glance was this redneck southern kind of man. When we were going through the SAG problems with the actors, he said to Ernest, "I don't believe that these people are acting like that. Don't they understand that we're trying to make history here?" You know, he was really upset. For a man who comes from somewhere totally different from us to understand what we were doing meant a lot. It's a sad comparison to make with the attitude some of the actors had. It's disappointing to think that the Black actors may not have grasped the importance of the project.

It was very sad to see the production come to an end, but it was a great feeling too. Even though we had so many hurdles, so many obstacles put in our way—I sound like the script now, like "Yoda"—we still got the movie made. We did, and that last night on the set, the last shot, I just looked around at different people, and as I looked at each person I thought about the experiences I had had with each one, and I looked at Spike. I thought of all the phone conversations Ruthe Carter—costume designer—and I had, waiting to begin preproduction. "Have you talked to him yet?" "No." "What did he say to you?" You know, the things that showed how really anxious we were to get on with it. And here we are now and it's over. There was no way I could have not been there for the whole shoot. I had to.

RUTHE CARTER (COSTUME DESIGNER) AND PATRICE JOHNSON (ASSISTANT COSTUMER) ▸

RUTHE ▸ Spike used to say that I eat all the time, which was not true. I mean, I tried to monitor my eating. Yes, I was going through trauma.

PATRICE ▸ He said he couldn't afford to have you in Atlanta because you ate all the time.

RUTHE ▸ He told Patrice we had to get more food for me.

PATRICE ▸ . . . You had a Twinkie in your mouth, that was the deal.

RUTHE ▸ Exactly. So I just want to set the record straight that I was not a glutton. I ate the same amount as a normal person. It was just that every time he saw me, I had food in my mouth.

PATRICE ▸ It wasn't your fault that you had Dunkin' Donuts every morning. . . .

RUTHE ▸ Towards the end, I think it was the last week, it was like the day before the last day of shooting with Kyme and Larry's love scene, I packed some things to send home and Kyme's sweater got packed.

PATRICE ▸ We got to the set to see how everything was going and as usual at five o'clock everything was going just fine. Come five-oh-five Ruthe gets this hysterical look in her eyes. She said, "The sweater, we need it tomorrow." It didn't click at first. Then I said, "Oh, my God, this is it. This is it, it's over"—because it's in a box, it's at airfreight, or it's in L.A., in which case Ruthe had to go to L.A. That was it—no other way—no one could know. No one could know.

RUTHE ▸ We were selling everything. Everybody was buying stuff and we had our list. You know, we were organized. It wasn't like we were just selling things at random, but the sweater was a big controversy from the beginning—whether we were gonna use it or not for that scene. But we were, because they walk from one scene to another and she has that on. So it was written down, it was just one of those wild things. So I got on the phone and called the air-freight people to try and get this sweater back. Well, when I first called he said, "Oh, yeah, I think the boxes are still here. Let me look in the back and I'll call you."

Yeah, that was before they knew that it was like flying out of Atlanta to L.A. He called me back and he said, "I'm sorry." I said, "Well you have to get that sweater. I mean it's really a life-and-death matter. I mean, it's my life here." All I could picture was Jennifer, my wardrobe person, flying off the handle—which she always did—and Spike coming up to me and saying, "Well, what

Of all the forty-nine shooting days none was as disorganized as the homecoming parade. I always try to be as organized as possible, so this scene was frustrating as shit. The car that pulled one of the floats couldn't be moved because the production assistant left the set with the keys. Actors were waiting at the production office to be transported. I jumped in a van, raced over there, and cursed up a blue streak.

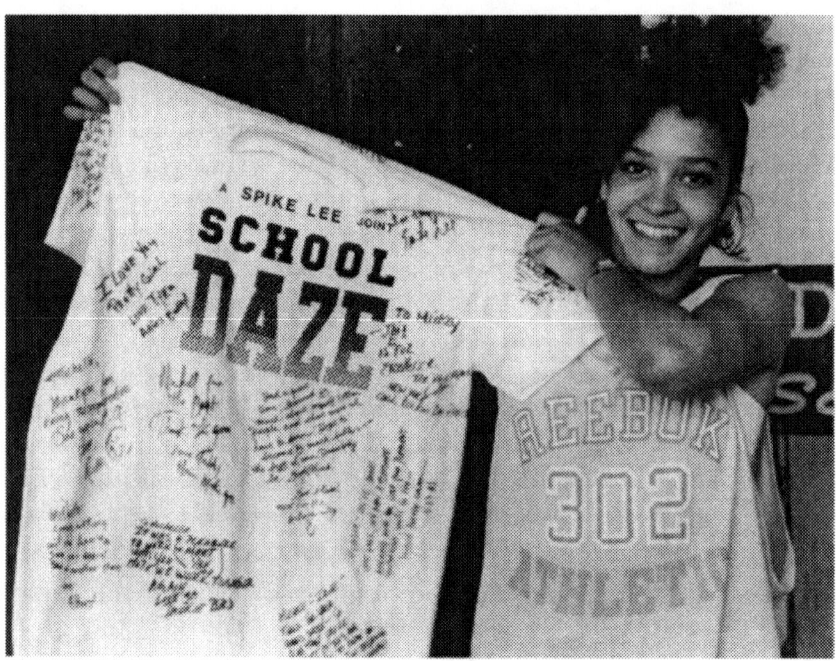

Michelle Whitney Morrison holds up one of the many different *School Daze* T-shirts. Films are only an excuse for me to design T-shirts.

happened?" and me having to tell the truth and fess up that I packed the sweater.

PATRICE ▸ It was a bloody mistake, but we couldn't let anybody in the wardrobe department know . . . because we had the Panic Patrol, that was Jennifer. And for the Panic Patrol, no matter what happened, if it rained that day, they would say, "Oh, no, and now it's raining."

RUTHE ▸ They would panic about everything. So anyway, he called me back, and he said there was no way, you know, that I can have it. So after I said it's a life-and-death matter, he told me that he would call his supervisor and find out if he could get it off the belt or something like that.

PATRICE ▸ But it was a very rare chance—this had never happened before. . . .

RUTHE ▸ Right, it was just like all arrows pointing to me—"You fucked up. You know it. Deal with it. Think of what you're gonna do now." I mean, it was like one of those items that's hard to replace —it's not like we bought it out of a store. We had it made.

So anyway, he said, "Okay, my supervisor has authorized me to take this off the belt, but you have to have the person with you who signed the check. I mean, signed the freight slip." Since Robi and I were sending things together, she had signed it. So it was a good thing that she was with Patrice and Jeffrey Cooper (a PA), who was driving. The airfreight man said, "You gotta get here by nine," and they weren't back yet—and it was eight o'clock, well, maybe a quarter to eight. So I met them coming in the driveway, jumping up and down . . . with my hands in the air . . .

PATRICE ▸ . . . saying, "You have to go to airfreight, you have to go to airfreight," and Jeff said, "Okay, I can take you. Where is it?"

RUTHE ▸ I swear, we were in the south of Atlanta, this place was way out. I mean hills, valleys, the whole bit. And here we were driving frantically, like ninety miles an hour. It started to rain and thunder and it was dark. So we were like going someplace for the first time and started to get lost. We were stopping at places, running into stores—the only place that was open was this Asian gift store. The lady in there gave me perfect directions, but we still couldn't find the place.

PATRICE ▸ We got really lost.

RUTHE ▸ So then it's about a quarter to nine, and I said, "We've got to call the freight company. They'll think we don't need it anymore —they're going home at nine."
PATRICE ▸ Suicide.
RUTHE ▸ So we stop at this pay phone and it's hard to hear and there are like Mack trucks going by, a million of them, and you can't hear and the guy says that he will meet us at the convenience store that we were at and drive us back. Anyway, so he drives us over there, the box was there, and we go through it, and I had other little things that I had, you know, packed and stuff, like little T-shirts and stuff, and I was just giving the whole staff gifts and . . .
PATRICE ▸ She said, "I'll give you anything, I'll give you anything— if you can just get this sweater. We're doing a movie; we've got all kinds of stuff I can give you—here's pajamas. You want pajamas?" It was so funny.
RUTHE ▸ So it worked out, but, uhm, by the skin of our teeth. It was like the most . . . harried moment of the whole shoot.

LARRY BANKS (GAFFER) ▸ The second day of shooting we did some car shots, and it took a little time for production and the ADs (assistant directors) to understand how long it was going to take to rig the car. Todd McNichol, the key grip, had said, "We're going to do this car and it's going to take us three or four hours to rig this car." And nobody could understand quite why it was going to take that long to hook the picture car up to a camera car and drag it along. But as we started to work they saw what was required—taking things off the car, and putting mounting brackets on rigging lights for the car, and rigging camera plates for the car, and all of that has to be done very tight and safely so that nothing falls off and nothing drops. We got out there before dawn and we got it all done by ten or so. We were getting ready to roll cameras in the camera car. Now it was obvious that Spike was used to doing independent productions, where you don't rely so much on your first AD, because I'd never seen a director do so much talking on the set. Roll sound, roll camera, move the thing, and action with the actors are usually called by the first AD. The AD gets sound rolling, gets the camera rolling, gets the camera car moving, checks with the director to see if he's ready, so the director only has to say "Action." I'm sitting on the camera car, and thinking, Wow, we've got a director here who's being first AD and director at the same time, not used to using a first AD. A little while after, I found out exactly why he wasn't. There was a language problem. We've got a camera car and a camera operator. He's sitting on the camera car and Spike's up there too, but this time he's sitting back. He's gonna let Roderick, the first AD at the time, handle it. Roderick, who's also on the camera car, looks at Spike and says, "Are you ready?" And Spike says, "Ready." And Roderick says, "Roll the car, action with the camera." The actors start talking, but the camera has not been slated yet. Ernest says, "I can't mark the camera until the camera rolls." The car's moving, it's already beyond the shot. Massive confusion. Everybody sort of cracks up and we've got to start all over again.

People say that the first AD's job is easy. But the coordination of all the information on the set is really what it comes down to, so the first AD's job can get very, very tricky. Particularly in a situation where you've got actors who are not in line of sight with the director. We had a silk hung on the dashboard to give a nice soft fill throughout the picture car. The reserve side of this is that nobody can see in the window to monitor what's happening with the actors. The actors are working with the director with a walkie-talkie, so that all they hear are these commands on the radio. So when they heard "Action with the camera," they figured that that meant for them to start their dialogue. But the camera was not rolling yet and sound had not started to roll. We did get through everything we needed that day. There were a few funny scenes but nothing that actually stopped us from getting where we needed to go.

There are a lot of things that have to do with the functioning of a set that you don't really learn until you spend a lot of time on a set. Who does what, for instance. Being a gaffer on the job, I'm in charge of providing light for the DP (director of photography), handling things that are electrical on the set. The key grip is in charge of set engineering, rigging, flags, and camera dollies. He's also in charge of rigging car shots. The props department brings the picture cars to the grips. But the grips handle the cars once they're brought to them. It's all pretty simple if everyone knows his job and has an understanding of what others do. Our props department hadn't had much experience on big features. Early on, one of the props people drove the picture car to the set and asked what to do with it. And we said, "Just leave the car there and we'll do whatever we have to do with the car. We will move it once it's rigged." Because once it's rigged, the moving of the picture car needs to be by someone who understands how the rig is set for the car. There are certain things that hang off the end of the car. It's very low; certain bumps it can't go over. A big argument went down between Todd and a props person driving the car. This person was insisting the car was props', and Todd was saying, "Yes, the car is props', but once this car is rigged, I run it until we take the rig off of it." Since props didn't rig it, they're not aware of all the holes that had been pinched in the floor, and the bolts down to the floor, and how the bottom of the car, which was twelve inches to the ground, would end up six inches from the ground. So one has to be very careful taking it over any kind of bumps. You could get inside the car and drive away if you didn't know better and half the rig would fall off.

Or somebody could fall off the camera car. The camera itself could fall off.

There was a very scary situation that happened the third day of shooting. We were still doing car rigs. I was sitting on the camera car. When we drove around a corner, there was confusion as to where the position of the cops should be. There were supposed to be two, one was supposed to be behind and one was supposed to be in front, but one had to be behind in such a way that we wouldn't see him through the back windowsill. Roderick had moved the cop who was supposed to be in front two blocks ahead of us to keep him out of the way. We were driving with the camera hung on the outside of the picture car; it's in a side-mount position, on what they call a tray table, hanging out the front window of the car, hanging three feet over the line on which the car was traveling. The truck was driving the car straight and inside the line. But now the camera itself was on the extreme left and it's hanging another couple of feet beyond the line. The driver was to keep over to the left side to keep out of the way of parked cars, and a bus started coming up on the left side. I looked at the bus, and looked at the first AD, and looked at the camera hanging out of the car, and I tried whispering to the first AD to get his attention. We were in the middle of a take. I looked over at the driver of the car, who was trying to keep the car as far to the right as he could without running over the cars on his right. But this bus was coming up with speed. I leaned my head out in a panic, to see if we were going to lose the camera. We missed that bus by, it must have been, four inches. Both Todd and I were tense, you know, holding on to the side of the car.

Probably the most difficult thing in dealing with people who do not have experience is that you end up with misinformation. Or they think that you don't need certain information or that you can do without certain kinds of equipment, certain kinds of knowledge. You have to be open to learning everything and not hold back anything. Work out of what you really need to know. But it's impossible to tell what you're gonna need on a shoot until you've had the actual field experience. I have always looked at doing a film very much like going to war. It's a strange kind of look, but a film crew is like your infantry, your first line of attack, the people who sit down and work at the boards. They work out their theories about how many pages they think they can do a day, based on what they think about a location, and all this information. But what happens is that this is given to the grips, the electrics, the props, and the camera department, and we all have to make that come together. We've got to find a place to put the camera or find a way to rig it. We've got to find places to put lights, design intricate and complicated rigs to position equipment so that it's not seen for wide shots and hidden for shots that are tight. So there are a lot of complex, tricky things that go on. Decisions that have to be made on the line. You've got your generals and your generals are working out of the office. But then you've got your reinforcements—like your key grip and your gaffer and your head of props and your assistant cameraman, who has got to get the camera to where it's got to go. You've got your captain of the crew, the DP; you've got the director, who is like the commander in chief of the whole army. But it all ends up coming down to the nitty-gritty and down to Todd and myself, the key grip and the gaffer. We have to answer questions like how are we gonna get lights outside of the third-floor window of the building because there's no place to put any inside that we won't see. And it rained last night so the ground is gonna be too soft to run the condor crane over, without destroying it. How do we transport on a train?

We had a condor crane one night that we could not get up a hill. It rained, and the motor of the condor was too weak. And it would not move on the mud and the grass. We spent two and a half hours trying to find a way to get the crane up. We literally could not get it up, so we literally had to redesign the entire lighting scheme of this exterior night shot to fit where we could get the crane as opposed to having it work according to the design we had already made.

Ernest and I had talked very early on about how we wanted to light the Death March. One of the things Ernest wanted was a "moon" that would light a vast area of the campus, and that we could kinda swing around to use for different angles and shots. So I sat down and designed a moon that had nine light maxi brutes, which come to eighty-one par lights, both mediums and narrows, that had to be hung in one rig so that they could all be operated as a single source coming through a thin piece of diffusion. With some blue gel to give the effect of a moon, the feeling of a moon. Well, I designed the lights that had to be in it, the cable that I wanted, and the shape that the rig had to be, and turned it over to Todd. He proceeded to engineer what type of pipe and how he would put that rig together so that we could raise it up. He knew what size crane we'd need to get up to about eighty feet in height. This became quite a big thing: what was going to happen with the moon, the cost of getting it rigged and of the large crane we needed to lift and focus it. We had to figure out what was going to happen if the weather changed while we were shooting, if we got wind. We had various other problems with holding that whole moon together. But we designed it. We set up the rig, and miraculously, except for a few setbacks, waiting for a few pieces of equipment that arrived late, everything worked out fairly well. It covered the area that we wanted it to. An area that was about 150 feet by over 100 yards and lit the entire field fairly evenly. This was the effect we were looking for and this was the effect that we had gained. Ernest was very, very happy with this, because he liked the idea of using large sources and getting moonlight he could manipulate and use. But we ran into weather difficulties with that shoot. We had wind problems and couldn't quite keep the light up as high as we would have liked to. And some things, the rain and cold weather, didn't make it easy for us. We lost bulbs and had shorts in our circuits because we had to leave the rig up for many days. We had to leave it outside, waiting for a clear day to shoot. Although we did cover it, it would get uncovered during the course of the day and fill up with water. There was a fair amount of little difficulties with the rig, but all in all it worked quite well, because it worked for the shot. At one point, we had two condor cranes working. One of them was an old condor crane, not as new and not as well put together as the other. We had built what I was calling quadrapods, which were twelve-by-twelve silks that were attached to the bucket with arc lights behind them. This was up about sixty feet in the air to work as a smaller moon.

This was the last day of shooting the Death March. We knew we had to finish up because production didn't want to pay for the crane for another night. Also, we were having problems on the campus as to what ground was whose, as we had been kicked off the Morehouse campus by then and we thought we were on Atlanta University turf. The two schools share a quad, though. It had been raining for a few days. The ground was soft, and moving equipment around had become a very complicated process.

Despite all the difficulties with locations and all the confusions caused by lack of experience, this film is in the can. Despite the misunderstandings. People with experience speaking in one language, and people who didn't have experience speaking another. Simple things. Todd and I would ask, "Are we coming up to the LFS?" and they'd say, "Yes." Then we would direct our crews to start wrapping up equipment. We'd get everything ready to go. Then those same people would say, "What are you doing?" I'd say, "This is the LFS, isn't it?" They'd say, "LFS?" "The last fucking shot!" "Oh, no, we've got many more shots to go before the evening is out." So I'd have to say to my crew, "Put down everything you've got in your hands and spread it out again. We're looking at more time."

It would seem that every department had its gremlins, you know. Something would, for no reason, not work, or would disappear. It happened to the grips the first week. Somebody stole twenty-one lead weights out of one of the jockey boxes. They just disappeared over one night. Nobody could figure this out. Lead weights aren't the kind of thing someone can walk off with. Those weigh more than you can put in the back of anybody's car. We're talking fifty pounds apiece, twenty-one of them—we're talking over a thousand pounds. Nobody could figure out how this could have happened. One night before this happened, somehow a lock on one of the jockey boxes was missing and so Todd decided to put the locks on everything else and figured that the lead weights were in no danger. Because who's gonna run away with a lead weight?

One day the camera department had its gremlins. They had trouble with magazines for no apparent reason. We were all in place for this twilight shot. The sun started setting, we were rolling the camera, it was time to get the new mag. The second AC pulled out a new mag and it's the wrong mag. The mag box is marked for 94 (film stock), but instead of having 94 it's got 47, which is a slow film. We're already down to the end of the day. The light is waning. By the time it took to go up to the car to load a fresh mag, we had lost all light.

So everybody had his share of gremlins. And I was waiting for mine to show up. I would go home every night and recheck my order of equipment, check what we were shooting the next day. Our schedule was changing, I was getting a new schedule approximately every three days on the picture. Our first shooting schedule didn't last for more than the first four days and neither did all my equipment orders and special equipment orders and special crew orders that I had set . . . that's it.

This picture sticks out for me for reasons that are not gonna show up on film so well. To begin with, this is probably one of the first musical comedies that's ever been done as a Black musical comedy and that has been done by a Black director.

The last musical comedy that I worked on was *The Wiz*. Sidney Lumet was the director, and let me tell you there weren't many Black people on that crew. In any part of it. I mean, Oswell Morris, the DP, was English; the gaffer, Norman Lee, was Jewish. There was nothing Black about it but the talent. *School Daze* is about a college environment that has not been dealt with as a subject of film, a phenomenon that takes place only on Black college campuses. And the whole political workings of it are something totally unique to the Black college environment. And so there are the obvious social and political aspects that make the project important. But there are other reasons. It's probably the lowest-budget musical comedy ever done. People may look at $6.5 million, and I'm saying this from experience. People look at $6.5 million and say, "Oh, that's big budget." But that's big budget if you're talking about a film that is basically talking heads, emotional conflict between people, walking around in an urban community. That's one thing. That's a good-sized budget for something like that. But it's not a big budget for something that has special effects, large set numbers, large exterior numbers, and musical numbers. There are many other things musical comedy calls for that make it a much more expensive and much more ambitious project to undertake.

That was one of the things that amazed me about Spike. I realized when Spike came into this that in many ways he was in over his head, given what all this was going to entail. But Spike has the unique ability to watch, listen, and learn.

It's an amazing ability, because there are very few people who can recognize that they are out of their element and then listen and learn what's happening all around. Spike didn't just listen to his actors, or listen to his DP. He was busy watching me while I'm setting lights. Watching Todd while he's setting up the crane. Watching others while they're trying to get props together. Watching Wynn rig a set. He got out there in the morning at the same time the crew did to see what was going on before the shoot began. He was there as things were being built, to see what it was going to take to put things together. And he was very open. You could say to Spike, "Look, Spike, this is going to take two hours." He wouldn't argue with you. He wouldn't say, "It can't take that long. We've got to do it now, now, now!" He'd say, "It's gonna take that long? Okay, if it's gonna take that long, then I wanna do something else now." And he'd go work out the rest of his schedule to fit. He had faith in the keys, you know, Todd and myself. He has a great adaptability. And, as I said, a willingness to listen and learn. So by the end of the project Spike was much more abreast of what had been going on, how things came to be on the film set, what position he was in, and what people did. When you do low-budget films, you don't see these jobs being done, because everybody kind of pitches in and does a little bit of everything. On a picture that is this large you have to be aware of everything. There's too much confusion happening, not to be aware. I have to know what's happening in my department. If anybody does anything I don't know about, then I've got a problem. I base everything on knowing. I talk to Ernest and it comes from me down to my crew. You know now if something comes in and forms a third angle, you know, it's likely to throw my whole scheme off. So I can't have anybody else moving, changing, or touching who hasn't been asked to by me.

Because the sets are very dangerous places. A lot of people don't realize that at first, but it's a very important thing to understand. I was working outside with over 200,000 watts of power. That kind of power with equipment hanging off the condor cranes and high scaffolds is dangerous. It becomes very important for people to be aware of what's going on around them.

For example, I had the prerigging crew come in and rig the lights one day. When we came to set, I had my guys test them. So we put the lights up. They were working, and we were lowering them down. As the operator tried to lower the next unit, using the controls from the bucket, the arm itself started to vibrate. The arm took a drop of about three or four feet. And that drop, with an arm extended out fifty or sixty feet, has got a lot of spring action. It's like a guitar string, you know, or something. So, so, so, it's rocking. The rocking motion starts shaking the head of the arc. The arc itself started vibrating back and forth. We wanted the guy to come down and try to lower it from the ground. But the whole rig started to shake, and then the chimney falls off. The chimney, which is about three feet of steel, sticks into the ground. It looks like an owl or something. Something out of *The Omen*. It just came and gouged itself into the ground. Mark, my best boy, ran over to pull it out, because his brother was in that bucket. He started instructing his brother how to steady the light, operating it from the bucket. I told Mark that he had better get back out of the way, because we were going to try to bring the light down using our controls from the ground. Mark's brother tried to come down again, using his controls, and the arm started to shake. I went to yell to him to stop, to stop trying to move it, that we would try to operate it from the base, because sometimes the controls are much smoother from below than they are from the top. As I went to tell him to stop, the arc itself, the neck of the stand, snapped, and the arc literally fell about forty feet and hit the one piece of cement that was out there in that quad of grass. It fell right on the edge of a walkway. It nose-dived into that walkway. Thank God for the movement of my crew. The generator operator knew to pull the power to the light, immediately, because the cables had been yanked out of the light when it fell, and they were floating around in the bucket and our man was still in the bucket. I didn't know what his condition was at that point. I knew he didn't fall out of the bucket, but I didn't know what happened to him. He wasn't saying anything at first. I sent Mark to operate the crane from the base, and I kept talking to his brother as we lowered it. His brother was all right. The arc had brushed him as it rolled off the bucket. At first he had tried to hold on to it, but he realized that that would be a mistake. Let the light go, but you don't need to go with it. Anything can happen. We don't like these things to happen, and we adhere to all kinds of safety precautions to prevent them, but things can still happen. Actors sometimes play games like walking under the cranes on set. But it's dangerous, no joke. If a screwdriver falls from sixty feet, it can kill somebody. Think about a three-hundred-pound light falling on you.

There was nobody near the light when it fell. No one got hurt (from below). We cleared the area before we moved the equipment. There were some actors coming down from the holding area at the time. They were on their way to the set and wanted to take a shortcut and walk under the crane. We stopped them and directed them another way. This was just before it fell. I told Randy Fletcher, our AD, to get somebody out there just to keep people away from the crane. "If you don't want to tell them, I will." People fail to realize how many lose their lives on film sets.

Joe Seneca and Art Evans getting minor instructions.

3

TAKE YOUR HAT, YOUR COAT, AND LEAVE, M-F!

—Morehouse College football chant

SCOUTING LOCATIONS

SPIKE ▸ Almost halfway through the shoot, with footage already in the can, the colleges of the Atlanta University Center decided to bar the School Daze Picture Company from filming on their campuses. The reason for the boot? They feared that *School Daze* would portray a negative (shit, that word again) image of Black colleges, and more importantly of Black people as a whole. You have to understand that historically Black colleges have been very conservative. They consider themselves the guardians of the integrity of the race. We tried to reason with them, in fact, negotiations with the schools had been going on since the previous November. But the alarm went off even before that, back in October 1986.

Before *She's Gotta Have It* opened in Atlanta that October, I came up with the idea of making the premiere screening a benefit for my alma mater, Morehouse College. I wanted to shoot *School Daze* at the Atlanta University Center the following spring and thought the benefit would get things off to a good start. Forty Acres would provide the print of the film, pay for the theater, the advertising, and the cost of printing the tickets. Morehouse would kick back and count the money. We planned to charge $15 a ticket, and the college would collect $6,000. We were sure that Morehouse would welcome the offer; we went ahead and printed the tickets. Morehouse turned us down.

The old, tired, conservative administration and faculty had heard that *She's Gotta Have It* was a pornographic film (a rumor that would haunt us throughout the shooting of *School Daze*). They didn't want Morehouse's good name to be associated with such a film. Even if the filmmaker was their alumnus. That hurt me a lot. I volunteered to put on the benefit. Morehouse does not have a $3 billion endowment like Harvard. It doesn't have enough money to turn down $6,000 flat.

Ultimately, a couple of friends of mine, Morehouse alumni working in the city government, talked to Dr. Hugh Gloster. They convinced him to do the benefit. Then we decided against it. But we did ask Gloster if we could shoot some footage at Morehouse's homecoming weekend that November, possibly to use in *School Daze*. So they invited us down and made a big fuss over us at the coronation and football game. We thought we were in, as far as the backing of Morehouse was concerned.

The week before the coronation my coproducers, Monty Ross and Loretha Jones, and I held a meeting with all the Atlanta University Center college presidents about shooting *School Daze* in the spring. Hugh Gloster, Dr. Donald Stewart, the acting president of Spelman, Dr. Meyers, a representative from Morris Brown, Dr. Elias Blake, the president of Clark, and Dr. Charles Meredith, the chancellor of the Atlanta University Center, were there. They asked to read the script. I told them no, and they left it at that. We went on to talk about contracts. They said they wanted a piece of the film. We ruled that out right away. But we came to terms on some other issues. Overall, it was a productive meeting. We were a go. We left thinking that the AUC lawyers would be in touch with Loretha.

We began shooting on the campuses in March without a contract, apart from an agreement signed early on with AU. After three weeks we still didn't have one. Heading towards our fourth week, we received a letter from the AUC's lawyer demanding that we stop shooting until the script was made available. We again refused and were barred from the campuses. Not only that, but the footage we shot previously could not, or so they told us, be used in the movie. At the time of this writing, Morehouse had still not agreed to let us use the footage shot on its campus. Morris Brown, however, gave a definite no.

There were so many rumors circulating around the AUC about the movie. Women at Spelman thought that Kelly Woolfolk—who played Vicky, football player Grady's love interest—had the role of a prostitute. The students were influenced by the propaganda being pushed out by the administrations. When I was at Morehouse the atmosphere was different. The student body was more vocal and certainly more political. We didn't take what the administration told us at face value. I think we would have been really upset if a young Black filmmaker came to our campus to shoot a film and got kicked off by the school. But there wasn't a whimper from any of the students at Morehouse, Spelman, Clark, or Morris Brown. In fact, we never had a chance to shoot anything on Spelman's campus. The acting president was quite adamant about us not being there.

I'm all for Black colleges. I'm a third-generation Morehouse man, and I hope my sons choose Morehouse. But there are certain things wrong at Black colleges and I address some of them in *School Daze.* To me, this doesn't mean that I'm putting forth a negative portrayal of these institutions. The AUC presidents were after squeaky clean images of Black colleges. I refuse to be caught in the "negative image" trap that's set for Black artists. Yes, Black people have been dogged in the media from day one. We're extrasensitive and we have every right to be. But we overreact when we think that every image of us has to be 100 percent angelic—Christ-like even.

MONTY ROSS talks about the first meeting we had with the college presidents back in November 1986 ▸ There was no battle plan. We merely wanted to shoot at the Atlanta University Center. So we went to the top people. We wanted to talk to them face-to-face, man-to-man, straight up. Even before we came down for the homecoming celebration they started with these rumors, "Is this going to be another *She's Gotta Have It?*" So we said, "Before this gets any further out of hand, let's sit down and talk." All the presidents came but one: Morris Brown sent a representative. It was over a nice lunch. But when the questions turned to money, Hugh Gloster really got upset.

The band that is in the film is actually the combined bands of Morehouse/Spelman, Clark, and Morris Brown colleges. All three band directors scoffed at our idea of combining the three. It had never been done before. It's strange, these schools are all a part of the AU Center, right across the street from each other, but rarely do they ever come together for a common goal. The credit has to go to my father, Bill Lee, and my aunt, Consuela Lee Moorehead. She wrote "Kick It Out Tigers," played by the band.

The Greek Show shot at Morris Brown's gym. Note the empty seats. A good deal of our time was spent moving the extras that were present from one section of the gym to the other, depending on which way we were shooting. On my next film I'll have a budget to pay extras. It's the only guarantee that the necessary bodies will show up.

We proposed to pay them a standard fee, $2,000 for each location, any costs, and reimbursement for any damages that occurred. Plus we wanted to give them the opening night premiere of the film. We'd rent the Fox Theater and turn the proceeds over to the AUC. Gloster wanted more money. He wanted a precentage in the film. He seemed to feel that Spike was going to make a lot of money, go off to Hollywood, and never be heard from again. Donald Stewart said, "Hugh, let Spike make some money first. We're talking about a guy with a first-time hit; he hasn't seen any real money. We can't make any demands on somebody who hasn't even made the film yet." And everyone laughed.

It was also Dr. Gloster who brought up the script. They were worried the film would be another *Animal House*. They didn't want illicit sex or any talk about the light-skinned, dark-skinned issue. Spike said, "Isn't Bill Cosby shooting on Spelman's campus this year, Dr. Stewart? Are you asking to see his script?" He said no. "Why do you have to ask to see mine?" Then Gloster said, "Because yours is a little bit of a different film. We know Bill Cosby and we don't know you." And Spike said, "But I'm from the AUC. I graduated from Morehouse. Why would I do anything of detriment to the school that I love?"

That was the first meeting. We didn't want to seem as if we were attacking them. So we tried to give them a lot of assurances, as many as we possibly could. Attorneys weren't involved at this time. We felt that the AUC is like a brotherhood. Whether you work there, are a college president, or are a former student, you are dedicated to your school. There's a camaraderie, there's supposed to be this bond. We didn't want to begin by involving lawyers and accountants. We wanted to establish that we're all friends. And we thought that they would say to themselves, "These are young people. They're coming to us because they want to shoot a film here. We understand that. And even if we do have some concerns about the images they will project, we'll hear them out."

SPIKE ▸ We assured Grace Blake and Matia Karrell before they started in Atlanta that the locations at the AUC were secured and that our relationship with the colleges was like father and son. Things worked out differently, of course. Grace and Matia ended up sitting through meeting after meeting trying to convince the college administrators of our honorable intentions, and how important their facilities were to our completing the film on time and within budget. Even Grace, who has more film experience than anyone on staff or crew, was taken aback at the deaf ears we found at the AUC.

GRACE BLAKE ▸ When I spoke to Monty before I got to Atlanta he said, "Oh, it's all taken care of. We know all these people in the government. There was a handshake and everything is fine." Once I came aboard I started asking a few questions and a few more questions and realized quickly that the locations were not tied down at all. At the first meeting with the colleges that I attended, I saw that something wasn't right. I just kind of sat there, looked around, didn't say much. When we came out I said to Loretha, "I think we have to stop taking Monty and the locations manager, Tyrone Harris, to these meetings. From the little that I've seen, the presidents are treating them like little boys, like students. They're giving them the sure-we'll-take-care-of-it, wave-of-the-hand treatment. I think we have to make this thing really professional. The two of us should be the only *School Daze* people involved." But even after Loretha and I took charge of the negotiations, it was yes and it was no, back and forth, and two weeks later before they would answer a phone call.

Loretha was handling the contracts. I said to her early on that we should go for a simple contract. You see, I have a one-page location agreement that I have used over the years. Take a ten-page contract to someone, to shoot in their house; they look at it and send it to their attorney. Take a one-page contract in simple language to someone, they read it, they sign it, and you've got your location. Plenty of location sites have been lost because of ten-page contracts. But Loretha was adamant about it. She was dealing with the AUC attorneys and that was out of my hands.

Atlanta University was terrific. We got lucky there. When Loretha first sent the contracts to all the schools, it was Atlanta University—the first campus we filmed on—that signed theirs. The others began to realize what was happening when they saw the "Divest Now" banners hanging from the Atlanta University administration building, and heard a few curse words from the actors. Earlier, during the rehearsal period, they had seen how rowdy the audience was at the auditions we held for the Greek Show. Then they must have said, "Wait a minute!"

But I really and truly felt that the contracts would be signed, that's why we continued to negotiate in good faith for so long. Some of the problem was that the colleges got greedy as we began shooting. Things started coming out in the papers in Atlanta about how *She's Gotta Have It* made so much money. I found myself telling people all the time, even crew members, "Look, if this was a white director directing this movie, the budget would be at least three times the size of our budget. We do not have the money." And we didn't.

The problem person at the AUC was Dr. Gloster of Morehouse. He was a troublemaker. The deal that Spike and Monty made with the colleges originally was that we would give them *X* number of dollars and the colleges would allocate it evenly amongst themselves. That's the way we were discussing it and the way Loretha was handling it in her dealings with the AUC attorney, Tony Axum. But all of a sudden Gloster says something to the effect that Axum does not represent Morehouse. We want to deal separately. Morehouse is the biggest college in the AU Center, and since we'd be shooting there the most, its administration said it wanted the most money. So now we're dealing with Morehouse on one hand and all the other colleges on the other. Then Gloster got back in with everyone else. He retracted his statements and went with the group at the very end. I think that the other colleges, Spelman, Morris Brown, Clark, might have been more willing to work with us had Gloster not been so resistant. He was truly concerned that Spike might drag down the reputation of the Morehouse man. Originally I felt that it was more money that they were after. But they changed midstream. I know that Gloster mostly wanted script approval.

Dr. Blake at Clark allowed us to use his college's gym to shoot the Splash Jam scenes. Then we went back to the other colleges to let them know that things went fine at Clark. We bought a new tarp for the gym floor and made a donation to the athletic department. Gloster was not impressed. Dr. Gloster said one thing that bothers me. He said, "You guys have that man playing the president of the college, the Black man with the beard. What's his name?" I said, "You're talking about Joe Seneca." He said, "Yes, he looks like a plantation man." I said, "A plantation man?" So then he looked around at his other flunkies and said, "Don't you agree with me? He looks like a plantation man. Presidents of colleges don't look like him." I said, "Are you real?" He said, "Yes." I let it go for a while, but the last thing I said before we walked out of the room was, "By the way, Dr. Gloster, for your information, the plantation man, he also played a president at the school that the Huxtables go to. You know, the family that gives you a lot of money, the Huxtables? You know, Bill Cosby?" I thought to myself, Here is a Black man teaching young Black men, a well-respected man, and he's saying Joe Seneca can't be a president of the school because he looks like a plantation man. At one point I thought of writing Dr. Gloster about what he had said, then I thought it probably wouldn't be worth it.

MATIA KARRELL ▸ When I first got to Atlanta Grace told me that Monty and Tyrone Harris had made the initial contacts with the schools. Monty was very optimistic about what they were willing to do for us. There was never a doubt, initially, in their minds that the schools would let them shoot there. Filmmakers are sometimes a little naive. They think people want them to film there. They forget that it's a business, and there are individuals and businesses that aren't enamored by the process. They don't have to have you there. We began with a positive feeling that things would eventually come through. Only the bureaucracy, paper, and lawyers were stopping things from happening.

The first meeting I attended was at Spelman during preproduction. We submitted a shooting schedule and a list of facilities on its campus that we needed access to at certain times. Maybe it was due to the way our unit manager worded it, but the administrators were put off by our proposal. We were being very open with them. You learn in filmmaking that the less owners of a location know, the better off you are. But we wanted to approach this differently. We thought, given Spike's relationship to the schools, we'd get a better response if they knew everything that we wanted and were going to do there. The approach did not work.

At one of the meetings a representative from Spelman said, "Why don't you come back in June when there's no one here?" And our mouths dropped. Does this woman understand that we are going to be shooting in a week? She said, "I don't even know why you want to shoot here. Can't you find someplace else?" Her attitude seemed to be that she had better things to do than deal with these people who want to make film. As if the film had nothing to do with anything in life. It was the first meeting that made us realize that Spike and Monty's connection to these schools made no difference in the minds of the people who ran them.

Because of the delay in contracts, we shot at a couple of the campuses without signed contracts. We got some complaints about it, and that's when rumors about the film—such as an actress from Spelman was playing a prostitute and orgies were being held in the grip and electric trucks—started circulating like wildfire. When we shot one scene in a hallway of one of Clark's dorms, it turned out that our locations department had neglected to inform the students the night before that we would be shooting there at 6:30 A.M. So here we are going into a women's dormitory at dawn unexpected. Word of mouth on us was very bad after that. The production has to take blame for such things. It's part of filmmaking. When you go into a location that doesn't belong to you, you're interrupting and interfering. You have to adhere to protocol and cause the least amount of flak possible, because you never know when you'll have to go back there to reshoot.

At one point, right before we were asked to leave the campuses, we were feeling sort of desperate. We had to get these locations. We're trying to do this for the director. We want to make it work for him, of course. So what are we gonna do? We made a decision, without informing Spike, to put a little video together to show to the colleges. We thought it was a safety measure. But Spike got quite upset. We assumed that we would make the decision to show the tape to the colleges, even though we knew it was up to Spike. We made the tape and had it ready in case we needed it, as a way of getting rid of the rumors and showing the quality of the film we were trying to make. We did show them the video. But they thought it was just an entertaining ploy. We included the scene where Ossie Davis, as the coach of the football team, talks about the devil in the opponents' locker room. The administrations really jumped on that; they were actually offended by the scene.

They were still dubious about the project as a whole. The only time they softened was at the final meeting when Spike started talking about his family, his background, and what Morehouse meant to him. It was an emotional moment for many of us in the room. He was talking truthfully and from his heart about what he believed in. I thought for sure there was going to be a change in how the administrations dealt with us, that is, until Spike had to leave in the middle of the meeting to start the day's shooting. The presidents had a how-dare-he look on their faces—Spike was just trying to get his film done on time.

It was a sad day when we got kicked off the campuses. During the final meeting with the colleges, the whole thing with the script reached a peak. The presidents were still questioning Spike's right to withhold the script. We were saying that showing the script would have been equal to censorship. What's gonna happen if you read the script and don't like it? What good will it do? You're probably not going to understand it anyway. Because the script is not final really until you see the film. We were trying to explain to them that the script is a work sheet.

After the break with the colleges, we were a little nervous about how Atlanta University would feel once it heard the decision the other colleges had made. But it remained separate from them. I think AU needed the money and was bound by the contract it signed with us early on in production. What we had to do was figure out how we could shoot at AU the stuff that we intended to do at the other colleges. So Grace and Loretha had a meeting with AU to talk about adding more shooting days there.

We were forced to reschedule locations and shuffle shooting days for the rest of the production. We were lucky to have a production designer like Wynn who could adjust. We sent Wynn out again and again to scout locations. This was almost the fourth week of the shoot, and he was busy doing other things—designing sets. Still, he was willing to go and try to find locations as good as those we originally had.

Overall we were fortunate to have a campus to shoot on at all. I don't know how Spike feels about the compromises we made in finding new locations. Nonetheless, that's filmmaking and these are the problems. So many changes had to be made that the standing joke was: What are we shooting today? Everybody would just throw their hands up in the air.

COLORED COLLEGE

BILL LEE (MUSIC SUPERVISOR) ▸ Spike and I weren't aware of it at the time, but we were simultaneously writing about our experiences at Morehouse College. I was starting my eighth opera, *Colored College*, at the same time that Spike was writing *Homecoming*, the script that later became *School Daze*.

When Spike decided to make *School Daze* a musical, he came to me and asked to hear the music I had written for *Colored College*, with the idea of using some of it in the film. It wasn't a bad idea, but I have a particular attachment to the opera. I wanted to let the *Colored College*'s compositions remain there. On occasion Spike and I have used music from other operas I've written to score his films. "Nola's Theme," from *She's Gotta Have It*, for example, was taken from an opera of mine called *One Mile East*. Actually, it's not an opera, it's a folk festival. It'll probably take two or three days to perform, it's that long. "Nola's Theme" was adapted from a selection of the festival called "Ye Little Old Folks Children's Concert Waltz."

I came to Morehouse straight from my hometown, Snow Hill, Alabama. I grew up in an all-Black community in Snow Hill and my grandfather founded a school there called the Snow Hill Institute. I felt a great sense of protection in my community. But as soon as I stepped outside my home, I had to put up this shield around me (just as I had to do later on at Morehouse). More than anything, I had to make sure I got back home without getting my head beat up. I had to make sure my yes-sirs and no-sirs were in the right place and that I used them to address the right people at the right time.

I went to Morehouse from '47 to '51; Spike was there from '75 to '79. The overall difference in the time periods has to do with the work of one man, Martin Luther King, Jr. I went to school with Martin Luther King. He was a senior when I was a freshman. Before King left Morehouse and went on to change life in the South, Black people were still riding on the back of the bus. Even young men like myself, attending high-class institutions such as Morehouse. We were big men on the campus. But as soon as we stepped off the grounds, we were looked at as second-class citizens or worse. And the instructors at Morehouse, the president, and the school ministers never confronted that.

Some of my instructors were still at Morehouse when Spike got there. I was under President Benjamin Mays, whom we called "Buck Bennie." Mays was a great man. He had the foresight to encourage some of the greatest minds to come out of Morehouse. Mays inspired Martin Luther King to achieve what he did. Many people were trying to discourage King, but Mays took King out of high school a year or two early and brought him to college. If it weren't for what Mays did, King might have been drafted in the Korean War. President Mays didn't lecture at school often, because his duties took him off campus so much. But whenever he spoke in chapel, he had a full house of students.

I was nineteen when I started at Morehouse. I'm glad I went at the time I did, because many of my classmates were veterans from the Second World War. I was in the company of older men. These men were five to ten years older than I. They had gone all over the world. It made a big difference in the atmosphere on campus. In fact, the thing I value most about my time at Morehouse is not so much what I learned in the classroom, but all that came of my association with the fellas.

My opera *Colored College* is quite a long piece. It's never been performed on stage. At the moment it is two thick books of music, dance, dialogue, and all the stories that go in between. My entire four years at Morehouse are crammed into those two books. There are various stories that go on throughout the opera. One involves two characters called Ghetto and Country.

I try to put on stage things that I've seen or experienced. And if I haven't seen or experienced something in my work, at least it's something that has been told to me. I happen to be this Country character. I come from Snow Hill, Alabama, and Snow Hill is way back in the woods, so that makes me Country. Ghetto is based on this fella from Cleveland, a lifelong friend who has passed away now. Ghetto and Country get to be pretty good friends despite the fact that the two have been raised differently and have different values.

Another one of the opera's stories involves the relationship between students and faculty at the school and their disagreements about the curriculum. The faculty has selected one route and the students want to pursue another. When I was at Morehouse, students wanted to read and talk about Black authors, but we were told to put that stuff aside. The school would have painted us as white as snow if we had let them.

Spike's great-grandfather, William James Edwards (I'm named after him) went to Tuskegee. He wrote a book called *Twenty-Five Years in the Black Belt* while he was there. It's part of Tuskegee's Negro Collection. I had never read the book, and I was hoping Morehouse would have it in its library. It didn't. I tried to get the librarians to get hold of a copy. They weren't too interested, but they were full of stuff like "Go read this Tennyson and this Emerson, and get yourself educated."

4

WANNABEES, JIGABOOS, AND WANNABOOS

THE CAST

LARRY FISHBURNE ("DAP DUNLAP") ▸ I'm a real verbal guy. Spike will tell you I talk too much. Before he decided to play "Half-Pint," we were talking about Larry B. Scott, a fine young actor. I felt that Spike shouldn't play "Half-Pint." Number one, because he had to direct the picture, and directing is a big job. You're in charge of a lot of people. I thought he was gonna spread himself thin. Second, Spike as an actor was brilliant in *She's Gotta Have It,* but I didn't know whether he could play another character. So I said, "Spike, I don't want to compete with Mars Blackmon." He said, "What are you talking about?" and then I compared characters I've played that were very similar.

I got over that, and subsequently he did something with "Half-Pint" that was similar to Mars, but it's not as high energy. When working in a Francis Coppola, Spike Lee, Alfred Hitchcock, or Cecil B. DeMille film, you're working with directors who are themselves the stars, which didn't click in with me at first. This is a Spike Lee film. So it's very important that his presence be there.

Before we shot the scene where "Half-Pint" tells "Dap" he's not a virgin anymore, I was telling Giancarlo, "Spike doesn't know, man. He can do this Mars Blackmon shit, but when he gets into this scene with me, we're going to be actors. I'm going to pick him up and slam him against the wall." I feel there are times as an actor when you take yourself to a point where you don't know any more than the audience does—are you acting or are you really this character?

So my thing was to take Spike to that point, see if he could hang. And he was in it! He surprised the shit out of me. Like when he started to yell (ad lib), "Get off of me, get off of me!" That's real shit, people do that even if the dude is bigger. My father used to pick on me like that, grab me, and I'd yell, "Get off of me." Then he'd really pop me in the mouth. Spike did great things with "Half-Pint."

One of my problems in the film was looking to Spike as my director. It was hard to make the transition from actor looking for the director's guidance to working with Spike as a fellow actor. There were lots of adjustments to make in terms of Spike as friend, director, actor, because there's a different way to deal with him in each role.

The first day of shooting we did the confrontation scene between the local yokels and students at the chicken joint. Spike set up the shot and we came out. There were ten of us, face-to-face, selling wolf tickets, looking at each other. We had marks to stand on and we weren't allowed to stray at all and it felt real unnatural. I've been called a natural actor, because I have to go with my instincts. And my instinct was telling me that ten guys hollering at each other would not stand toe-to-toe. I wanted to fix the scene, but I couldn't figure out how to articulate to Spike how it needed to be fixed. So I said, "Spike, can I have another one?" Can we do another take, after we had done three? His answer was no.

Usually what happens with a director is you try to feel him out and get to know his likes and dislikes. One of the ways to try to get things done is to do something the way you are asked to do it, and give the best you can. If that doesn't work for you, go to the director and say, "That doesn't work for me. Let me have one my way and see if you like it." This way you've tried it his way first. I got real upset when Spike said no; I just couldn't believe it, after I had done everything he asked me to do. He said, "Larry, it's like playing baseball. You're not gonna hit a home run every time." Baseball? And I thought, Well, I can't hit a home run every time, but I can *try* to hit a home run every time. As far as I'm concerned, every frame of film that I'm on is gonna be my best frame. I have to at least try to make it that way.

I'd tried to explain to Spike that the blocking didn't feel right to me. What he said was, "Don't worry about the fact that you don't feel good about it, it looked good. No one will ever be able to tell you were frustrated, Fish, because the camera angle is so def." Okay. Now, when the director says he's not gonna give you another one, you can't go to the DP and say, "Hey, crank it up, roll," so you have to sit and stew. So I sat and stewed. Then Spike came to me the next day and said, "Look, we can work together." It may have taken him a bit to figure out what I was trying to say because I didn't articulate it well. I was upset. When Spike said we can work together I thought, Oh, great. We gotta! We can't work against each other.

Another thing I told Spike that day was that I'm a newborn baby each time I'm out there. Meaning, "I don't know what to do unless you tell me. It's your film. My job as far as I'm concerned is to make you happy. If you know the film frame by frame before it's shot, then I've got to give you something that's at least close to what's in your head. If I'm not doing that, then you've got to let me know. If I am, let me know, even if you just look at me and raise your eyebrows."

Spike showed me the *Homecoming* script shortly after we met. It was really a story about a friendship between these two guys, "Julian" and "Slice," done in a series of flashbacks. It was a great story. There were scenes in the rain, all that good stuff. He told me he wanted me to do "Big Brother General George Patton." Of course my ego was hurt. I didn't say anything, maybe something like, "Sure, I don't mind." I would have been happy to do anything then. I was doing *Gardens of Stone* in Virginia in '86, and I don't know if I called Spike or he called me, but somehow we were on the phone. He said, "*School Daze,* 1987." I said, "Yeah?" He said, "Yep. Slice, you're it." I said, "Oh, yeah?" He said, "Yep." I said, "Okay, bet."

Another minimalist conversation with the coach. He's the sports freak so I call him the coach. I'm not a sports fan at all, which is why when he said baseball to me the first day, I flipped. So, I decided, if he's into sports, I'll call him coach. And maybe then he'll understand the relationship that I have with him. If he says, "You're on the bench," then I go sit the fuck down somewhere.

When I think about the characters I play, I first put together in my mind how I want the character to look. Then I go about getting all the stuff that I need to make the look happen. Once I've got that, it all falls into place. It's a liberty—developing the look of a character—that I have been taking now for the past five years. I did *Death Wish II,* and they hired five of us to play thugs. The wardrobe people weren't given time to put together a look for us. I think there were two actors, though, who already had their look together and had it approved.

I didn't think much about it. But then the wardrobe person came out and handed me this pair of plaid pants and a hat. One of those wool Applejacks in some monstrous tweeds. I was like, Yo, man, I can't wear this shit. What am I gonna do? I asked her where she got the clothes. She said, "Go over to so and so on Melrose Avenue; here's fifty dollars." So I bought myself a pair of green pants with a black stripe, a blue shirt, a red vest with black fronts, a big gray hat, and white military gloves. I had a magic wand, and one of the actors gave me some pink glases. From that film on I've always tried to have the look together before wardrobe even sees me. When I go shopping now, I even shop with future jobs in mind.

Most of my work, so far, has been as a supporting actor. That's always the best kind of work to me, because you have a lot or a small group of people working together. You all have this communion. The Fellas are just one great big personality, even though each character represents a different aspect of "Black life" on this college campus. As the more experienced actor, I tried to be the guy who says, "This is how you do so and so." And then at other times I tried not to be that guy. I tried to help in a way that I thought would be beneficial to them, to all of us. But a good teacher at times has to sit back and let you learn for yourself.

To prepare for the Wake Up sequence, I went through this whole process. I sat the Fellas down during the second week of rehearsal and gave each guy a book dealing with the history of African people on the planet—about racism and all that good stuff. I gave Kadeem Hardison a book, *The Things They Never Taught You in History Class.* I gave Eric Payne a book called *Freedom Rising,* by James North. North is from Chicago and spent five years traveling in South Africa. I told the guys to go through their books and pick out

Bill Nunn, who was three years ahead of me at Morehouse, made up some of the best ad-libs. He had the country football-playing "Grady McKissick" down to a T.

GRADY

I knew you were a Taurus. You look so good you ought to be on *Soul Train,* you know what? I'm gonna put you on *Dance Fever,* baby. [Unsnaps her raincoat.] Uh . . . uh . . . uh . . . uh . . . uh . . . uh . . . uh . . . look a'here, look a'here, look a'here. Come on over here, girl. Uh [they kiss], uh, uh.

VICKY

[Whispers.] Grady, we're not alone! [Pulling away.]

GRADY

That ain't nothing but a lumpy mattress, baby.

VICKY

That's your roommate in here.

GRADY

If you be quiet, they'll never even know. I'm a silent lover, baby, and if you don't scream, I sure won't holler.

VICKY

Will you let go?

GRADY

Ah, baby. Come on.

VICKY

Grady, get off me. Are you crazy?

GRADY

Naw, you're crazy.

some nifty piece of information that we all should know and pass it on. This would allow us to be down for the cause and knowledgeable about it in one way or another.

When we got to the Wake Up sequence, I figured that everybody in the cast would know how to react to my saying "Wake up." Not "Wake up, get up, you're sleeping." But "Wake up, we've been sleeping for four hundred years." Some people took the statement literally and then wanted to know how they performed. When I told them they didn't get it, they asked, "Why didn't you tell us?" That was the one thing that I was not supposed to tell them. They were supposed to know that one. That's the lesson we're trying to teach with this movie.

I also brought down some lecture tapes on racism and mental health by Dr. Frances Cress Welsing. During the rehearsal period, I had everybody, the Fellas and all the women, Jigs, come to the apartment and listen to them. I told everybody that this is information that we all need to know and should pass on to the Wannabees—offscreen. I thought it would create tension. It creates some kind of tough emotional stuff. So I was trying to get everyone to walk up to these folks that were playing Wannabees and drop these little thoughts on them. Because at the end of the movie, we're all supposed to be in the same space mentally.

Another reason for the gathering at my apartment was that our group needed to sit down and be together. The feelings of alienation that the women felt certainly weren't imagined. They had some beefs and it was a good place for them to air them. One was that they were never given the opportunity to play together in the film, while the Gammas and the Gamma Rays played together throughout. Makeup, their hair, and their wardrobes were concerns. So I told them about the cover-your-own-ass school of acting I learned on *Death Wish II*.

The saddest part of that meeting was finding out that Laurnea Wilkerson's mother had died. We were playing a tape and things were going very well. Laurnea had a bad headache and someone took her back to the hotel early. Turns out Grace Blake was waiting for her with the news. James Bond ("Monroe") volunteered to collect the funds that we all chipped in so that she could travel and take care of whatever needed to be taken care of at home. I would like to commend James Bond officially for that. Outstanding work, 007, outstanding.

At our first rehearsal session, Spike said that he wanted the film to feel as if it was all ad-libbed. When I read the script, I knew that was gonna have to happen anyway, simply because of the way it was written. It was written, to me, as a skeleton. It was very much a blueprint, the foundation of a building. Spike is the architect. He takes his tools and he draws up the sketch of this building. We are the construction company that comes in to build it, under his supervision. The ad-libs came out of Spike's faith in our understanding of the story.

It's nice to get that type of freedom. For me, it was the first time I had been given as much. I'm used to having a director hold me back. Francis Coppola would give me some stuff to do, but he would still hold me back just a bit. But with Spike, it was, "Here's the ball." And when that happens to you for the first time, you think Oh, God! What am I gonna do? After I got over the fear—"Oh, shit, I got the ball," I said—okay, I'm gonna run with it. How am I doing, coach? So that's what the ad-libs were about.

I did one ad-lib that was too sick. It was something like, "Let's do the glocose connection." Spike said, "Enough of that." But at least he gave me the opportunity to try it. Another favorite ad-lib I got to do is in the scene where I'm in the shantytown talking to my people. It wasn't an ad-lib per se; I was quoting Dr. Welsing—"All you have to do is get a bus and take it to like any downtown inner city, with a sign saying all the fried chicken you can eat, all the drugs, all the alcohol you want, and Black folks would get on the bus." Bill Nunn ("Grady") did some incredible ad-libs. And I don't think he even got loose. I know there's more where that came from. "Collard greens and Wilson Pickett. If you don't scream, I won't holler!" That's Bill.

I feel as though I put a lot of work into the film, so it's really more than a film to me. What's important is that it inspires all of us to continue to make films in the tradition of *School Daze*. It shouldn't be unusual that a group of young Black people can get together and make a brilliant film about their own experiences, and their own existence in this country, or any country on the planet. It shouldn't be an eyebrow-raiser. You know, it should be like, Yeah, that's right! We're making a film. Oh, really? Can we help you? should be the response. It shouldn't be unusual that we can make films. It shouldn't be unusual that we can start a country. I think it is that we all understand that. It lets us folk know how important, how intelligent, how creative, how resourceful, how beautiful and marvelous, wonderful, and how perfect we are.

ROGER SMITH ("YODA") ▸ I was in Minneapolis doing a season there with the Guthrie Theatre's acting company when Spike Lee's *She's Gotta Have It* came down the pike. I sat through it twice, loved it, and said, "This is important, I've got to get hooked up in this somehow." So I started doing research, calling around, asking folks who is this Spike Lee guy, where can he be found, what is he doing next? Then I heard about *School Daze* and I thought there must be a role in it for me. Fortunately the timing was right. By the time I came back to L.A. from Minneapolis, they were holding auditions.

I had planned a trip to Hawaii for the week to get "colored." Not for the *School Daze* audition, but for myself, after having been in Minneapolis so long. I had an initial reading with Robi in L.A. and she said, "Okay, great, we'll have you in for a callback for Spike." Spike was on his way to town and his time was limited; he was seeing people on certain days and that would be it. It was either stay in L.A., audition for Spike, and miss my trip to Hawaii (the ticket was nonrefundable), or go to Hawaii and blow the film. I almost went, but at the last minute I got a doctor's excuse saying I was deadly ill and the airline changed my ticket. I auditioned for Spike after all, and obviously, I'm glad I did.

I was asked to read sides for Spike, sing a song, and do a comic monologue. I sang "La La La La La Means I Love You," a cappella, and told a dirty joke. Wasn't sure if the singing part was really serious. I was hoping not. I can rap, but I'm not a great singer. I gave it my best shot and ended up squeezing some rap into it anyway. My joke went like this:

Last night I was with my old lady, we were making beautiful love in the park, and a police officer came and shined the light on us. I got up and hit the police officer, bam. And he said, "What did you hit me for?" And I said, "Because I was making beautiful love to my old lady here and you came and shined the light on us." And then my old lady got up, pulled up her panties, and hit me, bam. I said, "Baby, what did you hit me for?" She said, "Honey, 'cause you hit the police officer." I said, "What do that mean? I was making beautiful love to you and he came and shined the light on us." And she said, "Honey, the police officer done you a favor, you been eating grass for the last half hour."

Yes, Spike laughed. I guess then he realized I was ill enough to do what he needed done for the frat-brother roles.

I've never been in a frat and I didn't go to a Black college, although my older brother did. He and my father were members of Omega Psi Phi at Howard University. My brother is eleven years older than I am. When I was a kid, I would hear him doing these chants. They didn't make much sense then, but I remember them pretty vividly. So I put that family experience together with a sense of the militaristic nature of the whole thing and I went with it. The social element, that was really no problem. I grew up in Jack and Jill—a social organization with chapters across the country devoted to the children of affluent Blacks—and I was able to draw on that.

In high school I was president of clubs called Vogues and Esquires, which is like the senior group of Jack and Jill. All these kids have grown up together and their mothers are friends. I went before the mothers and told them I thought it should be disbanded. By the time kids got into ninth and tenth grades, they'd already made their social contacts, and anything beyond that, I argued, was just forced. I caused quite an uproar, but I didn't lose my title, because I was the people's champion! So I guess you could say I'm very familiar with the Black social hierarchy that Jack and Jill and the frats represent.

I didn't do anything drastic before leaving L.A. as a way of preparing for the role. It all came together at the reading of the script we had that first day of rehearsals. Just sitting around that long table with everyone, soaking in the atmosphere, the people from all over, the energy, it was truly like going back to college. That was the greatest challenge for me, and probably why I attacked it so aggressively. I had been out of undergradute school for ten years. And I knew I'd have to commit myself gung ho in order to be believeably juvenile.

I came up with this heavy-duty thing for my character, "Yoda," since Spike asked me to coordinate the Gammites. I tried to align him with a certain sense of politics and history. Whether or not that comes through after the edit is another story! But it was a choice I made, and I think it served me well. I came up with the idea that "Yoda" had been in the military. Actually he had taken part in the invasion of Grenada and got into college on the GI Bill. All of which made it believable that "Yoda" was older and wiser than the rest of the Gammites and they looked up to him. I decided that politically he had become frustrated with the military while in Grenada. So when we see him in the film, he's aligned with the Fellas rather than the Wannabees. (In the sequel, "Yoda" will become "Dean Big Brother Almighty" and reform the entire fraternity system!) There were also a few things I tried to work in, in terms of the improvised dialogue. When the pledgees went over, at the Death March, I made a point of cussing out Margaret Thatcher and Ronald Reagan. And when I got my Gamma shirt, I said, "Fuck the Ku Klux Klan, I'm a goddamn Gamma man."

Monique Mannen (ensemble Gamma Ray) and I missed the flight for the actors from L.A. to Atlanta by about two seconds. We were practically banging on the door of the plane. We ended up on an evening flight (which was cool, because we sat behind Isaac Hayes), and when I finally got to the hotel it was quite late. I didn't get to meet folks until the next day and missed out on all the rumors about the "segregation" of cast members into different hotels.

Now about that segregation, I think it may have served to create more animosity toward Spike than amongst the actors. I never thought there was any true animosity between the so-called Wannabees and Jigaboos. However, there was certainly a kind of recognition of the possibility of that animosity. It seemed to work as a kind of shock therapy for some folks. My imagination is so warped that I don't need stuff like that to get myself going. But for some people it may have been helpful.

The conflict really was a conflict of artistry. There was true conflict among the Gammites, because you've got eight guys, including Spike, who work in completely different ways; guys who have different levels of physical training and approaches to developing a character. There were guys who had done films, and those who had more TV experience. Some had done almost nothing but classical theater. And there was a wide range of ages and experience.

There was extraordinary pressure, physical demands, psychological demands. We had some guys at each other's throats. As leader of the group and as a guy who doesn't like to see people get hurt, I had to chill this out a number of times. We had serious conflict between Dominic (Dominic Hoffman, Gammite "Mustafa") and Kirk (Kirk Taylor, Gammite "Sir Nose") simply because of the different ways they worked. When we did the dog-walk sequence, which was our first day on camera, those two had a screaming match. There was taxing physical activity involved in the scene and it was cold that day. People were telling other people what to do and what not to do left and right.

Kirk and Dominic's thing was a silly little human type of conflict that happens when people are under pressure like that, and when guidance of the thing is still in its developing stage. We got a lot better as the time went on. We made a point to get together every day, even when we weren't called to the set. We'd get together and do physical warm-ups, vocal warm-ups, sometimes improvisations. Or we'd just play some football or basketball.

Spike basically handed things over to me. He said, "You're in charge of the Gammites. I don't have that much time and I can't spend it all with the guys, so it's gonna be up to you to coordinate these things." He got together with us once and went through everything we had to do in the script. We had a list of things to accomplish: the roll call, the method of marching, the dog walk, the method of addressing the Big Brothers. These were very intricate steps that had to be rehearsed on a daily basis. I was proud of what we put together. If we hadn't had all that rehearsal time, it would have been pure chaos in front of the camera. And that's what the frat thing is about, organization, as we learned from the real Greeks in Atlanta.

I believe Spike is the only one of the Gammites who attended a Black college. Eric went to Brown, Dominic went to Santa Cruz. But at some point we all had contact with someone who had gone to a Black college. My nephew was on line at Morehouse at the same time I was on line. He'd come to me every Tuesday and Thursday, hiding out from his big brothers, and crash in my hotel room. I picked up a lot from him: the fatigue, the persecution, the whole head trip they put you through. His going over coincided with the Gammites', it was practically simultaneous.

I have this great theory that *School Daze,* the film, will prove to be a very interesting comment on culture. Here's the example: The Gammites, the pledgees who are supposedly Wannabees, are perhaps the most African men on campus, culturally that is; their sense of kinship, bonding, their sense of movement, rhythm, the chants, call and response, addressing the elders. It's all very African. They've got all this happening, but they see themselves as Greeks (or on the float at the parade as Egyptians, which is getting closer!). On the other hand, you've got "Dap" and the Fellas, who are talking Africa, who are looking at Africa from a political perspective. This paradox is at the heart of the dilemma as African-Americans—the unification of the political and the cultural. That's what I feel Spike's entire operation, Forty Acres and a Mule, is doing, and we all need to be about that.

When I went to see *She's Gotta Have It* for the first time, it was with a group of white actors from the Guthrie who felt the film was hilarious, yuk, yuk, yuk, a great comedy. I happened to have seen a whole lot more in there. I thought, Yes, it was amusing, but there was so much more in the film in terms of what it had to say about where we are now, where we've been, and where we could go. Something which wasn't apparent to my comrades, for obvious reasons.

Whether or not you deal with Jesse Jackson, you have to consider the history of his coming down to Atlanta to bless *School Daze*. And what that invocation had to say about the responsibility of our generation. It says we have to make good on the struggles of those who have come before us. We're the first generation to have grown up with integration legally as a fact. We were exposed to the social and political upheaval of the late '60s, early '70s. But the movement continues in different ways now. One of the major arenas it continues in is in the media. The media battlefield.

Robeson said the artist must elect to fight for slavery or freedom. I've made my choice. The sacrifices and struggles of those who have come before me must now come to pay off. One thing Jesse Jackson said was it's not enough to have opportunity these days. For our generation, it's not enough to go to New York University, it's not enough simply to go to Yale. At some point you have to make good on your potential, on your promise. And I see an example of the fruition of this promise happening with this project.

It was extraordinary that actors like Joe Seneca and Ossie Davis were pulled into this project. It must give them satisfaction to know that the work they've done will continue, that when they're gone, another group of people, even more dedicated, more strident, more organized, will continue the work. That's one of most important facets of this project. No matter how much money it makes, there is something that can never be taken away from this project: It brought the generations together and it dealt with issues that are usually only dealt with in the kitchen. And it was done expediently and in good taste.

ROBI REED ▸ The color and class issue that the film explores was a very real thing for the actors, and it started early on with separate hotel arrangements—the Jigs at the modest Ramada Inn and the Gamma Rays and all the male actors at the plush Regency Suites. At the auditions I spoke with various actors about the issue, and they said, "It's only a movie, we can step away." But many weren't able to. There were some Jigs who gave Tisha a hard time, just disliked her, refused to see beyond her character. The dark skin/light skin thing had a noticeable effect on them and the Gamma Rays. With the Gamma Rays it was about acting like "superior beings."

Tyra Ferrell (Gamma Ray "Tasha") is very Black, very culturally aware, very much into being who she is. She was adamantly against Black people changing the color of their eyes with contact lenses. But then we cast her in this role, the darkest Gamma Ray. She made such a personal adjustment. She went and bought a pair of blue contacts even before she got to Atlanta and wore them around town in L.A., just to get used to it. She became this very difficult person. I know Tyra personally and I know she's not who she played in the film. But in Atlanta I couldn't stand her when she was "Tasha," which was most of the time. The Jigs felt left out and mistreated the entire shoot. They had qualms about how there was never as much time spent on their hair and makeup as there was with the Gamma Rays. They never understood that was just the nature of the roles. But it really bothered them, so we had to go to the makeup and hair department and ask them to spend a little more time with the Jigs, even if they weren't actually applying any more makeup.

It's a very sensitive subject, class and color. And I think the majority of the people on the shoot thought they were beyond it. They were forced to examine it, though, and many realized they weren't as far removed from the issue as they thought.

JOIE LEE ("LIZZIE LIFE") ▸ The first week of rehearsal was horrible actually. I felt really out of place and I wanted to go home. Spike was trying to create this friction and I was resistant to it at first because it didn't seem natural. The first day of rehearsals when we broke for lunch he had everyone separate into their groups. I had wanted to ease into it naturally, stay on the outside and look in, but

The Gamma Rays. Weaves and blue contact lenses.

"Da Natural Sisters."

Spike wouldn't let me. He was kind of growling over my shoulder, pushing me to make myself known.

Spike had a good idea, it was great in a way, to create friction between the groups from the beginning. And I know there were more people who found it easier to jump into the situation than I did. Not knowing the people who were on your side and not knowing those on the other side, and having to build a relationship with the Jigs and conjure up this animosity for the other group, was very difficult. I kind of wanted to hang out with my brothers. That's how lost I felt and it took me some time to adjust.

I was trying to bring something to an individual character and it seemed as if it was more important to represent a Jigaboo rather than this one character, and it made the first week difficult. I got lost in this war game. Everything I worked on—building a character—was just completely shot down. It was more important that I be a Jigaboo rather than "Lizzie Life," this character, who is perceived as a Jigaboo by others. And was being a Jigaboo a perception of the Wannabees or was I a Jigaboo at heart? And just what was a Jigaboo?

Something like this isn't gonna happen so often, an all-Black cast and a strong cast too. There were so many beautiful people involved, and I think people just went crazy, men and women. It seemed that the interest of the males really did lie in the lighter-skinned women. The men were running after the Wannabees as if they were the last women on earth. And we (the Jigaboos) took it to heart. It's not that we wanted to establish relationships, it was more like friendships. It was hard to get to know anyone outside of our group, particularly males, due to the fact that the Jigaboo women were all at one hotel, while the male and female Wannabees and the Jig men were all at the other hotel. Alva, who played "Doris," and I would have conversations in Atlanta about feeling like a Jigaboo on and off camera. We felt we weren't wanted, felt conscious of our physical appearance: the shade of our skin, the texture of our hair. We weren't Wannabees, and the Wannabee women were fine, you know?

Our sense of Jig community began as soon as we started rehearsals for "Straight and Nappy." After rehearsal, the Jigs would get in one van and go to the Ramada and the Wannabees would go to the Regency. During the eight-week period, we spent a lot of time riding in the van to the rehearsal or the set. A lot happened on those rides,

A family portrait: my sister Joie, my grandmother Zimmie Shelton, and myself. The shooting of the film took a heavy toll on my grandmother. She knows everybody in Atlanta and the break from Morehouse put her in a sticky situation. T. M. Alexander, a big man on the Morehouse board of directors, is a lifelong friend and was the person with whom I was clashing. He advised President Hugh Gloster to give us da boot.

and one thing was finding out that we were all adamant about not being able to spend time with the Jig men.

ALVA ROGERS ("DORIS WITHERSPOON") ▸ We Jigs were getting shafted. It was as if we only had each other. It was just like real life. Spike was trying to make this one point and he made us become a stereotype.

JOIE ▸ The Wannabees, I felt, were pampered.

ALVA ▸ They were very pampered.

JOIE ▸ They were extremely pampered, and we were just out there.

ALVA ▸ So we said, "Okay, well, if Teddy Jenkins, our hair and makeup artist, is not going to do our hair, let's get together and help each other out." The hair, the makeup . . .

JOIE ▸ The costumes . . .

ALVA ▸ We wore our own things on camera. We'd ask each other, "Do you have something I can wear at the football game?" We used to eat dinner together, order Chinese food, practice dance steps on the hotel balcony. And we'd have rap sessions in Eartha Robinson's room, 'cause we said, "We have to talk about this, we have to get our shit together."

JOIE ▸ When we met in the morning for rehearsal in the lobby, we had some great rap sessions down there. Most of these were completely spontaneous. While waiting for the van we'd start talking about each other, our feelings and the other cast members. We needed to release a lot of stuff. We felt as if we were not being treated equally, so we created a support system.

ALVA ▸ We gave each other compliments and hugs.

JOIE ▸ There was no malice, just intensity, enduring this hostile situation every day. We made each other laugh. It was the only way.

JOIE ▸ There was a period when none of the Wannabees would come over to the Ramada.

ALVA ▸ None of the Wannabees except Paula Brown—Gamma Ray "Miriam"—and Michelle Whitney Morrison—Gamma Ray "Vivian."

JOIE ▸ Paula, Michelle—who else came over? We don't want to leave anybody out.

ALVA ▸ Tisha came over a couple of times.

JOIE ▸ It was interesting, because by the end of the film no one cared. All the attitudes just leveled off. But people did carry their characters with them beyond the set. It got to be kind of ridiculous at times. That came out at the Greek Show when we kind of traded those lyrics . . .

ALVA ▸ " . . . your eyes are blue, but you ain't white, your hair is straight, cause you pressed it last night."

JOIE ▸ That verse blew the Gamma Rays away; they took it very, very personally. All these chants were improvised. And the Gamma Rays were looking at us like, Are you playing a character or not? Some of them were so upset, in tears even.

ALVA ▸ That was the night of Spike's birthday party, too. Kyme said to us, "Come on you guys, let's get together. Let's party. Let's not take this to heart." But lots of people didn't go to the party that night.

JOIE ▸ Yeah. I think "Tisha" was upset at what the Gamma Rays yelled at the Jigs.

JOIE ▸ Michelle was upset too because she didn't want to call us monkeys and baboons. When I heard their verse, in character, I thought it was hysterical. There was something very deep, yet something very comical, very humorous about it. I tried to put it in character, which is to say the Jigs would not even stoop so low as to respond to something like that. But it pained the Wannabees to say those things. Apparently the Gammas and Gammites had composed the verse for them. But I thought it was great, how we fed off each other and composed these chants at the spur of the moment.

ALVA ▸ Shortly after the Greek Show, the Gamma Rays stopped wearing their weaves all the time, some of them at least. For a long time though, quite a few—I don't know if they had a choice or not—kept their weaves on even off camera.

JOIE ▸ Which is funny, because when they first had the weaves put in, they were complaining all the time.

ALVA ▸ One was complaining all the time, but she kept that bad boy in the whole time; she left with her weave.

JOIE ▸ Yes, she left with that weave.

TISHA CAMPBELL ("JANE TOUSSAINT") ▸ Kyme and I were the only two girls around for the first week of rehearsal. So there was an immediate bond. I'm glad that we were together, because we established a friendship that has lasted. We were both nervous at first. Kyme wanted to know if I was really a Wannabee. And I kept hoping she wouldn't think that I was. I was nervous about going down to Atlanta, period. I was the youngest in the cast and this was my first adult role. It was also the first time I'd been cast with so many women. I'm eighteen and I've played teenager roles for a while. I realize now that people take me differently when I'm playing a teenager.

It was hard for me to play this character, but I wanted to do it because it was different from the roles I usually play. The thing about my character, "Jane," is that she could be so easily "vamped out." She's already stupid, okay. But I didn't want to play her stupid. I wanted to put an innocence in Jane. There's this innocence that people see in me, and I tried to put it in Jane. To make her naive, rather than stupid; confused, rather than whorish or sluttish. When it came to "Julian," her man, I tried to make "Jane's" innocence really show through. When she's with the Gamma Rays, that's a different story. That's when she becomes her own woman. She's their leader and she's stronger with them. I think that was because she had to stay on top of herself to keep "Julian." I hated "Jane." I still hate her.

There was one time when I honestly felt that I was this character. We were filming the Greek Show and I knew that I was she, and I began to hate the Gamma Rays, the Jigs, and hate myself. It was one of the Gammas who actually came up with the rhyme about the Jigaboos that the Gamma Rays shouted in the Greek Show. If we'd had the time, I think we would have made up something ourselves, something that wasn't so harsh. To me, both rhymes felt uncalled for. I looked over towards them (the Jigs) when we had finished chanting. There must have been this expression on my face of anger mixed with hurt. Tracey Robinson (ensemble Jig) called my name, not "Jane," but Tisha. I looked, blinked my eyes, and looked again, and she said, "We know you're a Jig, we know you're a Jig."

I guess she was trying to get me out of it because I was sinking. I felt myself becoming this character and I knew I had to stop it. I mentally separated myself from everybody and became really quiet. I wasn't talking to either group. This was right before one of the Fellas grabbed my head and the fight broke out. It seemed like I was the cause of it, which made me feel worse. After the Step Show, after it all happened, I went outside the gym by myself. I couldn't stand being around everyone for another minute. I was really upset and about to cry when Kyme caught up with me. We talked for a while. She said, "I hated you at one point because it was so real."

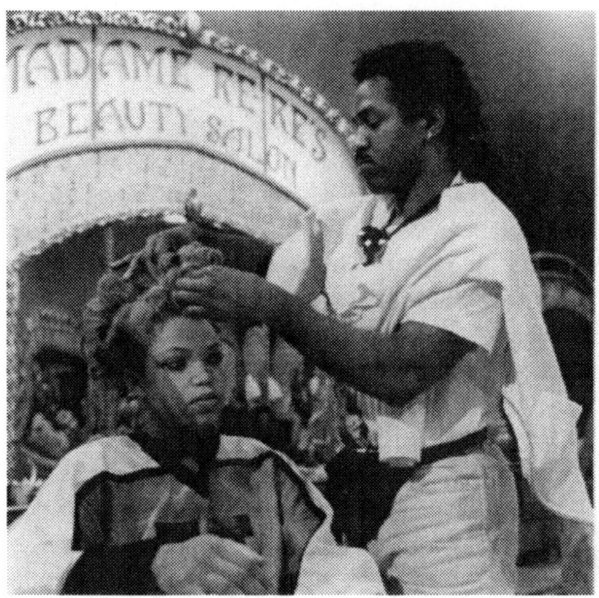

Hair-makeup person Teddy Jenkins does Tisha's do. The Jigs complained that Teddy ignored them. I do know for sure that Ms. Campbell got the most attention from Mr. Jenkins.

The Gammites get the "wood" from "Big Brother General George Patton." The scene as it is in the film is considerably shorter than it was scripted.

We just held each other and I promised myself it would never happen again.

What made it so real was the separation between the two groups. Spike was so slick. I didn't really think about what he did until it was finally over. Kyme and I kept wondering when we were first separated, Why would Spike separate the women?

There was even a sense of separation within the Wannabees. The Jigs were so close, I was jealous of how close they were. I wanted to be that way. I wanted to be close to somebody, I guess the Gamma Rays. But I always felt in the middle, like I wasn't with anybody. When I think about it, there could never have been this closeness between the Wannabees; there were too many clashing personalities. Spike knew what he was doing. He and Robi cast the hell out of this movie. The actors were so real to me. The only one of the Gamma Rays whom I really hung out with off the set was Jasmine Guy, Gamma Ray "Dina." I always wanted to go over to the other side and pass for a Jig! But I understood what I had to do, and I had to be a Gamma Ray, I had to.

Method acting is fine, it works for me in my ways, but there is a time when you have to turn your character off—especially a character like "Jane." You have to turn her on and off like a light switch. I could not be this person, I could not be a Wannabee. I have no problem with being Black. Black isn't a color to me, it is a culture. I'm Black and I'm proud of it. There's no difference between being darker or lighter, to me.

I'm the lightest one in my family. My brothers have always teased me about it, called me a little white girl and all this other stuff. And to this day I've always wanted to be darker. And to this day they still call me white girl! It may seem like light-skinned people act a certain way—want the long hair, want the blue eyes. I know it was exaggerated for the movie, but it's not so with every light-skinned person. There's another story that needs to be told.

Whenever the Gamma Rays—the actresses—tried to have a meeting, it was the same as the one you see on-screen, very unorganized, everyone had her own views. I didn't help at all, because Tisha isn't a good leader like "Jane" the character. Tisha could not take control of the meetings offscreen. What's weird is I heard the Gamma actors' meetings were similar. That everyone had his own views and the meetings wound up nowhere. Most of our meeting time was spent trying to justify that we weren't the bad guys. Spike told us we weren't. But in the script it just seemed that we were. We tried to say that our characters weren't Wannabees; they were just trying to get ahead in life, go to college, and better themselves. We wanted to say that the Jigs were too rebellious and impatient. It was hard for me to sit through meetings where this was said because I felt that neither group was the bad guy.

When Kyme and I were first shown around the Atlanta University Center, we met some members of the Delta Sigma Pheta Sorority Incorporated and they explained the organization and their views. They said they'd give the shirts off their backs to a Delta, that they loved each other. The bond between them seemed similar to the one the Jigs had. I asked them about Alpha Kappa Alpha Sorority Incorporated and how I could meet one. They said the AKAs are Wannabees, that they are always dressed and they go around thinking they're better than other people.

Another thing the Deltas said was—excuse me for this—but that the AKAs will "dick" each other around. That they aren't as close as the Deltas are, and there's always jealousy between them. I never got to talk to any of the AKAs. I did ask the Deltas, "Are all of you dark-skinned?" And they said no. And I said, "Are all the AKAs light-skinned?" They said yes. I guess we are divided that way.

I asked my best friend, who goes to Howard, if this stuff was still an issue there. She said that she was walking down her dorm hall recently and she heard this girl say to her friend, "I don't like my new roommate, she's too dark." It's shocking, but it's still alive.

LARRY FISHBURNE ▸ Giancarlo and I are buddies, pals. We work differently, but we're sensitive to those differences. Despite them, we look for the same results: strong, powerful performances. Very intense performances. It's the way we arrive at them that is different. Giancarlo's method is a lot more physical than mine. For *School Daze,* he started working out, training physically, to prepare for all the Step Show stuff and to be commander in chief of the quasi-military organization, Gamma Phi Gamma.

While we were in Atlanta, Giancarlo went down to Little Five Points and ended up in an antique store. He has a thing for school chairs—the old ones with built-in desks—and this shop had a bunch he liked. He also saw this sawed-off bat and thought, Wow, this would be good for my character. He bought the chairs, didn't buy the bat, but mentioned to the proprietor of the store that he might want to come back for it.

Giancarlo couldn't take all the chairs with him at once, so the next day he asked me to pick up the two he left. I went down, asked the guy about the chairs, and he said, "Yeah, they're right there." I saw the little bat near the chairs and I said to myself, Man, this would be just right for Giancarlo, it would work perfectly with his character. I bought the bat for four dollars and went to Giancarlo and said, "Yo, here's your Little Darling." He had it spray-painted and it's in the film.

We just know each other that way. It's a very unusual thing we have. We've always wanted to work together again since we did *Cotton Club*. Giancarlo played one of my bodyguards. We were getting ready to shoot a scene in the backstage of a theater. Wooden beams were all around the place and there was this ice pick stuck in one of the beams. Immediately I thought about Giancarlo, how it would be really hip for his character. So I grabbed the ice pick and took it to him right away. For the next couple of weeks he was walking around with this ice pick in his jacket. He'd do this thing where he'd lean over (he had these red glasses, they added to it) and open his jacket a bit and give you a peek. It got so scary that the prop guy took the ice pick away from him. I was with Giancarlo when the prop guy came to confiscate it. Giancarlo left the room in a hurry. Three minutes later he comes back and he's got the ice pick again.

THE CREW

LARRY BANKS (GAFFER) ▸ My crew was split fifty-fifty. Carl Johnson, my third electrician, and myself are Black. Mark Moore, who was my second, and John Massey, my fourth, are White. There were no problems with my immediate crew. We were relatively tight in that sense, although we weren't much of a hanging-out crew. My guys all would go their different ways when the day was over. Mark was on his way to the country. His wife is a stewardess and he was always trying to catch her for a couple of hours before she got on a plane. John was headed home and Carl would sometimes hang out a bit. But he would split for home after a while. I can't forget Pete Peterson, the generator operator, who is white. If there was such a thing as a crew person of the year award, Pete would win. If there was any kind of problem, if something would break down—anything from the transmission of the truck to a light—Pete would take it apart and fix it. He could take that generator apart piece by piece and put it back together. He was one of the sweetest people on the whole crew. I had young Addison Cook driving the truck for me. Not much experience, but lots of youthful arrogance. The only person his arrogance didn't spill onto was me. Because he respected me. Everyone else, he looked at like a dirty dog.

I would hear certain things from Todd McNichol, the key grip, things that would get back to him. Todd himself is used to working for and with Black people. Coming from New York, one of the people who trained him is George Patterson, out of NABET—the National Association of Broadcast Employees and Technicians—and he is Black. Because Todd is white and his entire crew was too, he was privy to talk that I wouldn't hear. No one on the grip or electric crews, to the best of my knowledge, had ever worked for a Black DP or Black director before. And though they didn't have to deal with Ernest or Spike directly, both crews had to deal with me, as a Black gaffer, because gaffers in pictures generally have to direct both the grips, in terms of where their services are needed on the set, and the electrical department. I never had any problems, but there was a bit of an undercurrent happening, a challenge to see if I really knew what I was doing. I had more experience than anyone in these departments, so there was never any real conflict, but there was that sense of challenge.

It's hard to say because some of it may have been based on the jealousy and annoyance that guys in the South feel whenever a picture comes into town. They get the jobs as best boys and on the crew, but they never get the jobs as the keys, because everybody brings their keys from out of town. They bring them from New York and they bring them from California, but in most cases they don't pick up their keys in Atlanta. So there's always this unspoken resentment for the out-of-towners.

So Todd would talk to me about some of the things that he'd heard from the grips, some of the comments about Black people. You've got to realize that this was a first-time situation for them in many ways. They hadn't worked on a Black film and they definitely weren't used to Black humor. There was the Black humor in the movie, the Black humor used by Black people around the set, and the Black humor that some of the white crew members started throwing around. It became a little bit of a game for them, to see how far they could go.

It started the first day of shooting; it was the scene where the Fellas meet up with the town folk in the restaurant and there's a conflict, Black against Black. There was a funny line which everyone kept running back, "What time it is," then they'd laugh. The grips kept repeating it in this overdone Black southern accent, as the actor had done. They'd say, "What time it is," then yuk, yuk, yuk.

When we shot the Greek Show, there was some real tension then. The two groups of girls, the Gamma Rays and the Jigs, were catcalling to each other from the sidelines. One line was, "Who wants Gamma Ray, everyone's had a Gamma Ray." But the line that the grips kept repeating was something like, "Went to the zoo to find a Jigaboo, saw a nappy-headed thing and it looked like you." (Note: Actual verse chanted by Gamma Rays at Greek Show was "Who wants a Jigaboo? Why don't you check the local zoo? 'Cause we spent the other day at the local zoo. And they had a big, nappy beast and it looked like you. And we looked up at the cage, it said Jigaboo.")

Certain white crew members kept running that stuff back and a few people got pissed. They didn't want to hear those words coming out of a white person's mouth. They didn't want to hear those lines thrown back at them. I guess the whites thought they could get away with it as long as it was in the film.

My third electrician works out of Atlanta. He found himself in a weird position because he works with these people a lot and has to continue working with them. He would get very quiet around that kind of stuff. I don't think he felt comfortable with it, but at the same time, he couldn't jump, he couldn't say, "Take that language and shove it" or "Do that when you get home, because I don't want to hear it."

So we had our tensions, but none of it ever surfaced very far. Because, let's face it, on the set there are rules and etiquette. When it came down to it, everyone toed the line, came through with what he had to come through with. So if there was an ill feeling, it never spilled over to, "I ain't gonna take that kind of shit from a nigger."

Everybody played a little bit of the dozens, though. The crew, they'd joke with you, they'd play with you. A couple of times I had to throw a joke out myself just to let a person know that I wasn't letting his stuff go by, just to say, "You're not the only one who can joke about stuff like that. It can come back to you."

BARRY BROWN (EDITOR) ▸ The feeling that I had when we were all down in Atlanta was one I used to get a long time ago in theater, especially in summer theater. It was a feeling of people pulling together for something bigger and better. And it was a feeling that I hadn't had for a long time, not since I was a teenager. I loved being close to it. I didn't realize I had it until Marty, my wife, verbalized it. Marty came to Atlanta to visit a couple of times and she was so jealous. She said, "This is like working in the theater again, everyone's like a family." It wasn't really a family, but there was that sense at times.

Someone on the production came into the editing room in Atlanta one time and I was really pissed off. He said something about me being the coolest white guy he ever met. He meant it as a compliment, but it was a kind of insult. It was someone who didn't know me, so I shouldn't have taken it one way or the other. I should have just kicked him out. Every now and then I'd get questions like "How are white people gonna react to this picture?" "As a representative of the white race . . . " How would I know? Am I the quintessential white person? Spike doesn't think of me that way. I don't think he does. If he did, he'd never have me edit his film.

I never really think of *School Daze* as a "Black film." I just look at it as an editor would look at any film—is this scene funny, is it not funny? Is something touching, is an actor in character, did an actor deliver the line well? Or did he flub it? Is there an energy coming across? Is this love scene working or is there something I don't believe about it? *School Daze* is no different from any other motion picture in that respect.

The characters in the film represent so many different types. "Dap" reacts and thinks in ways that many campus radicals would. I've been in a lot of situations were I was riding around in a car with five other guys on top of each other, all the time ranking each other out, talking about their sexual powers, about the other person's mother, about the car they're riding in; the same as "Dap" and the Fellas did. *School Daze* is to me as much about the human condition as any other picture. But so was *She's Gotta Have It.* Any good motion picture is, whether it's made in India or Japan or America. Some white people I know marveled at *She's Gotta Have It* and said, "Wow, even I can relate to these characters." These sorts of statements disgust me. Why the fuck shouldn't you be able to relate?

RANDY FLETCHER (FIRST ASSISTANT DIRECTOR) ▸ I guess I dealt with more people overall than anyone else on the shoot, except the director. There were some racial slurs, and I'm not the type to back down, smile, and grin. That was the mentality of one crew person in particular. I handled it just as I would handle it if I were on 125th Street. If you think because I'm a different color than you that I'm any less of a man, then we can step behind the trucks.

I did see some tensions among the white women crew members. Before the cast came in, they got attention, but when the cast arrived, there was a bunch of beautiful Black women to compete with. It must have hurt. I think most of them had worked on predominantly white films before. Ours was basically a Black crew. And no one was smiling, grinning, and asking them to go to dinner, which is the usual occurrence on a film. It was as if their womanhood was threatened, that's my theory.

I had a couple of run-ins with white women crew members over job responsibilities and little things like helping to clean up. Towards the end of the shoot they seemed more frustrated than anyone else working on the picture, and I don't think it was because their jobs were harder than anyone else's. All of us were tired. All of us went through the same thing.

WYNN THOMAS (PRODUCTION DESIGNER) ▸ There were no major racial problems with the art department. Working with me was the first time any of them had worked for a Black production designer. I don't think my set decorator wanted to do the project, at least initially. First of all, she wasn't getting paid what she normally does. It was several hundred dollars less than she was accustomed to making and she's worth it. She's a fine decorator. I felt she was a little leery of working for me when I first me her. After the first three weeks, and she could see that I knew what I was doing, she relaxed. Her whole persona changed. At the end of the shoot she came up to me and said, "You know, Wynn, you are the most talented designer I have ever worked for."

I think there is this assumption that we are not as talented, and that's when racial situations arise. This happens to me often. I am almost always the first Black production designer or art director that a crew has ever dealt with. And you have to prove yourself right away with them, all the time. Or at least convince them that you can talk. One of the things that we have to be in this business is articulate.

One thing that happened early on, in the first or second week of production, was a confrontation of sorts with a crew person of mine, a white woman. She was putting up some props in the storage area in the back of the production office. The entire set-dressing crew was there plus the props department. I said to this person, "Can you come here and do something for me or come help me with something?" She said, "I's 'acomin', boss." I turned to her and said, "Don't ever say that to me, don't ever talk to me like that." And I never heard words like that for the rest of the shoot.

MATIA KARRELL ▸ When I first got to Atlanta, Tyrone Harris, locations manager, picked me up at the airport and I think he was in a little bit of a shock. He said something like, "Oh, I was expecting a sister." Then he was fumbling and apologizing and I said, "That's okay, Tyrone." When we got to the hotel we went up to the desk together and he asked for my key. The clerk gave us two keys. Tyrone started to laugh, a laugh that only Tyrone has. Then he told the clerk he wasn't with me and gave him back a key. It was as if he was enjoying the experience. And I'd just gotten off the plane. I didn't know what was going on.

I don't see myself as white, I just don't. And what's funny, what was interesting to me, is that it's like a luxury, in a sense. The luxury of being white is that you don't think in color, of your own color. When I talked to Tyrone, everything was about the Black man, Black skin. It's always there. Somehow it would always preface his experience.

Monty and I had the hardest time understanding each other. I didn't realize my effect on him. I treated every dealing as a business exchange. It wasn't a power trip. But I had to realize that here's a man putting himself up as line producer. He has little experience, but he wants to be good and he wants to do a good job. I have the utmost admiration and respect for Monty because he really wanted to learn. He respected Grace a great deal. Learning from her, I think, was different from learning from me, 'cause she's Black. I had to learn not to let out my frustration and my fatigue and attack Monty on the basis of his inexperience, because I saw that it affected him too much. I don't know if I should even be saying this, but we had sessions where we each lost it a little bit. I would cry, I mean. Tears would well up in my eyes, 'cause I wasn't happy in our arguments, but they were arguments that no one wins and no one wants to win. No one even wants to have the arguments. But they come out in the circumstances and under the pressure and stress of making a film. All of sudden you blow up at each other.

Monty and Tyrone were in my office towards the end of the production and we were discussing how to make a location work. I don't remember what the issue of concern was, but I said something to the tune of "Is this Filmmaking 101?" Monty got very upset about that and I had to apologize later. I had to make him understand that my frustration was a bigger frustration. It wasn't directed at them personally but at having to take up slack in so many areas. Sometimes Tyrone would say things like, "Is this so bad? I didn't do so bad, did I, for a Black man?" Or he'd refer to himself as one of "us Black men." I guess I'm very lucky to have had that experience, you know.

Tyrone needed a lot of acknowledgment—"You're doing well, Tyrone." "It's wonderful, Tyrone." And at the same time I think if he had been a more experienced locations manager I wouldn't have had to expend that energy. But it's okay because it made me remember why I wanted to do the film. Spike, he's in it for all the right reasons. And it made me think about life in bigger terms. Sometimes you have to remember that life is not a business, that filmmaking is not just a business. It's a business about people.

DOWN SOUTH

ADDISON COOK (ELECTRICIAN) ▸ I went through an intensive workshop through New York University's School of Continuing Education. Came out in December 1986 with a dynamite film, best film in the class, *Texas Road*, and that brings us to the point where I met Spike. We were sitting in Du Art film labs, my friend Jeff Fererzeig, who was the producer of *Texas Road,* and I, and Jeff was eating a cup of clam bisque when lo and behold we see Spike walking up to the COD counter. Much to my chagrin and surprise, my friend Jeff yells out for everyone in the immediate area to hear, "Spike Lee is with us," he says with upraised hands. Spike is wearing his brown leather jacket and his Mets hat, and he just sorta turned. I was real embarrassed and said to myself, Oh, shit, I can't believe he just did that.

We went over and introduced ourselves and I told Spike that I lived in his neighborhood—I knew he lived out in Fort Green somewhere. We told him about *Texas Road.* We'd both seen *She's Gotta Have It* and we told him how much we liked it, which was true, we did. We told him we wanted to crew out for him on his next project. We were both out of work, so we figured what the hell. Spike was really nice, a lot more approachable than I had imagined. So as the clam bisque dripped off Jeff's chin, Spike told us to drop a VHS copy of the film and our résumés into his mailbox and we'd take it from there.

Actually I had seen Spike about two months earlier, watching the New York marathon just down the street from my apartment. I think he was with Larry Fishburne and Giancarlo Esposito, and we all know what happened to those wizards. I was going to approach him at the time, but all these people were coming up to him taking pictures. I thought, Shit, I don't want to bother him. People must do that to him every day. And why would he keep me in mind, some privileged white boy slumming it in Brooklyn?

I got a call in February from Randy, Randy Fletcher, who was transportation captain at the time; he asked me if I wanted to work as a production assistant on *School Daze* and could I come down early. I had listed all this director, writer, producer, B.A. Columbia junk on my résumé, but I guess the hook was I can drive any vehicle up to four axles, and they needed drivers. Could I come down in two days? I said, "Yeah, fine." He reminded me that they were hiring me as a local, and I'd have to find my own place to stay. Of course, over the phone I was saying, "Sure, no problem, no problem." But really I was scared shitless, thinking, How the hell am I going to find housing in Atlanta?

I couldn't have been so worried about it, 'cause I packed my bag that night and threw all my possessions into my fairly drivable Mercury (which later blew up on me towards the end of the production). I threw my bed into my car too, thinking, Wherever I end up, I'll get a good night's sleep. And I drove nonstop to Atlanta. Got in about nine o'clock the next morning and started driving for *School Daze* that afternoon.

I ended up driving for two weeks during preproduction, driving these vans, Ford Aerostars, which handled like sports cars, driving them about eighteen hours a day back and forth from the two hotels to the airport. I learned the whole city in a week. I spent a lot of time with Ernest Dickerson, driving him around to the camera tests and discussing cinematography. I was putting in twenty-hour days, not that everybody else wasn't doing the same.

Matia said to me a couple of days before our first day of shooting, "You're going out with those guys and loading up the five-ton electric truck." I said, "Oh? No kidding." She said, "You've driven a five-ton, haven't you?" I said, "Oh sure," but at the time I wasn't aware it was a split shift. I'd driven a split shift about seven years ago or more, so I was a little nervous.

Fortunately, when I got out to P.S.A., the equipment house, there were two greasy biker-type, motorcycle-helper, rat-bag kind of guys who gave me a few tips. One guy took me out in the parking lot for a test drive. He was saying, "This is a great truck, it's a great truck, she's called Jamie Lee, and she's got a brand-new motor, she really hauls ass." He gave me an impromptu driving lesson on the split shift, which ended up being easy to drive and a lot of fun. So that's how I became the driver of the electric truck.

If you don't know it, the drivers are always the first guys to get to the set and the last guys to leave. Very long hours, and we were not getting a union rate or anywhere even close to scale, but the experience was worth it. It seemed the norm that both the drivers of the grip truck and the electric truck would have their balls busted at least three times per hour about anything. We were the rookies and we took a lot of heat in a friendly sort of way. I was often reminded that I was from up north.

Carl Johnson, the third electrician, made sure I kept the truck in order and pretty much adopted me as a redheaded step-child. He had a lot of patience with me, because the electrics would send me to bring a piece of equipment to the set and every once in a while I'd bring back the wrong thing. They'd just laugh and laugh and laugh, but Carl would show me the right thing. He'd always say,

"Ad, you'd never make it in Alabama." I could never tell if he was serious or not. Another one of his sayings was, "Ad, you're a hell of a dog and one of these days we're gonna get you a bone." Bring you up to the big house. It was sort of a master-slave relationship. With juxtaposition that I was the slave and he was the massa.

I was born in Jackson, Michigan, a small town in the south-central part of the state. In my elementary school we had maybe one Black kid. And then in high school it was racially mixed, but there was a lot of racial hostility, the lines were definitely drawn. I guess what I'm trying to say is I wasn't apprehensive but I was curious about the racial makeup of the crew. Driving down, I kept thinking, What's it going to be like working in a situation where most of the people are Black? Turned out I found it very much to my liking and I was certainly a lot more at ease than I had anticipated.

I had dinner in New Jersey with this friend of mine and his family, all Italians. This was before I left for Atlanta. They thought I was crazy—"Oh, you're gonna be with all those Black people?" And I said, "Yeah, it's gonna be great." They couldn't believe I was doing it. "Well," they said, "if you come back we won't blame you at all."

Atlanta has some great alternative radio stations; I would have these punk rock or new wave stations all the time. I'd pick up some actors from rehearsal, they'd pile into the van, and almost immediately I'd hear, "Addison, what is this shit you're listening to?" They'd make me switch to a funk or soul station. I got pissed off one time because I'm a blues fanatic. Now, blues is definitely important in the Black experience, right? Twice people in the cast made me turn off the blues. The second time I turned around and said, "Hey, what's wrong with this music? Why do I have to educate you about the blues?" It wasn't a thing for me, but I was sort of surprised. But what the hell, I was just a driver. No big deal in that.

Everyone just accepted me, as far as just a white guy on a predominantly Black film, as just another guy from Brooklyn geting a lucky break. I ended up living with Mustafa (Mustafa Kahn, production assistant), who was a friend of mine I had met in film school, and Eric Oden (assistant auditor), both Black guys, and we had a blast. We hijacked a bunch of Kool-Aid and beer and had our little house in a totally Black neighborhood, Grant Park, and we had a ball. I taught Eric a song by the Ramones called "We're a Happy Family," and it was just the funniest thing he'd ever heard in his life.

Mustafa and I, we'd go home late at night after working on the shoot, and just say, "Hey, it's great we're working on this, that we got a chance." We'd think of the film class we just completed that December and name anyone in the film class and say, "They'd die to work on this." At the same time, from a filmmaker's point of view, there's Spike Lee and it's his deal. Boy, I'd love for this to happen to me someday, with my own story. So we were very envious, but at the same time all the way appreciative.

Fact is, if I hadn't worked on *School Daze,* I'd still just be another sluggo to come out of some film school with a little twenty-minute movie I can't do a thing with. And you're not going to have too many experiences like *School Daze* in Atlanta. I said to Carl one time, "Everybody's so nice down here in the South. It's not like Brooklyn at all, where everybody's ready to jump in your face for looking at 'em sideways." And he goes, "Ad, you know why everybody's so nice down here in the South?" And I said, "No, why?" He said, " 'Cause we all got pieces, and everybody knows that if one motherfucker gets out of hand, the other motherfucker is gonna shoot him."

5

THE LOOK

THE LOOK OF THE FILM

SPIKE ▸ I think Ernest and I accomplished the visual look we wanted for this film. We wanted the camera to always be moving, whether on a dolly or a crane. The camera moves in this film are really good. The camera's like a character itself, dancing around people.

ERNEST DICKERSON ▸ Spike and I got together during preproduction and we drew pictures. We came up with ideas of how we wanted to approach certain shots and scenes. I think I did a lot more of this on *School Daze* than on previous films because Spike was tied up with the actors. But I knew pretty much what he was going for based on our preliminary discussions. I came to Atlanta at the start of the two-week rehearsal period, but nobody saw me at the production office because I was in the hotel drawing storyboards.

One of the things that I wanted to do was work out a nice way of introducing each new character. An example is how the Gammites interrupt the Divest Now rally at the beginning of the film. First you hear, "It takes a real man to be a Gamma man, and only a

I gave the actors freedom to create their own characters. Guy Killums ("Double Rubber," Gammite #3) took advantage of it. It was his idea to wear a pair of prophylactics around his neck. Above, he sports a pair of them as the new craze in eye wear.

Otis Sallid.

The most close-knit group in the film was Da Fellas (left to right): Branford Marsalis, James Bond III, Kadeem Hardison, Bill Nunn, Larry Fishburne, and Eric Payne.

Traci Tracy, Branford Marsalis, and Laurnea Wilkerson.

Gamma man is a real man." The feet of the people at the rally step aside and then the Gammites' feet come marching into the frame. The camera slowly tilts up, so we take in all of their costumes and end up on their faces as they go by. Here again, we wanted to keep the camera moving, trying to keep a lot of movement within the frame, just keeping up with that homecoming energy.

A motif we used throughout the film was two people in profile, "up in each other's face." That was a conscious decision. We wound up having more than we originally planned for. You see it in the parade, with the two groups, the Gammas and "Dap's" people, on either side of the banner. You see it right before "Straight and Nappy," when Kyme and her girls bump into Tisha and the Gamma Rays in their dorm hallway. It's there again in the Kentucky Fried Chicken scene where "Dap" and his boys have a run-in with some local yokels.

As a cinematographer one thing I have to do is create a mood or suggest how characters are feeling through light. Back in my still-photography days, I did a lot of shooting with Kodachrome, which is a very fine-grained color slide film. The warmth and the light that I saw when we went down to see Morehouse's homecoming reminded me of Kodachrome. It has a tendency to make reds pop. The overall feeling I decided to go for in *School Daze* is very Kodachrome, very bright colors, popping. Bright colors are a very Afrocentric thing. If this film was taking place at a white school, I'd probably use more subdued colors. Even the camerman Nestor Almendros said that you can't put bright colors on white people. It makes them look ridiculous. You can put all the colors in the rainbow on Black people and they look absolutely beautiful.

There's hardly any white light in the whole film. We used bastard amber gels on our lights quite often, 'cause they warm things up a bit. We also put lights on dimmers pretty frequently. As you dim the lights down, they get warmer in color temperature. I like the way warmer lights look on Black skin tones. Black people have red, yellow, or orange undertones, so a warmer light brings the skin to life. I used a softer light on the lighter-skinned ladies because their skin reflects so much more light. Browner-skinned ladies can take a harder light. On all the ladies I used a net—a black stocking that I had stretched on a frame to put in front of the lens. It takes the hard edge off.

There are a lot of color contrasts in the film—meaning colors on opposite ends of the spectrum. The Gammites have a scene that takes place in the boiler room of one of the dorms; they're hiding out from the Big Brothers. The Gammites are in the foreground and they're lit by an orangy light, while the light in the background is bluish. You see color contrast again in the Death March scenes—the orange color of the torch flames and the blue of the moonlight.

All of our nights in the film are bluish, which is a Hollywood standard, but we made them bluer that most. Normally I don't like to go as blue, but for *School Daze* it seemed to complement what we had to say. The colors overall are a bit surreal. They're a bit overdone on purpose, 'cause it felt right for the film, what the film was about. I can't really give you a technical reason for it. It's intuitive. You know, things either feel right or they don't.

THE SHOTS

SPIKE ▸ There ought to be a study done on how many questions a film director is asked during a shoot. With a film of this size and scale, a director gets faced with thousands of questions a day. It's said that if the brain were receptive to all the stimuli that is out there, a person would have a nervous breakdown. When I'm directing I try to operate with this in mind. I tell people only what they need to know to do the jobs they were hired to do. Otherwise I'd be spending the entire shoot answering questions.

I got into a lot of static with my script supervisor this time around. It's her job to ask for a shot list every day and I didn't have one every day. We wanted to be open. For some scenes you want to see what the blocking is going to be like, you want to see the actors go through it on location, and then you want to look things over with your director of photography. I would have a shot list for big scenes with lots of extras, though. But the little stuff, things that are not going to involve many shots, I rehearse them, then I took at them. I don't want to come on the set all the time with a predetermined idea of what we're gonna shoot. There's no spontaneity to that.

ERNEST DICKERSON ▸ We spent plenty of time planning coverage for *School Daze,* but we weren't locked into it. There are always scenes

—certain dialogue scenes, for instance—which are almost impossible to storyboard. Often it comes down to getting on set and letting the actors rehearse, seeing what they do, and then working around that. More times than not, we found ourselves letting the coverage come organically out of what the actors did.

A film becomes an entity unto itself. You look at what you shot the day before, and then you look over what you planned to do with a scene you're shooting today, and then you make changes. Sometimes it is something new that an actor is bringing to his character which makes you want to change your concept of the scene. You can't always live with a fixed shot. You have to let the film almost make itself. If the film is proceeding right, it'll take on a life of its own and you'll see certain things develop that you didn't see before. Spike and I were always trashing ideas we had months before.

Take the scene where "Big Brother Almigty" dumps "Jane." We had several shots planned. When we saw Giancarlo and Tisha rehearse on set, we realized we could cover the scene in one shot. We let the actors really go at it, instead of breaking up their performance with editing. If the performance is strong enough and the lighting is dramatically correct, often the storyboard goes out the window.

I had storyboarded the entire football game. We knew exactly what we were going to do; we had three cameras planned and a big crane. Then Ossie Davis came and did his bit out on the sidelines, looking at the game. Spike came over and whispered in my ear, "You know, I'm not going to shoot the football game." So our concept went from shooting an entire college football game—staging a wild, elaborate, funny game and really getting inside it—to something totally minimal, cutting it down to the point where there are no shots of the game itself. Spike felt that everything happening on the field could be read on Ossie's face. And Ossie was playing it to the hilt. For Spike to decide that takes a lot of *cojones* (balls).

There was also trouble with the colleges and we couldn't go to Morehouse's stadium to shoot any more football scenes anyway. But Spike talked about de-emphasizing the game long before that. He said that most of the action at homecoming games was in the stands anyway.

SPIKE ▸ In the final scene of the film, we call it "Wake Up," I wanted to show that the people at Mission College had come to some kind of realization, some kind of meaning, some kind of truth. (I had the Gamma Rays take out their weaves and their blue contact lenses for this scene.) And when "Dap" calls everyone out of bed, they come because they've realized something, not just because they're being summoned. That's the way I wrote it. And I hope it comes off that way. It is a metaphor for the sleeping that we as a race have done.

There's this line in *Joe's Bed-Stuy Barbershop* when two of the thugs come to the shop to get "Zachariah Homer" and bring him to see the numbers kingpin, "Nicholas Lovejoy," played by Tommy Hicks. "Zachariah" is asleep in the barber's chair and the two thugs say, "Wake up, the Black man has been asleep for four hundred years." That's what the Wake Up scene in *School Daze* says; it's about who we are, where we've been. And to me that's what this film is about. Our need to come together. Black people are sometimes like crabs in a barrel. In my case, if a Black person tries to do something, I will support it. On the other hand, though, if people are doing things I don't agree with, I will speak out against them. That doesn't mean that I don't support Black people or I'm being that crab in the barrel.

The crisis in *Homecoming,* like in *School Daze,* is when "Julian" tells "Jane Toussaint" to have sex with "Half-Pint." The difference in the first script is that the Gammites, "Half-Pint's" line brothers, come into the room after "Half-Pint" and run a train on her. Somehow word gets back to "Slice" (he was "Slice" then), and he has this big fight with "Julian." The script ends with "Slice" trying to make it to the president's house to tell him what's happened. He's about to be stopped by the Gammas, but the football team and the rest of the student body protect him. It was too much of an *On the Waterfront*–type of ending. I guess you can draw a comparison between *She's Gotta Have It* and *School Daze* in that it's a sexual act that transforms things; it's the kicker that puts the final thing in motion. In *She's Gotta Have It,* it's "Jamie's" rape of "Nola," and in *School Daze* it's "Slice," now "Dap," finding out that "Julian" coerced "Jane" into going to bed with "Half-Pint."

When I came back to do *School Daze,* I knew I wanted a different ending. I had an ending in my mind, but it was fuzzy at first. I knew that I wanted it to be the coming together of everyone in the film, everyone on the campus, a microcosm of Black people all over the world. On the other hand, there was the danger that it might be-

Why must we be like dat, always the cat must be da Gamma dog in us.

Spike Lee and Ernest Dickerson.

come one of those "We Are the World" things. So it was a delicate situation. I hope we don't lose it at the end. Even though *School Daze* is a musical, it's realistic for the most part. The end is a total change in tone. It's surreal, but I think it's very uplifting and optimistic.

Ernest wasn't really sure how he was going to shoot the ending until we did it. Barry also didn't have any ideas about how to treat the Wake Up scene. When it came time to cut the scene, I was out of the editing room shooting a video for Anita Baker, "No One in the World." Barry kept saying to me, "Spike, you gotta be here." But we worked it out. I came back that night from the shoot after Barry had cut it and looked it over. It was great. I made a couple of suggestions, left a note on the Steenbeck, and the next day Barry made the changes. That was it. When we showed it to Ernest he was kinda disturbed because he felt that there wasn't any continuity to the light. We told him that it's a surreal scene, and first and foremost we had to go with what was best dramatically.

I think there's going to be a lot discussion about whether people like the ending or don't like the ending, and what the ending means. I'm sure some people will say, "I like the film up till the ending. That's where he fucked up."

ERNEST DICKERSON ▸ We didn't shoot the Wake Up scene until practically the end of the shoot, and I was worried the whole time about what we were going to do with it. It's surreal, but I had to make it surreal within budgetary limitations. If our budget had allowed for it, I would have had the whole campus re-created, almost like a fourth perspective, on a soundstage. Like in the film *Mishima*. Some of the scenes in the piece were straight out of his literature. There's one towards the end of the film when the assassins have canceled their attack. There's this beautiful surreal setting in which the clouds and the ground are blown out of perspective. I would have gone for something like that.

Given what I had to work with, what I decided to go for was a very bright and intense sunrise, like the dawning of a new day. The day Wake Up was scheduled to shoot, we had actors flying in from L.A. and from New York to be in the scene. Weather reports said it was going to be a beautiful day. Well, I woke up that morning, walked out onto the hotel balcony, looked up, and there was nothing but clouds. It would have been physically impossible for me to re-create sunlight over that big area. I had to call up the production manager and say, "Matia, we can't shoot this scene today." When I got to the office and everyone was going round and round like crazy doing replanning, I felt a little guilty about it. But I had to do it.

I hear about other DPs who routinely call off shooting days. It's something that a DP should be able to do, but again, we just didn't have the budget. If the weather isn't exactly right for Kurosawa, if he doesn't have the right cloud formations, he won't shoot. He'll wait for days and days until he gets the right formations and ground fog to shoot. That's a luxury. But that's how you get beautiful cinematography. You wait and you wait. In America you can't do it, because you've got to pay people while they're waiting.

I think in the final printing we still have to work on what we shot. Print more color into it, more orange, and play with the brightness levels. I'm a bit disappointed with what we have. I think I didn't take it far enough, but Spike's happy.

THE SETS

SPIKE ▸ Wynn Thomas was the production designer on *She's Gotta Have It.* He did that work with practically no money. On *School Daze* he had a decent budget—not a ton of money—but we gave Wynn the ball and he ran with it. The sets he built for the film are great—"Straight and Nappy," the Gamma house, "Dap's" room, and the coronation. He had this sequence of interconnected backdrops worked out for each number of the coronation. We ended up cutting one of the dance numbers, "Sun Is Rising," from the film.

WYNN THOMAS ▸ To design a film like *School Daze,* I knew I had to prepare the audience to see a musical: a stylized film. The scenery can't be altogether realistic. When you look at the film, you see that everything is on a slightly large scale. The dorm rooms are overdecorated. That's intentional, because that's taking a realistic set and exaggerating it, so that when all of a sudden you have musical numbers, the audience will accept the possibility of that. But there's something sort of romantic and stylized about the script, even if it weren't a musical, that calls for an exaggerated type of scenery.

One of the problems I had with designing the coronation set was how not to get too theatrical, how not to get too big, because it's a college show, after all. So I kept my ideas simple and familiar and came up with a celestial theme. There's certainly nothing sophisticated about that. When it came down to working with the painters I told them not to make the set too wonderful, too pretty. Painters refer to things as being tight, they mean very polished. Well, I didn't want it tight at all.

My design, as always, had to work for a number of people. Not only was I dealing with Spike and Ernest, but I had to consider the choreographer's needs too. What solved the design puzzle was the idea of a circle. We start out with this small circle in which "Buckwheat," the MC, comes out à la *Star Wars*. We see the same circle as a moon shape behind the dancers in the "Sun Is Rising." The circle grows once again and becomes a sun. Then finally the circle expands completely to become a pop night backdrop for the Gamma Court's number, "Be Alone Tonight," and the coronation itself.

One of the most difficult design problems for me was the actual crowning of the queen. When I saw Morehouse's coronation with Spike the November before, it was kinda drab and uninteresting. But I remember seeing a mirror ball on stage and thinking how corny. But when I came to design the coronation, I felt that I had to use something that a college student would go out and buy. This being the movies, you can't keep the scale. So instead of having one mirror ball, I put a wall of them behind the queen as she's being crowned by the president. When the mirror balls move, they look like stars, so the whole thing fit into my celestial theme.

The parade floats were fun to design. One of the things I wanted to express through the fraternity floats, and the Gamma Phi Gamma frat house in particular, was that many members—"Brothers," they call themselves—become our major leaders, e.g., Martin Luther King, Jr., Andy Young. When we see these fraternity men in the script, it's during a hazing period. It's not the most positive image we could see of these men; they're doing some awful things to their pledgees. As a production designer, one of the stories that I wanted to tell subtextually was that these guys are smart. Which is why the Gamma float evolved the way it did. The idea of a pyramid opening up is a sophisticated one. I wanted to say that these guys are thinkers, engineers; they would put together something this extravagant each year to present their women.

As for the look of the fraternity house, I wanted it to evoke a sense of tradition. The dressing and the accessories in the house are almost stuffy. There's a look of old money, especially with the photographs. It was important to me to suggest a Black academic tradition. It had to express a sense that this environment was spawning a tradition of Black leadership despite what happens in the script.

The Alpha Phi Alpha fraternity was our research model. We consulted some of its historical material, but primarily we looked at the fraternity's photographs. Ironically, there was no Black frat house in Atlanta to visit. They have existed in the past, but the fraternities these days have not opted to use their money that way. There were many white fraternity houses in the city we could have used, but I chose to make up the house, especially the interior.

The production designer is responsible for the look of the film, and when you work on a film of this scale, you need a strong art director to execute your ideas. Your set decorator, also, becomes an extension of your eye. It comes down to trusting that person and hoping he has the same vision of the project that you have. It's the same with my relationship with Spike. He doesn't dictate what the set should look like, but I'm sure he hopes that I will give him something in keeping with his vision.

Spike is very concerned about dressing details. I don't think to this day he ever liked the Snoopy phone that we put on the set of "Rachel's" room. I was trying to introduce some playful elements. Who is to say that "Rachel" wouldn't have had a Snoopy phone as a young kid that she brought with her from home? Blacks are Americans and we partake in the same sort of consumerism, the same sort of pop icons. So, why not? The idea for the phone initially came from my set dresser, Lynn Wolverton. But I think she was absolutely right-on there. It's those details that give the film an extra texture. It says something more about a character.

For the set of "Dap's" room I designed and had this glass lamp made. It has a barbershop pole inside it that twirls around. Spike rejected it, which is fine; it's his choice. But again, I felt that it was important to introduce something that had some humor in that room. The room had a lot of political stuff, all fine and appropriate, but we all carry a past. Sometimes there's a carryover: silly things from our childhood, when we weren't so politically astute.

THE DAILIES

SPIKE ▸ I always want the actors to view dailies. But first, you want to see what you've got for yourself. Ernest is like a lot of DPs; they're very nervous about how their stuff looks. They don't want anybody to see it before they do. So once Ernest felt assured that everything coming back from the lab looked well, we opened up dailies. I think the dailies helped a lot of actors. For those who hadn't done film work before, they saw how a film is put together and they could see their performances. It wasn't until the end of the shoot that we had a full house come see synced dailies. Eventually, it became like a party. We'd send out for pizza, beer, and soda. Everyone had a real good time, cheering each other on. I think it was the realization that the film was coming to an end for them.

We started screening silent dailies at the production office. We had a projector shipped down from New York, and in the big room that we used as a rehearsal space during preproduction, we put up a rinky-dink screen and soundproof boards around the projector. It wasn't the best of conditions to see dailies, and my brother Cinque, who was apprenticing, and Meredith, the assistant editor, were terrible projectionists. We were always teasing them. Eventually, we went to a screening house to see synced dailies. Barry had to struggle with Matia and Grace over money to book the place he felt was best. Finally he had to come to me about it.

So we went to the place Barry picked out about twice a week. Since we didn't begin right away, we had a backlog. On Sundays—our only day off—we'd have four of five hours of dailies. That's really too much. And when we were working nights, I would come into the office early. If we had a five-o'clock call, I'd be in at two. I'd sit down with Barry in the editing room, and he would show me stuff on the Steenbeck.

BARRY BROWN ▸ If you just look at the number of scenes and the amount of really good footage that was shot in eight weeks, it's really phenomenal. You have some very tasteful musical numbers, and some scenes involving hundreds of extras—Splash Jam, the football game. There is an incredible amount of versatility in this motion picture. There is stuff that ordinarily one wouldn't get for the money it cost to make *School Daze*.

Certainly there were little technical problems, like finding out that there was a blue haze on some of the film shot on the last day, or finding out that Morehouse wasn't going to cooperate anymore and that we couldn't go back there and get any more football footage. These are little things that can be worked out. I looked at the footage and thought, Now, this is great. But the thing I was most worried about was: Am I really up to this motion picture? Am I gonna be good enough for the film?

The first time I saw the scene where Ossie Davis ("Coach Odom") is watching the football game happen from the sidelines, I had to just sit and watch. If you cut a scene like that, you kill it. This was a case where the writing was great, the performance was superb and was shot beautifully. It's a three-minute-long scene. We have something like four cuts. It probably could have been done with less than four cuts. As a filmmaker, and an editor, I respect and marvel at a shot that can last a long time without any cuts. It's first-rate filmmaking to have a sequence without cuts that is so compelling.

What was being captured on a day-to-day basis was impressive on the whole; really impressive. Everyday there was something to be awed by. From the very first day, shooting the scenes in the fried chicken place with the Fellas, there was something rare happening within the frame. The actors were so much in character that even when the dialogue veered from the script, they never lost it. The camera had become a fourth wall.

ERNEST DICKERSON ▸ The film that we made for $6 million, I think somebody else would have made for $20 million. For us, this meant things had to work right the first time. With $20 million, we could have gone back and done something like reshoot our biggest production number, "Straight and Nappy." I'd love to do that, just rethink the whole thing. Woody Allen might have had a six-month shooting schedule. Then, farther down the road, he'd have three months set aside to reshoot. So he could rethink everything. We didn't have that luxury. Six million was certainly the biggest budget that we've ever had, though. But it was no safety net. Or the safety net was close to the ground. So, when you fall, you still hit the pavement.

6

THE MUSIC

SPIKE ▸ My mother took me to Broadway plays and I went to see my father in jazz clubs in the Village when I was five or six years old. I was brought up around music, and whether I do musicals or not, music will always play an integral role in my films.

I didn't begin with the idea of making *School Daze* a musical. I wanted to make a film which took place on a Black college campus during homecoming weekend, and from that material, the music arose. There is always so much music happening during a homecoming. The subject matter of *School Daze* really dictated that it be a musical.

Neither Island nor Columbia objected to the idea of a musical. Though Russell Schwartz, the president of Island, wanted to cut some of the numbers to trim costs. When I was still with the company, one of the major issues to resolve was the money for the music. Even before I wrote the first draft of *School Daze,* I knew I wanted a separate budget for the music. Island Records gave us only a $7,500 advance to distribute the sound track of *She's Gotta Have It,* and we had to fight to get that. I didn't want to be tied to Island Records or Columbia for the *School Daze* sound track, so I made a deal with Manhattan Records, a division of Capitol EMI.

I think the idea of a musical really struck a positive note with Columbia. I guess they know singing and dancing Negroes sell. But *School Daze* was not going to be another *Wiz*. It's an original work for film, whereas *The Wiz* began as a play with an all-Black cast adapted from the film *The Wizard of Oz*. The film translation didn't work for me. Critical mistakes were made in casting and it was overproduced. They went for box-office names, like Diana Ross, instead of actors who could do a believable job. Ms. Ross was too old.

School Daze is not a traditional musical; actors don't just break out of nowhere into song and dance. In many musicals you can always tell when a song is coming because the dialogue gets corny. I wanted to integrate the music into the movie. One traditional musical piece in the film is "Straight and Nappy," which is meant as a prototype MGM musical number. People sing in the other numbers because they are performing in a show or are accompanied by a band—where the setting is realistic.

My father wrote the score, acted as musical director, and contributed two featured songs. My aunt Consuela Lee Morehead, an accomplished pianist and composer in her own right, assisted him. Unlike my previous films, we had input from other songwriters.

SONG BREAKDOWN (BY ORDER OF APPEARANCE)

1. **"I'm Building Me a Home"** (opening credits)
   Old Negro spiritual arranged by Uzee Brown
   Sung by the Morehouse College Glee Club

2. **"Perfect Match"** (background music)
   Music and lyrics by Lenny White
   Sung by Tech and the EFFX

3. **"Straight and Nappy"** (featured music)
   Music and lyrics by Bill Lee
   Performed by the Wannabee and Jigaboo ensembles

4. **"Be Alone Tonight"** (featured music)
   Music and lyrics by Raymond Jones
   Performed by the Rays (Tisha Campbell, Jasmine Guy, Paula Brown, and Angela Ali)

5. **"I Can Only Be Me"** (featured music)
   Music and lyrics by Stevie Wonder
   Performed by Keith John

6. **"Kick It Out Tigers"** (featured music)
   Music by Consuela Lee Morehead
   Performed by the Morehouse/Spelman, Clark, and Morris Brown colleges marching bands
   Recorded live at the B. T. Harvey Stadium, Morehouse College

7. **"Da Butt"** (featured music)
   Music and lyrics by Marcus Miller and Mark Stevens
   Performed by the E.U. Band

8. **"Be One"** (featured music)
   Music and lyrics by Bill Lee
   Performed by Phyllis Hyman and the Bill Lee Quartet

9. **"We've Already Said Goodbye"** (end credits)
   Music and lyrics by Raymond Jones
   Performed by Pieces of a Dream with Portia Griffin

"I'M BUILDING ME A HOME"

Anybody who went to Morehouse College knows about the Morehouse College Glee Club, one of the greatest glee clubs in the world. The director, Dr. Wendall P. Whalum, passed away in July '87. He and my father were classmates and were in the Morehouse Glee Club Quartet together. I've always wanted to use the glee club somehow in my films; with *School Daze* we were able to. The script calls for the glee club to sing a song on camera by Olatunji called "Betelehemu." This is a song they do at Morehouse and Spelman's

On the set with Anita Baker, the "No One in the World" music video.

Sound recordist Rolf Pardula and Bill Lee.

annual concert every Christmas. It's from Yoruba and features drums and tambourines.

During the rehearsal period we decided not to shoot "Betelehemu." It was clear the film was going to be too long and we could do without the scene. "Monroe," one of "Dap's" boys, is a member of the glee club. There are numerous references to his being late for glee-club practice. We were going to see him rehearse with the club after the Fellas' run-in with the local yokels.

"I'm Building Me a Home" is my favorite song in the glee club's repertoire. It's one of those old, old spirituals, and when I was at Morehouse, Uzee Brown, composer and musical instructor at the college, always sang the solo in that deep baritone of his. It's his arrangement of the song that plays over the film's opening credits and photo montage—"I'm Building Me a Home" being a metaphor for the growth of Mission College and the history of Black people in America. The song was recorded at RCA Studios in New York while the glee club was on its annual spring-break tour in March '87.

From the start, I knew that I wanted all the idioms of Black music in this movie, all idioms. We've got spirituals, funk, R&B, go-go, jazz. I had an interesting experience during our first weeks of editing the film. Manhattan Records is distributing the sound-track album. (At this moment they are; when this book is published, who knows?) Gerry Griffith, the head of Black Music, or what they call it now, Urban Contemporary, pursued the deal for them. It was between Manhattan Records and Warner Brothers. I decided on Manhattan because there was a guy at Warner Brothers who wanted the title "Executive Producer" on the album, and he had nothing to do with it. I said no, that's out. So we went with Manhattan Records. Bruce Lundval, who for years ran Blue Note records, heads it up. I think they will do a better job, because they need it more. Warner Brothers is too big for me.

Well, I went to Manhattan Records, and as I played them the songs, Gerry Griffith looked very worried. I gave him the script when we signed the deal. He kept asking me, "How does this song fit within the context? And is this song a period piece?" I had given him a script to read in advance of this. Finally he came out with it: "My neck is on the line. I've been telling everybody we have a hit album and I don't know if we really do. We need another single." Griffith suggested recording a song with a group on their label, Pieces of a Dream. So we'll see—if they come up with something I like, it might be included. (I ended up soliciting another Raymond Jones composition, "We've Already Said Goodbye.")

We had nothing to worry about, I thought, as far as singles were concerned. "Be Alone Tonight," could be released first, "Da Butt," second, and "I Can Only Be Me," the Stevie Wonder song, third. They'll probably try to push that Pieces of a Dream song as number three. I would think that they'd want to push the Stevie Wonder song, but Griffith said it wasn't hit material. We shall see.

We got to discussing whether the album was going to sell or not. I said, "Look at *Little Shop of Horrors,* the film was a modest hit, and the album sold well." He wanted to know how many copies it had sold. I picked up the phone and called David Geffen. Geffen himself answered. I introduced myself. I told him about my negotiations with the record company and asked how many copies of *Little Shop of Horrors* were sold. "Three hundred thousand," he said. "Without airplay and without a single?" I asked. He said, "That's true."

If they sold 300,000 copies with no single, no video, and no airplay, I told Gerry, I know the least this album is gonna go is gold—500,000 copies. People are gonna buy this album. Gerry said, "All-right, but you don't want the songs in the order that they appear in the movie, right?" I had to think about it. I decided not to, and he felt good about that. "If we have 'I'm Building Me a Home' as the first song on the first side," he said, "people are gonna take the album back." I don't necessarily agree with that. Look at some other sound-track albums that went platinum. *Fame* is one. You had a couple of songs on that album that weren't "hits." They even included a gospel number.

My feeling is that people will listen to good music if they're given a chance to. And there's enough mixture on this album that it's gonna sell. Some people thought *She's Gotta Have It*'s jazz score would turn young audiences off and that was not the case at all. In fact, Nelson George, who's the Black Music editor of *Billboard,* and the recording artist Mtume both brought those concerns to me about *She's Gotta Have It.* They felt a more contemporary score would sell the picture. I disagreed with them then, and I disagree with them now. This whole formula of putting music in movies is horrible. To get a hot producer, a hot artist, and have them do a title song so the film will sell is bullshit. I'm never gonna do films like that. I just don't work like that.

People ask me if my films are always gonna have jazz scores written by my father. Well, it really depends on the film. There are gonna be films where my father will not write the score, because there will be films where we need a different sound. There are just certain types of music that my father does not write. He would not want to write a song that WBLS would play on the "Rap Attack." My father and I talk about this all the time. In *She's Gotta Have It,* when "Mars Blackmon" rides his ten-speed down the hill, my father wanted to write something for that scene. He had some bebop in mind and I said, "No, we're gonna use Strafe's 'Set It Off.' " Finally I had to say, "Daddy, it's just not gonna work; bebop isn't the type of music that Mars Blackmon would listen to." My father does not play music that's electrified. Never in his life has he picked up a Fender bass; he calls his music "tone as is."

"BE ALONE TONIGHT"

"Be Alone Tonight," sung by Tisha Campbell with backup vocals by Jasmine Guy, Paula Brown, and Angela Ali, might be the first single. I met Raymond Jones, who wrote the song, through his good friend Geoffrey Garfield, who is also a good friend of mine and was "Dog Number 12" in *She's Gotta Have It.* Geoffrey tried to help me raise money to complete the film. Raymond played piano in the group Chic. He has since gone on to make his name as a songwriter, penning a number of hits for Jeffrey Osborne.

Geoffrey took Raymond, another mutual friend, and me to dinner at this Ethiopian restaurant in the Village. I gave them the prospectus for *She's Gotta Have It* and I tried to talk them into giving me some moolah. Neither of them felt the film would get distributed and had no reason to invest in it.

When the film became a hit, Raymond, like many other would-be investors, became very apologetic but came to talk to me. I told him I was interested in working with him; that I wanted him to do some music for *School Daze.* I met Raymond and he played me some songs while I was casting for the first time in L.A. in January '87. We drove around L.A. in his black BMW as he played me demo tape after demo tape. When I heard "Be Alone Tonight," I knew it would be vicious! Dolette McDonald, one of Sting's backup singers, sang lead on the demo. I said to Raymond, "You gotta give me this song."

I wanted him to turn it into a 1960s' Motown number. Take out all the synthesizers, add real strings, real drums, and a real Motown tambourine. Everything sounds the same. I don't care what anybody says. There is no way a synthesizer sounds as good as a real instrument. Real strings are more expensive, but so be it. The demo of "Be Alone Tonight" was all synthesizers.

The tracks were recorded in L.A. before the shoot, and Raymond came down to Atlanta during the rehearsal phase to oversee the recording session for the vocals. He came in early on a Thursday, slept that morning, rehearsed with Tisha and three backup singers for a couple of hours that afternoon, recorded that evening, and was gone the next morning. The four actresses had to rehearse with me in the morning and early afternoon, so the most of the time they spent with Raymond was over dinner at a soul-food place called the Beautiful Restaurant.

I have always liked Raymond's music. He has a gentle voice; not his singing voice, but the voice inside him. The recording session lasted from about six in the evening to close to midnight, and Raymond worked the four of them every minute. They were very appreciative at the end, full of praise for his arrangements and his clear sense of what he wanted. Though they had an instrumental tape to practice with for a week, the girls were given the vocal arrangements only the day Raymond arrived. I guess that's not unusual for backup singers. The pros just go into the studio and knock it out after one sing-through. Many times they're left up to their own devices to come up with the background sound.

People are really going to be surprised when they find out that the girls who performed the songs in the movie actually recorded it. But for me the true standout in this number is Otis Sallid's choreography. About midway through the dance rehearsals for "Be Alone Tonight," Otis felt that the feeling had gone out of the dance. The four dancers had mastered the piece technically but, he felt, had lost all the sensuality. So Otis gave them a little session, teaching them exercises to put the feeling back into the dance. Apparently the girls were hesitant at first, but they did manage to work things out by shooting time. On camera, they do come forth, as Otis would say, with some "major" butt rolls.

Tisha Campbell throws down viciously in "Be Alone Tonight"

with her singing and her dancing. It was my idea to have that talkie bit where she breathes à la early Diana Ross, "Boy . . . you know I love you." With their outfits and hairdos, the girls really look like a 1980s' version of Martha and the Vandellas.

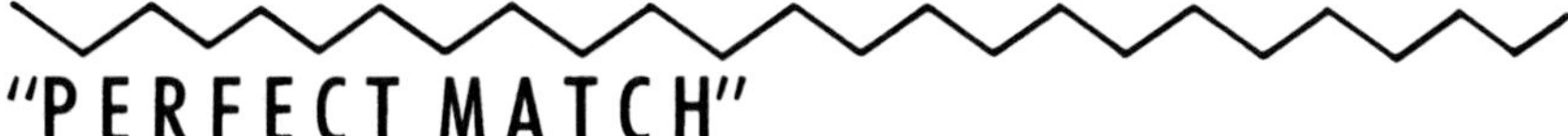

"PERFECT MATCH"

While we were in preproduction, still working out of the Brooklyn office, I got a call from the drummer Lenny White. He said, "Spike, I got some songs for you. Come on by; I'm in the studio now." He was recording at a studio in Bed-Stuy over on Fulton Street. I went by there and I picked up his tape. When I heard "Perfect Match," it was a godsend, it mirrored "Jane Toussaint" so much. It had to be her theme song. The words, "I've always been looking for a perfect match," that's "Jane" talking about "Julian."

You hear "Perfect Match" two times in the film; the first time is when we meet "Jane," she's alone in her apartment flipping channels with her remote. Then we hear it during the love scene between her and "Big Brother Almighty." The song begins with a refrain from "Love Is a Many-Splendored Thing," which comes over "Half-Pint's" scene at the dorm. He's trying to bring a girlie back to the frat house, but gets his "face cracked" instead. He's just sitting in the lounge looking like an idiot and you hear that. Then we cut to Jane propped up in her plush pad reading *Essence*. (This last scene was cut.)

Lenny White's new group, Tech and the EFFX, performs the piece and it was supposed to be on their debut album. It'll make their second album instead. Terry Blanchard, the jazz musician, does a trumpet solo. I heard Lenny wanted to get Miles, but he wanted too much money. Terry also plays lead trumpet on "Straight and Nappy." The dueling trumpet and sax you hear during the instrumental break, that's Branford Marsalis and Terry Blanchard.

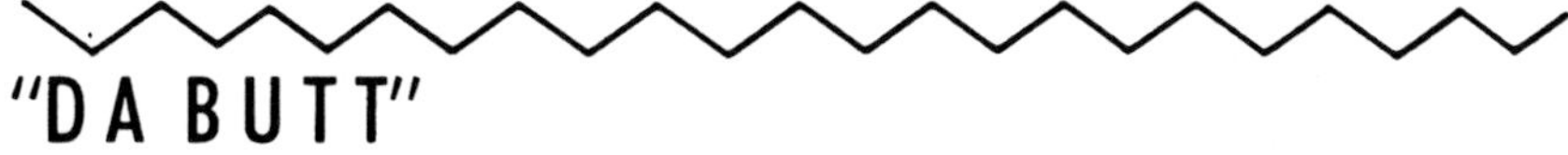

"DA BUTT"

This was another one of those instances like "Straight and Nappy," where I had an idea, had a title, and went to a songwriter to realize it for me. Marcus Miller is a talented young musician and songwriter. He's known more and more as a producer, having coproduced a few of Luther Vandross' albums and Miles Davis' *Tutu*. Marcus is a veteran studio bass player as well. I wanted "Da Butt" to be the film's big party song. Even before I set Marcus up to write the song, I had made up the dance, "Da Butt." I've always wanted to make up a dance. It's always fascinated me how popular dances get started, where they come from, who makes them up.

After I completed the Miles Davis video for *Tutu* in November '86, I went about getting in touch with Marcus Miller. This woman I went to school with knew his brother, so I was able to reach him that way. It turned out that Marcus had just seen *She's Gotta Have It* and was down. He had never done anything for a movie before, so he was fired up. I suggested that we use E.U., a go-go band out of D.C., and Marcus had no problem with that.

The go-go band that gets the most publicity, the most play, is Trouble Funk. For my money, I'll go with E.U. The band was still with Island Records when *She's Gotta Have It* opened in Washington, D.C. Island gave a big party for the film down there and E.U. played. Them go-go bands, they can play three hours straight, nonstop, serious funk. They're bad. And I said to myself at this party, I gotta use them in the movie. The guys in E.U. are young and hungry, and I was happy once again to round up some talented people who haven't been given a shot. When I called Johnny Mercer, E.U.'s lawyer, in November '86, he was very enthusiastic about the project, and later that month I got the band and Marcus Miller together. In January four members of the group came up and cut the record with Marcus.

When I first told Marcus about "Da Butt," he said, " 'Da Butt,' 'Da Butt,' what kind of title is that?" I told him it was supposed to be a fun record, and if you heard it on the radio or on your stereo at home, you'd think that it was recorded at a party. So the night after Marcus and the four guys from E.U. recorded the tracks, I called my friends and a couple of folks who were going to act in *School Daze*. They came down to the studio to record the party sounds. We had a good time doing that stuff. All of us got into a debate about how we should handle this call-and-response bit where people from different states yell "We got da butt." We never did get that together.

The Wizard of Oz is one of my favorite films. So I told Marcus I wanted to use that chorus from the film, "Oh we oh, oh oh, oh we oh, oh oh." So he played the song and I showed him exactly where I wanted it and he slipped it in. While we were shooting in Atlanta, Prince's *Sign o' the Times* LP was released. I went out and bought the CD the day it hit Atlanta record stores. I remember because it was a Sunday, our only day off. Prince has this song on the album called "It's Gonna Be a Beautiful Night." Wouldn't you know he used that same *Wizard of Oz* chorus? I was lying in bed listening to the song, and when I heard the chorus, I jumped up and ran around the room screaming, "What the fuck is this?" I guess Prince likes *The Wizard of Oz* too. I decided to keep our version of the chorus in.

"Da Butt" is one of two songs that play at the Splash Jam. The whole premise of Splash Jam is that it's a beach party in a gym. You can't get into the gym unless you're in a bathing suit and sneakers; you just can't get in. There was a scene in the script showing people without the proper attire being turned away at the door, but we didn't have enough time to shoot it, nor did we end up needing it.

We got our best turnout for extras during the two days we shot Splash Jam. The Clark College gym was packed with guys in their swimming shorts and women in bikinis; the students came through like champs that time. While we were setting up, before we brought the extras inside the gym, Otis Sallid was outside teaching people how to do "Da Butt." There's one shot that I think is fantastic in this scene. The camera cranes up just as the crowd bends down low dancing. The frame is filled entirely with Black limbs, nothing but a sea of Black people, sweating, gyrating, to the beat y'all.

"I CAN ONLY BE ME"

I've loved Stevie Wonder's music since something like the fourth or fifth grade when I started listening to the radio. There's a friend of Stevie's named Dyanna Williams, who is a dee-jay in Philadelphia on station WDAS. I was introduced to her by Nelson George. I told Dyanna that I would like to meet Stevie Wonder, she called him a couple of times, and finally I got a call from the man himself. Stevie was in British Columbia at the time, on his *In Square Circle* tour. He said he wanted to meet me and "see" *She's Gotta Have It.* I had

Island Pictures send him a cassette, and before one of their concert dates, everyone on Stevie's tour group watched the film. Stevie called me back during the show's intermission to say how much he liked the film and that maybe we could do something together.

I got a call from Stevie in November '86; he was about to end the tour, the last show was in Columbia, South Carolina, and would I come down. It was OK with him if I brought a guest, so I said, "Come on, Monty, let's go." Stevie paid for everything, booked our flight, put us up in a hotel. It was a great experience, meeting him, talking to him. He feels your face, that's how he tells what you look like.

We also met Carmen Efferson, who's an associate of Stevie's. She was very gracious to me and Monty, and we've stayed in contact since.

So I told Stevie that I would really like him to do a song for *School Daze*. I asked him at first for an up-tempo song for the coronation; this was before Raymond Jones gave me "Be Alone Tonight." Stevie said he would deliver, but it's legend that he takes his time to do stuff. He has his agenda and that's just the way he is. People were skeptical that he would ever do a song for us.

Once we got into preproduction, it was apparent that I was gonna have to tell Stevie to hurry up. The song needed to be recorded to use as playback when we were shooting. I called him and said, "I've got to have this song by such and such a date." He said he didn't think he'd be able to do it. He had a new album coming out and many things to do. I resigned myself to the fact that I wouldn't have the song. Then after a couple of days Stevie called back and asked, "Do you still want that song?"

In early March, after we'd begun shooting, I got another call from Stevie. He was on one line and Keith John, his backup singer, was on another. Keith is the son of Little Willie John and has been with Stevie for the last seven years. They have similar voices. Stevie himself is an admirer of Little Willie John. I listened on the phone as Keith sang "I Can Only Be Me."

I said, "Okay, this is it," but in my mind I knew it wasn't quite right because it was synthesized. So, as I listened, I was agonized. Here's a great, great, great artist who's doing me a favor. How can I tell Stevie diplomatically that this is not right for this film, that he has to go back to the studio and do it with a grand piano? I finally came out with it. There was silence on the other end of the phone. I wanted the song to be like Stevie's old stuff. This song had synthesized sounds too big, too overproduced. "Let's keep it simple. Simple is always the best," I said. "Stevie, I really feel stupid, but I have to ask you, can you find it in your heart to go back into the studio and just try it with the piano?" He said, "Okay, Spike, I'll try it."

It would have been nice to have Stevie sing the song himself, but he's always having contractual problems with Motown. Having Keith sing was fine though, and it gave me another opportunity to give someone talented but unknown a little exposure. When we shot the coronation scenes, Keith flew to Atlanta to sing "I Can Only Be Me" on camera. The song is intercut with three scenes: Keith singing on a bare stage; "President McPherson," played by Joe Seneca, crowning Miss Maroon and White—Miss Mission College and her court; and "Dap" and "Rachel" making love.

At one point I tried to get Jimmy Jam and Terry Lewis to do a song for the film, but that never materialized. They're so busy. Everybody wants them to work; they're booked up for four or five years, I hear. I never even got to talk to them. I was in touch with their manager-agent, Clarence Avant, who is one-third of the trio of Griot. That's a film company that also includes George Jackson and Quincy Jones. Clarence Avant wrote me a threatening letter in the fall of '86, telling me that if I had any sense, I would stop talking bad about Michael Jackson, Whoopi Goldberg and her contact lenses, and *The Color Purple*.

Ironically, though, when I was in L.A. the June after the shoot, I went to see game six of the NBA championship games. When I walked into the Forum I saw Whoopi. I walked up to her and said, "How you doing?" At first she didn't recognize me, and then she took off her sunglasses and said, "Spike . . . Spike Lee . . .?" We hugged and there was no animosity between us. At halftime, we had a picture taken together. Who knows, that might end up as one of "this week's photos" in *Jet*.

"KICK IT OUT TIGERS"

"Kick It Out Tigers" was one of the hardest numbers to pull together. It's the fight song played by the marching band and recorded live at the football game. The hard part was getting three school bands together as one. We had Morehouse's band (including Spelman), and Clark and Morris Brown students. It had never been done before. All I can say is that we were lucky to be able to shoot the scene before the AUC gave us the boot. When we first brought the idea to the band directors, they looked at us like we were crazy, like we wouldn't be able to pull it off. With only two or three rehearsals, my father and aunt were able to get things together. Another marching band plays briefly in the film, the Booker T. Washington marching band from a local high school in Atlanta. It's their fight song that begins the parade.

A highlight of our cast trip to Morehouse's homecoming was seeing the Morehouse and Howard University marching bands have a face-off at the football game. Morehouse's drum major is the same guy you see leading the Mission College band in *School Daze.* He's an incredible dancer. Just with the expressions on his face and all his little gestures, he looks like a tin soldier. He does this dance called the Reebok, which you see people do in other parts of the movie.

The actors came up with a number of little songs during the shoot, some of which made it into the film. Roger Smith, who plays the Gammite "Yoda," did a reggae rap about his fellow Gammites that we wanted in the boiler-room scene but had to cut later on. The Gamma Rays and Jigaboos each put together a group song. I wanted to work these into the film, but again, there was no time. The Gammas came up with a little verse the day we shot the parade. When "Jane" and her court emerge from the Gamma pyramid, the Gammas sing, "Gamma queen, she's so fine, Gamma queen, blow my mind." The Fellas came back with their own version, "Drag queen, she's so fine, drag queen, blow my mind."

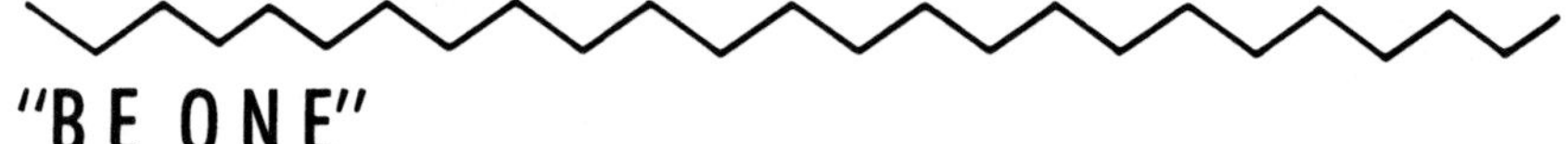

"BE ONE"

"Be One" is the slow jam that plays during the Splash Jam. I wanted to have a scene in the film where people danced to a slow record, so I gave my father a scenario and he came back to me two weeks later with "Be One." "Be One" was recorded in February of '87 at RCA Studios in New York. I was in Atlanta with key members of the cast, but I came back for the session. The student extras in Splash

Jam loved "Be One," which is like a 1940s-style torch piece, as if it would have been a slow song by the Isleys or anyone. Phyllis has a big following.

Patrick Ewing, basketball player for the Knicks, knocked on the door of my father's house one night as my father, my aunt Consuela, and I were going over "Be One." Consuela had moved into my father's house from Snow Hill, Alabama, to work with him on the music for *School Daze*. It turned out that my father's next-door neighbor was one of Patrick Ewing's best friends. His friend told him that I lived next door—I actually live down the block from my father—and he stopped by to meet me.

BILL LEE ▸ Spike told me he wanted me to write a love song, but he didn't want it to be like the other love songs. I agreed with that, because somewhere along the line, lyrics have gotten stuck on, "I love you, baby," and haven't gone much further than that. There are many more words that you can write. I've written operas—nine jazz operas—that deal with many things other than "I love you, baby." I try to draw on what my experiences have been.

When I was in junior high school in Snow Hill, Alabama, we had a basketball team. This was the early forties, the years of the Second World War. We went to a tournament nearby at Miller's Ferry. So we stepped on the floor and right away our first player made a spectacular pass to me from the center of the floor. The crowd went wild. Then I heard somebody telling the crowd, "Be one, Gloria, be one." We played the rest of the game, and all that day the crowd was yelling, "Be one." I finally heard the rest of it, which was, "Be one, go on and be a fool, go on and fall in love." It turned out that they were telling Gloria to fall in love with me.

I hadn't thought about that much until I started to write this song. But it was those lyrics that inspired me to write "Be One," which Phyllis Hyman, a great singer, was engaged to sing. She came over to the house, and at first I had it in the wrong key. When I had written the song, it wasn't decided who was gonna sing it. The key itself doesn't matter to a musician, because he can always transpose it. And that's what we did; we transposed it to her key, where she could be comfortable. But first she asked me to sing it.

Now, let me just say this, let me take this time to explain how I feel about a new piece of music. If a composer writes a piece of music, I think he should be able to give his interpretation of it. As a singer, you may look at a piece of music on paper, dry paper, and come up with the wrong feelings even if you do have the right tempo. You may come up with an interpretation that may be your experience, but not the composer's experience. I'm not saying you shouldn't bring your experiences to it, but since he composed the song, at least give him the benefit of the doubt and listen to what he intended.

I explained the lyrics to Phyllis and sang it for her, not meaning to limit in any way what she wanted to bring to it. She said, "Okay, change the key for me and let me try to get this together." We taped it, she took it home and made the song hers. Her interpretation turned out to be very beautiful and we had a good time with it. We didn't have to stay in the studio any time at all. I think we made two takes. Phyllis herself was pleasantly surprised that we could get it in that amount of time. We used a small combination of instruments, but it was a very full sound. I played bass, Joe Chambers played drums, there was Harold Vick, a very wonderful tenor, and Consuela on piano.

SPIKE ▸ Since the success of *SGHI*, people constantly ask, "Are you happy, are you sure?" My answer is still yes. I'm doing what makes me happy. And I say my prayers every night that I'm able to do the thing that makes me happiest and make a comfortable living too. And people ask, "Why film?" Well, I think because it encompasses all the arts, photography, music, acting, dance, you can put all that stuff in a film.

I probably could have followed in my father's footsteps, but I rebelled against it. He never pushed me into it, not any of his children. Whatever we wanted to do with our lives was fine with him. He and my mom just stood back and gave us encouragement. Moms dragged me to Broadway plays, and had to take me home in the middle of *The King and I,* because I cried. All that singing, music, and dancing scared me to death. But that's where I started to like musicals. On becoming a filmmaker, I knew that I'd want to try to do a musical. One of my first Super-8 films was a four-minute dance piece, the dancer was Melody Ruffin, and the song was Patti Austin's "At the End of the Rainbow." Melody had done it for the Morehouse coronation I directed. So we came back a month later to shoot it. By the way, Jasmine Guy, who plays "Dina," a Gamma Ray, danced in that coronation. She was a freshman in high school at the time.

In *SGHI* I tried to incorporate a musical number, the duet in color. Of all the reviews I read, this one scene received the most mixed response. I liked it then and still do. Island Pictures made several hints that it should be cut. One reviewer said, "Vince Minnelli is turning in his grave." That hurt. We tried it again in *School Daze* with the "Sun Is Rising" number and during the editing it got cut. It's a good dance number, but the film was too long. Barry and I spent a lot of time in editing trying to make the piece work. But alas, it still had to go.

When I think about it, *School Daze* really isn't a musical piece. But it's not a comedy or a drama either. *School Daze* is a complex hybrid of all the above. It's a hard film to describe in a sentence. But I strive not to make films that can be boxed in and categorized —unlike these "high concept" Hollywood movies. What is *School Daze* then? Maybe it's just a Spike Lee Joint, better than *SGHI.*

ERNEST DICKERSON ▸ One of the reasons I am a photographer, or a cinematographer, is because I'm a frustrated musician. People always ask me if I can play an instrument and I say, "Yeah, I play a camera." It's true. I think that music and photography are the same thing. See, music is vibrations that are picked up by the ears, cinematography is vibrations that are picked up by the eyes. When we shot the Miles video, we were doing some Super-8 stuff of him playing out on his roof and Miles just like leaned down and started playing to the floor. He just played to the floor. I said, "Miles, why do you play to the floor?" He said, "Oh, I'm bouncing sound off the floor." He said, "It makes it softer." I said, "Well, Miles, I do that with light." He says, "What?" I said, "Yeah, when I want to bounce light, I get a white board and bounce it off the board. It makes a softer light." Photography is light vibrations and music is sound vibrations.

To me, the only art form close to film is music. It's not literature, because literature is something that you have to cycle, you've got to work it out in your mind, you've got to think about it. But music

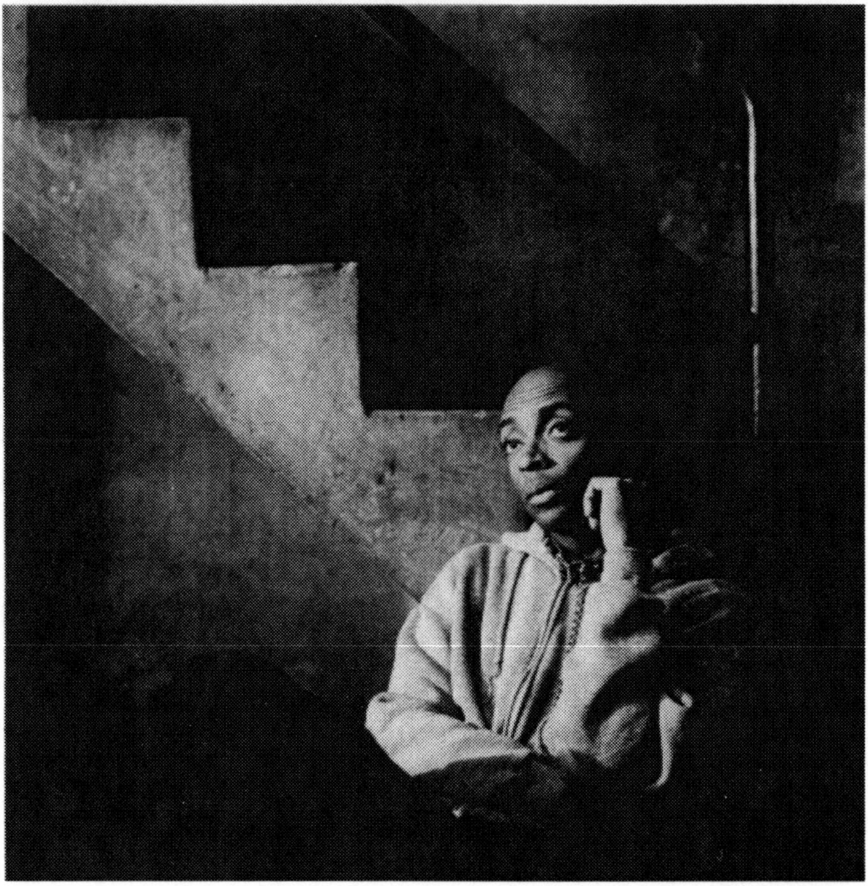

The actual production of a film, to me, is the killer. It's so physically taxing. I could stay in bed for a month just recuperating.

Barry Brown with Spike Lee.

you don't and film you don't. With music, it can give you subject matter to make you think, but in it's purest form, it just hits you. It just overwhelms you. Film works the same way. It's like direct access to the brain, either through the eyes or through the ears.

One reviewer said *She's Gotta Have It* was the closest thing to visual jazz he had ever seen. I don't think we were thinking about it while we were doing it, but it's sometimes that Spike and I used to talk about as possible. I mean, something we could really get into it—similar feelings—and play with concepts and stuff. It would be great, you know, if we could do for film what jazz has done for music, make it more spontaneous.

I think there's a lot of surrealism in our work. *She's Gotta Have It* has moments of surrealism. The filmmakers whose work we love the most do these things, like Martin Scorcese. He'll play with time, provide different perspective of time. We do that too. We replicate in film how one person's concept of time is different from the rest, or how when you have an experience that is intense, time for you slows down.

There's a scene we did in *School Daze* where "Half-Pint" goes to the dorm to try to find a girl because "Big Brother Almighty" tells him he has to bring a freak back to the frat house or he'll drop him from the line, and "Perry Sardner" (played by Kasi Lemmons) comes walking in. She's so beautiful that we shot her walk towards "Half-Pint" in slow motion. This happens again with "Grady," the football player, and "Vicky," the girl he meets at the Splash Jam. It's something that I feel all the time whenever I see a beautiful woman. Time slows down, you know.

The scene when "Dap" and "Rachel" make love, the lights are out and there's just moonlight coming in through the blinds. "Dap" starts kissing her neck. I had it worked out so that the light coming in through the blinds starts to move. All of a sudden the blinds patterns move over their bodies very slowly. It's almost like the world is rocking. It's totally apart from reality, but it's emotionally correct, it makes you wonder what the characters are feeling. It's that expressionistic thing that I think we put in our films that is in jazz. Just going straight for the feeling. Forget whether or not it's technically correct. Is it emotionally correct?

BILL LEE ▸ Spike and I have had the experience now of coming up with the best results, of working together on films. It's a very unselfish thing to do, in that the work itself is unselfish. 'Cause you just want to get what's best for everything. What's best for the movie and for the scene. And though you might have in mind that you want some music there, Spike might say, "Naw, I don't want music there." And you might have composed what you think is a great piece of music, but it may not fit there. And you have to put that piece of music aside. But I've had the experience of knowing that Spike is the director and that his final decision is just that. We've come to pretty good terms on that.

I haven't gotten to really talk about how much I enjoyed working with Spike on this. On the whole thing. And how happy for and proud I am of him. Right now we are just in the middle of doing the work. And all the accolades and everything else, all the praises—they will have to wait till we get all this work done. But that's one of the things that I'm happy about. That we do have the work to do. And I think it's work that the world needs done. That's been one of my quotes that I've kind of adopted. My grandfther said that there's a lot of work out there, but the work that you really want to do is the work that the world needs done. Plenty of people get up in the morning to do a whole lot of work that nobody needs. So I think the world needs this work we're doing.

Why do I think so? The movies, which are one of the major ways to influence people's views and rearrange people's thinking, have been misused so. But Spike is putting a real picture up on the screen for people to relate to. He's putting it back on the right track by being truthful. Anytime that Harold Vick (jazz saxophonist) can be identified as Harold Vick himself, representing himself on the screen, I think that's a great advancement. People can see this great, great man and hear his great sound come out of an instrument and know that it's him, that's truthful. See, a lot of time you may see somebody up there mocking, but it's actually not him. So it's a great stride. There are other things that are very innovative about what Spike is doing with movies. As time goes on he will be even more innovative.

I think Spike and Ernest, too, are musicians. Because the feeling that they have and the natural way they do things is actually a musician's way of doing them. With that rhythm and that lyricism they have. Just the phrase that Spike did when he said, "Please, baby, please, baby, please, baby, baby, baby, please." The way he said it, it comes out rhythmically even. So I look at Spike and Ernest as musicians, and if they had wanted to continue being musicians they would have been great musicians. Ernest says he started playing music when he was small. And I know Spike started playing when he was small, because I would direct him.

Spike Lee, my son, I'd call him the Charlie Parker of the movies. 'Cause Charlie Parker broke the chains that bind the music, and Spike has done the same in moviemaking. And they both lift up the world by doing so. The reason I'm saying all of this is because I think that musicians, especially jazz musicians, are the most talented men on earth; they are the closest to the spirit. They are the ones through whom the spirit is speaking. And I think they are closer to God than anybody. They're closer to nature and nature is God. So they're closer to the plan. A jazz musician has the practice of knowing what's right from wrong. He knows when he's played a bad note, he's had the constant practice of knowing the imbalance and the bad feeling that you get from playing a bad note and that feeling you get from hearing a bad note. So in his actions he knows what's right and wrong. And his dealing with people. He can make decisions on the spot, just very intuitively. But that comes from giving yourself up to the music. And if you follow the music, it'll lead you down the right road.

MUSIC MEETING

SPIKE ▸ The next step on my whirlwind tour of meetings around the offices of Columbia was the music. Sitting around the conference table were Bones Howe, Bob Dingilliam, Tom Andrews, Jane Alsobrook, Katherine Moore, Ed Russell, Dennis Green, and Gerry Griffith from Manhattan Records. What it came down to was Manhattan signed the deal for $350,000. We had gotten a $175,000 advance already and they weren't satisfied with the material on the album. Gerry said "Da Butt" was the only single. Then Bones Howe from Columbia echoed those sentiments. I was being asked to put another song in the movie. To put another song in the movie that had absolutely nothing to do with the film. Asked to put another song in the movie that had absolutely nothing to do with the film solely for the record sales. People can say what they will about a song promoting the film and the film promoting a song, but the shit has to be integrated.

This recent practice of having ten songs by the ten top-selling artists for a sound track SUCKS. It's the worst kind of fucking filmmaking. I hate it. And I told Gerry Griffith, made it plain, that *School Daze* is not that kind of film. And I told him that from the start, before the deal was signed. NO, NO, NO. I ain't having it. I did him a favor by putting his group, Pieces of a Dream, in the film. There has to be some integrity somewhere. The songs in this film and the sound track are "Be Alone Tonight," "Da Butt," "I'm Building Me a Home," "Be One," "We've Already Said Goodbye," "Perfect Match," "Straight and Nappy," and "I Can Only Be Me," plus possibly two selections from the score my father's writing. All the pieces are an integral part of the story, the film as a whole. I'm not gonna stick some terrible shit into it to guarantee something that can't be guaranteed. I made a conscious effort to have music in *School Daze* that doesn't sound like the shit you hear on the radio today. I'm a true believer that people want to hear good music; the album will sell, period.

7

"STRAIGHT AND NAPPY": GOOD AND BAD HAIR

SPIKE ▸ "Straight and Nappy" is the most ambitious piece of music in the film. I told my father in the fall of '86 that the big number in this movie would be a song about straight hair as "good" and nappy hair as "bad." It would feature the two groups, the Wannabees and the Jigaboos, each singing about the virtues of their hair type. The minute my father played it for me I knew it was a winner. We had to finagle with the lyrics a bit, but my father is very open to suggestions.

There are a couple of lines in the song that he actually asked for my input on. I suggested the word "kitchen" in the lyrics, and the line, "Look who's getting new today," both of which he hadn't heard before. I've heard the term "kitchen," as relates to Black hair, used many ways, but Meredith Woods, the assistant editor, gave me the most convincing definition. When you're getting your hair straightened, the back of your neck is the most sensitive part. The hot comb really feels hot back there, so they call it the kitchen.

Another explanation I heard comes from frying chicken. You get those bits of fried flour in your pan of oil, little crackly things that look like the little nappy curls near the hairline.

Although I came up with the titles of "Straight and Nappy" and "Da Butt" and the ideas behind the songs, I'm not a songwriter. A good talent is knowing when you can't do stuff and knowing who to get to do it for you. You merely convey what your vision is to them, what your ideal is.

I wanted the sound of this song to be big, so we had a fifty-piece orchestra record "Straight and Nappy" at RCA Studios in New York on February 5. While we were still with Island Pictures, and out in L.A. casting the picture, I met with Otis and played him a demo with just my father singing and playing the piano. He wasn't too thrilled with the song and said, "I don't know, Spike."

Otis had a partner who's a songwriter. He's written pieces for the group Teen Dream; Terry Whitlow, one of the Jigaboos, is the lead singer. Otis tried unsuccessfully to sell me on some songs written by his partner. I was unwavering. Later, when I played Otis the orchestra version of "Straight and Nappy," he began to see the piece in his head and told me he liked the song after all.

After my father rehearsed the twenty-four actresses for a week in Atlanta—plus a few local singers called in to fill in for those with less than perfect voices—we recorded "Straight and Nappy." We also recorded another song, which was later cut from the film, "Turn You Around." We had a complete reading of the script on the first day of rehearsals for the full cast (minus the day players). And when we came to "Straight and Nappy," I played a tape of the instrumental version. My father got up and sang all the parts. He danced up a storm, spinning around the room. On the last line, "Good and bad hair," he looked like Judy Garland. He had his arms stretched out and he hung on to those last words until everybody broke out into applause.

There was much discussion between Otis and my father about the interpretation of "Straight and Nappy." My problem with my father was that he didn't let go of the songs. There comes a point where you have to let go of them. I had faith that Otis was gonna do the right thing. But my father didn't know him and was afraid that this song, this piece that he wrote, which he loves, was gonna be tortured. We had a big meeting during preproduction which turned into a knock-down-drag-out battle. I was sitting at the head of the table mediating.

My father would yell; it would come back to Otis, and he'd yell. My father's worry was that Otis was trying to make it too much like a Hollywood film—too much like *West Side Story*. He thought that Otis would leave none of the negritude in the dance that was inherent in the music. My father felt that Otis didn't understand the type of dance that came out of the period he was drawing from.

Otis was very accommodating. He really bent over backward to make sure that my father's wishes were carried out. I can't really see any other choreographer doing what Otis did on this film. Many people would have told my father, "Later for you." Otis opened up the rehearsals so my father could see, and gave him a lot of input. The first time my father saw "Straight and Nappy" in the dance studio he walked out before the song was over.

My father, I think, was being overly sensitive. He didn't want Otis to do any choreography before he got there. He wanted to be in on it from the beginning, which was just impossible. We didn't have the time or money.

There was a point, though, where my father turned the number over to Otis completely. He was on set when we shot the scene, but he just observed. And when we showed him the edited version in New York, he was pleased.

It was three hard days shooting "Straight and Nappy"—a Friday, Saturday, and a Monday. There was so much dancing to be done. Tisha and Kyme danced with injuries. Kyme reaggravated her knee, which wasn't in good condition when she arrived. Tisha sprained her ankle the first day and didn't tell anyone about it until late Saturday night. And that Monday night was the last day for all the women in the film, except Tisha and Kyme. I gave them all copies of *Their Eyes Were Watching God* and *The Women of Brewster Place* with a note written inside. We had champagne on set, and there was a lot of crying and stuff—not done by me, though. People were sad to go.

"Straight and Nappy" is my favorite number. I love "Be Alone Tonight," but I think "Straight and Nappy" is more cinematic. Otis was tremendous. He is a great choreographer for the camera. One of his major strokes of genius in "Straight and Nappy" is his use of fans. The Jigaboos carry Vivien Leigh fans and the Wannabees have Hattie McDaniel fans, both from *Gone With the Wind.* Otis bought them in a gift shop in Atlanta and he didn't tell me about them before he incorporated them into the dance. I came to rehearsal one day and the dancers whipped them out and surprised the shit out of me.

Even though my father objected to the *West Side Story* comparison, I still saw this production as a gang fight, and the groups as teams. So I wanted them to be in uniforms of some kind. During preproduction in New York, Ruthe Carter was trying to get me to be more concrete about the costumes. I finally said I wanted to go with hockey jerseys, with a big *W* for Wannabee and a big *J* for Jigaboo on the front. She worked on that, modified it, and added those skintight pants, and the matching running bras and dance shoes.

I like the contrast between the contemporary feel of the costumes, the big-band swing music, and the old-time set. It would have been too much to have the actresses dressed up in 1940s garb. Everybody involved thought at one point or another that we should just go ahead and make it a period piece, but I decided against it.

BILL LEE ▸ It must have been back in the fall of 1986 that Spike gave me the first draft of the script. I kept asking him and he'd say, "When I'm through with it, I'll let you see it." Then he gave me a second draft around January and we talked about where he wanted some featured music. He told me about a piece called "Straight and Nappy" that he wanted me to write. It was supposed to be a big production number. At that time it was just a little seed.

Well, "Straight and Nappy" rang a bell with me. It's inherent in our culture, the good and bad hair thing. I was down at the A&P, ran into somebody, and was telling him about this piece I was writing called "Straight and Nappy." One of the clerks, a young man, overheard, and he said, "Straight and nappy, I don't know anything about that." I said, "You don't?" Now, he had just gotten all his hair cut off. So then there was a little fella bagging, you know, one of the little kids bagging the grocery bags as we came through the line. So I asked the clerk, "What kind of hair does he have?" He said, "Oh, he has good hair." And sure enough he did have good hair. It wasn't kinky, it wasn't nappy. So I said, "I thought you didn't know anything about that?" He knew plenty.

So it's in our culture, and I've been hearing it all my life and I'll continue hearing it. There's a poem, I don't think I've ever recited it before, but I'll recite it now. It is from one of my operas called *Baby Sweets,* and it goes like this:

There's still such a thing as good and bad hair
Niggers just went 'round the corner and came right back, they ain't gone nowhere.

When we say "straight and nappy," we refer to a criterion which Black people use to defeat or to praise; we use it as a weapon, have used it very effectively over the years, and will continue to, as far as I can see. When I first told Consuela, she said, "Oh, now, you got that one." So I know already she has an attitude about her hair. In fact, most people have an attitude about their hair. When I was coming up, I thought white people had good hair. I thought they didn't have to do anything to it, just get up in the morning and walk right on out the door, while we have to struggle with trying to get the comb through our hair without breaking all the teeth out.

It was fun writing "Straight and Nappy" and rehearsing it and recording it with the young ladies who performed it. They all identified, but some of the young ladies had not heard the terms I used

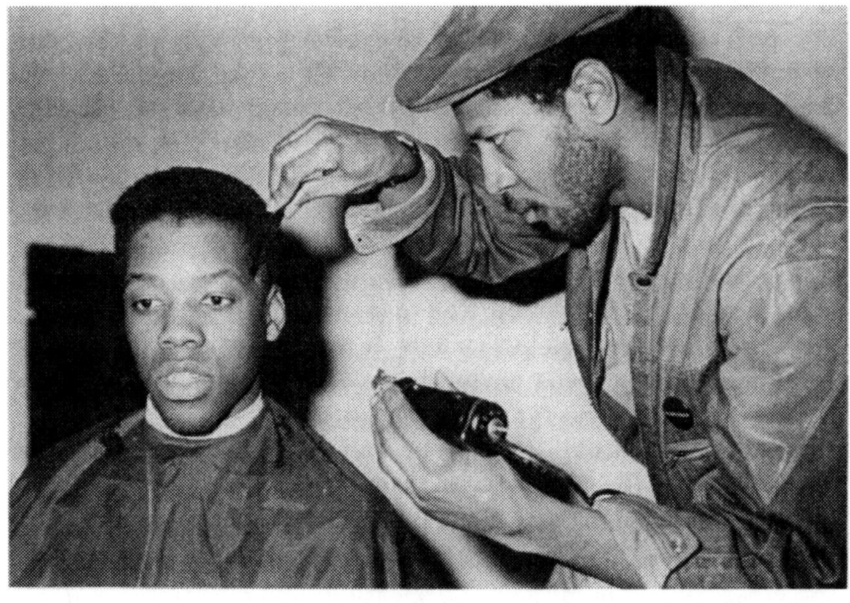

Larry Cherry—who's my barber—hooks up Kadeem's head. Larry also cuts Wynton and Branford Marsalis, Bernard King, Noel Pointer, Dave Winfield, and Willie Randolph. His styles are called, "It's a Cherry."

in the lyrics—sandyspurs, cock-ca-bugs. Some are poetic license—some for rhyme and rhythmic effect. So we went through every line of the song and discussed each. Cock-ca-bugs are little sticky plants, about as round as a peanut. They really don't serve any purpose other than to stick to your clothes. A sandyspur is a weed that grows and has these stickers that come out on the end of it. You don't have to wait for them to dry up and get brown to become hard. They're hard and brittle even when they're green. They come in bunches at the end of a bush and are such that you can throw them at somebody. If you walk barefoot in the South you are liable to get one painfully caught in your foot.

So we went through every line of that song and discussed each one. As a music director I advised them to have a really good understanding of what they're singing. As we worked on the number, I told the ladies that if the lyrics have no meaning to them, then they have no meaning to the people who are listening. But all of them had something of their own experience to bring to the song.

"Your hair ain't no longer than this [finger snap]." Yeah, we used to say that. And you got "cain't cha, don't cha hair . . . Cain't cha comb it and don't cha try." We talked about how some people neglect the kitchen in trying to keep their hair up. In fact, maybe they're not neglecting it, maybe it just knots up back there. Maybe they just can't do anything about it. I remember somebody would come up to you and say, "You better get that ole nappy, hey. Don't you think you better go get some of that ole nappy stuff cut off your head?" That would crush you right then. You'd say, "Aw, man, I got something like that sitting on top of my head? You mean am I the possessor of something that bad? Oh, well, let me go 'round here and get it cut." Because you're really offending people, man, if they're looking at you, and your hair is just making the whole world go all lopsided. So tighten up. You're the cause of all this confusion. Yep, a lot of things been put on hair. It just brings to mind some of the things that we spend too much time on. There's no such thing as good and bad hair as far as I'm concerned. All of it's good.

I think I was walking alone, up and down Myrtle Avenue in Brooklyn, when the melody came to me. It came in snatches. And I had to get to the piano to patch it together and make it make sense. It's strange sometimes how music comes. I kind of rely on the spirit. The creative part is mysterious, spiritual, and mystifying. I don't really understand the process myself. I just leave myself open to be an instrument for the music to flow through.

It took me a month to complete "Straight and Nappy." I'm not a fast writer, and a seven-minute piece with a fifty-piece orchestra is a lot of music. But I never shirk the work. I always enjoy it. Spike would rather not hear it until I think I've come up with something presentable. Because it's not fair to him or to me. I may have a good idea, but until I've worked with that idea, it may not sound right. And if Spike listens to it and doesn't like it, then I've lost a good piece of music that maybe later on we could have used. It's the same way with his work. He doesn't like to present a piece of work to me until he's satisfied that we can get the best results from having looked at it. That's why he doesn't want me to see dailies, only the rough cut. That's how we've worked on all of our movies.

Spike told me that he wanted me to get together a large orchestra to record "Straight and Nappy." I selected the pieces myself, French horns, trombones, trumpets, saxophones, flutes, strings, and a rhythm section. It came to fifty pieces. I felt very proud and fortunate to have an opportunity to be working with all of them, the greatest musicians in the world. Some I'd never met before or heard play. But I had confidence in the word of the musicians who recommended them. All of their cooperation and determination to do the work was just overwhelming.

We didn't overdub the sections we recorded in that session. We recorded live, something that is virtually unheard of these days. Now the violin section comes in first, then the rhythm section, or maybe they'll just bring the bass player in and begin. Musicians end up listening to recordings where they don't know who they played with, or never saw them.The first trombone player never sees the second trombone player.

We're at a point right now where the synthesizer will knock all the musicians out of work. They can take one of these electrical synthesizers and replace a whole one-hundred-piece orchestra. The musicians don't feel good about that at all. I have always felt that electronic music would somehow hurt the industry. Not only the quality of the music, but hurt your pockets also. They used to laugh when a bass player couldn't bring his upright bass to a job, but had to bring his Fender bass instead. Now they don't even bother to call us; they just ask one man to bring his synthesizer. So when we had the opportunity to record "Straight and Nappy" with a full orchestra, the people at the studio couldn't believe it. They couldn't believe that somebody was going to use a fifty-piece orchestra.

WYNN THOMAS ▸ The first week of preproduction, instead of my going down to Atlanta to look for locations right away (I was kind of anxious about getting down there and finding them), we had a week of concept meetings. Spike, Ernest, myself, the first assistant director at the time, Roderick, and the costume designer, Ruthe Carter. We sat around and talked about the script. It was a wonderful exchange of ideas. The only thing that we knew about "Straight and Nappy" at that point was that Spike wanted it to be in a beauty parlor with oversize props. Spike also told us that it was going to be a confrontation number like "America" in *West Side Story*. It ended up not being like "America" at all. We did look at several musicals during those meetings, just for us all to get a common vocabulary. But I don't think we ended up using anything. I knew at that point that I wanted to use mirrors on the "Straight and Nappy" set. How I was gonna use those mirrors, I really didn't know. We were all waiting to hear about the music.

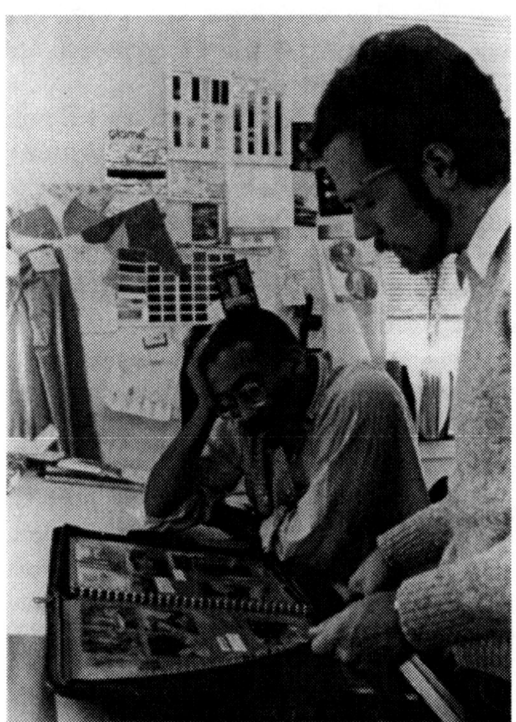

Wynn Thomas (left) and Alan Trumpler, Art Director.

We had all read the script prior to these meetings, but it didn't say anything about "Straight and Nappy." All it said was it was this "major MGM production number." The piece ended up evolving over several months, really. "Straight and Nappy" was probably the biggest challenge for everybody in the movie. Since nobody really knew what it was going to be, what it was supposed to be, the whole process became very much a strong collaboration. When the music came, I was totally shocked, because it was not at all what I thought it was going to be.

I had anticipated a musical number, you know, like "America," which is very Broadway, very overorchestrated. I didn't expect it to be jazz. So when I heard Mr. Lee's sort of very jazzy, sort of Gershwinish, '40s composition—I don't know how to categorize it—I was stunned. I was surprised and I didn't know what to design. Because in my head I was designing a set that would have functioned for a Broadway musical. For a while his music was the stumbling block. I didn't understand how it fit into what we were trying to say with this particular number, at least from the impression that Spike had given me. Spike was surprised by it too, I think, because I remember him saying something about how we were going to have to change our thoughts on "Straight and Nappy" a little bit. [Author's note: I was not surprised. I saw it as a jazz piece from the start.]

Part of the design problem that I had with the piece was time, since I didn't actually design it until we were shooting. My day was full of supervising, taking care of the immediate problems. I was also procrastinating because I didn't know what it was supposed to be. Nothing was coming into my little head. The more I listened to the music, I said, "All right, I've got to deal with this." Then I went to a couple of rehearsals with Otis and Spike. And I noticed something. My initial ground plan on that set was a big circular room in which the actors would revolve around each other like cats. Otis was working with something that was more linear. So I began to see that space as the one to work with.

One of the ways the music influenced me was that it was very fluid. As a result I said, "This should be a room that is rectangular, but no straight lines. It is a room where nothing is square, everything should be circular somehow." I began to investigate art that was fluid—certainly art nouveau and some Edwardian art. Then I began to see in my head all these sort of wonderful sculptures that were very loose. I said, "What if I do a sculpture with straight hair and one with nappy hair and use these sculptures somewhere in the room?" Once I hit on the sculptures, the whole thing sort of clicked, came to be. I knew that I could use the hair to create an arch, for example. And once I solved that, the whole look evolved for me.

Another design problem that I had to solve with "Straight and Nappy" was Spike's use of hockey jerseys as costumes. He wanted the Jigaboos in these red, orange, purple things and the Wannabees in white and gray. Both Ruthe and I hated the idea of using those jerseys. But they were ordered and it was something that Spike really wanted. Both of us said, "Ugh, God, this is terrible." Without knowing much of anything about the piece, without knowing the music, he wanted these sports jerseys with the women's names on the backs. I hated the colors. But at that point, both Ruthe and I realized that this was something that we could not change.

Ruthe must have said something to Spike about my disliking the jerseys, during the rehearsal period in Atlanta. Spike came into the office and said, "I want to see what you have so far for 'Straight and Nappy.' " I hadn't worked it all out. I had my initial quarter-inch-scale rough sketches, that was it. I showed him the initial shapes, and one of the things we talked about was the fact that costumes would be an anachronism in the space. Once we agreed on that, that they wouldn't make sense in whatever space we put them in, things were fine for both of us.

The ideal way of working is that you come up with your set first and everything else should evolve from there. That's the ideal. Obviously Spike felt very strong about these jerseys and wanted them. But it was only when we agreed that they would stand as an anachronism that I could accept them. Until that point I was trying to encourage him to go with something else.

So I brought two samples of those jerseys into my design room and said, "I've got to design some colors around these things to make the costumes work." That is where the color pallet I used on that set came from. I ended up with those sort of broad lavenders and golds, choices that would contrast and complement the jerseys, particularly those the Jigaboos would wear. Anything will work with gray and white. But I had to get something to work with the bright colors or they would have been an eyesore.

The colors that I used in that set, the lavenders, those greens, those three turquoises, were colors that I had never used before and

I was petrified. I worked very closely with my scenic designer Brian Schultz, and I would say to him, "Paint me one piece in this color, paint me a swatch, because I'm not sure of it." I would go to the soundstage every day to see how things were progressing and see these colors and not have any idea of what they were going to look like. I had never used such broad color before, such colorful colors before. In the movie business you normally have to be very conservative about color. You don't want it to stand out too much. You want the scenery to recede in the background. Here color was used as a very bold element of the set and at the same time managing to complement the costumes and all the skin tones.

Ernest was very helpful in making me feel secure about the colors for "Straight and Nappy." We had a big meeting just about color. Initially I was going to do the purple cyclorama in a traditional cyclorama color, a light blue. It was Ernest who suggested using purples throughout the rest of the set and painting the cyclorama a deep purple. I think it was a fine idea for pulling the whole set together. We didn't have to saturate it with light in order to get a feeling back there.

Ernest was very supportive. You have some directors of photography—Gordon Willis is famous for this—who go to a production designer and say, "These are the colors you are using." Neither Ernest nor Spike has ever done that. They've always been very open and receptive to my color schemes.

When it came time to give the salon in "Straight and Nappy" a name, I went to Spike. Since we'd see the name on-screen, I wanted to make sure that he'd be happy with it. This was supposed to be the definitive Black woman's beauty salon. And when I think about the history of Black women's beauty salons, I think about Madame C. J. Walker. So that's where the "Madame" came from. We named it "Madame," Spike added "Re-Re."

Lynn Wolverton, my set decorator, was very helpful in suggesting ideas for the set dressing. We were over budget by this time. And to make the oversize props we had in mind would have been too expensive. It involved making molds, and that was cost prohibitive. So Lynn went out and found all these wonderful jars for me and we painted them to match the set. We had to limit the use of wig stands because wig stands are very expensive. But both of us decided that we wanted outrageous wigs and other colorful items to dress the set. We spent almost $8,000 on chairs. At first, the company covered them with the wrong fabric in the wrong color. We had to send them back and start again.

I was nervous about the entire set for the longest time. I was showing everybody else stuff before I showed Spike. It was a set that I just didn't know about, but once I got the idea of using the sculptures as a unifying element, I was home. Then it was just a matter of showing things to the Lees.

Bill Lee and Consuela Lee Morehead had particular ideas about the way they wanted things to be choreographed to their music. I personally don't believe that's something that they should have had a say about. We had all been instructed that "Straight and Nappy" was to be MGM musical material. That says broad, theatrical dancing, something in the tradition of musical theater rather than something jazzy.

I think the Lees were upset when they saw what Otis was doing, so upset that we had this meeting the week before we started shooting. One of the things I like about Spike is his concern with letting everyone express his own point of view. And that's what happened at this meeting. To me, there are times when collaboration is fine and there are times when someone has to say, "No, this is what it's going to be." Spike eventually did that. But we spent two hours meeting before that happened.

Those open discussions put Otis in the awkward position of trying to satisfy the Lees rather than just satisfying Spike. Otis should not have to work for the people who write the music. We all work for the director, Spike. We're all collaborators to a point.

"STRAIGHT AND NAPPY" GOOD AND BAD HAIR

Music and Lyrics by Bill Lee

A Chorus—Wannabees and Jigs

Talkin' 'bout good and bad hair
whether you are dark or fair
go on and swear
see if I care
good and bad hair

B Wannabees—1st Verse

Don't you wish you had hair like this
then the boys would give you a kiss
'bout nuthin' but bliss
then you gonna see what you missed

Jigs—1st Verse

If a fly should land on your head
then I'm sure he'd break all his legs
'cause you got so much grease up there
tell me, dear, is that a weave you wear

C Wannabees—Bridge

Well you got cock-ca-bugs
standing all over your head

Jigs

Well you got sandyspurs
rather have mine instead

Wannabees

Well you're a Jigaboo
trying to find something to do

Jigs

Well you're a Wannabee
Wannabee better than me

INSTRUMENTAL DANCE

D Wannabees—2nd Verse

Bad hair is only good for one thing
if you get a lick, back it'll spring
caint cha, don't cha hair stand on high
caint cha comb it and don't you try

Jigs—2nd Verse

Don't you know my hair is so strong
it can break the teeth out the comb
I don't have to put up at night
what you have to keep out of sight

Wannabees (Bridge) repeat
Jigs repeat

INSTRUMENTAL DANCE

E Wannabees—3rd Verse

Your hair ain't no longer than [finger snap]
so you'll never fling it all back
and you 'fraid to walk in the rain
oh, what a shame, who's to blame

Jigs—3rd Verse

Don't you ever worry 'bout that
'cause I don't mind being BLACK
go on with your mixed-up head
I ain't gonna never be 'fraid

F BRIDGE

Wannabees

Well you got nappy hair

Jigs

Nappy is all right with me

Wannabees

My hair is straight you see

Jigs

But your soul's crooked as can be

Wannabees

Look who's getting NEW today

Jigs

Look anywhere you please

Wannabees

Not at that kitchen of yours

Jigs

Mind out what you say

G Chorus—Wannabees and Jigs
Talkin' 'bout good and bad hair
whether you are dark or fair
go on and swear
see if I care
good and bad hair

(repeat 3 times)

Tag

go on and swear
see if I care
good and bad hair

(repeat 3 times)

WHAT MUSIC VIDEOS HAVE TO DO WITH IT

SPIKE ▸ I've honed my filmmaking abilities in many ways by making music videos. It's something that doesn't take up a lot of time. You don't have to devote a year to a music video; it's a week or two at the most. It keeps you sharp, because, admit it, if a filmmaker does one feature every two years, that's great. I want to do stuff between features. And I want this stuff to be film. Television doesn't appeal to me much, and I don't want to get into that world of commercials where ad-agency executives stand over your shoulder saying they don't like that color of blue or the way this cornflake is shaped. So music video is a happy medium.

A week or so before we finished the rough cut of *School Daze* [July 21–25], I did a music video for Anita Baker, photographed by Ernest and edited by Barry Brown. It's Anita's fourth single, "No One in the World," and her fourth video. It was ironic in a way, because Anita Baker was my first choice to sing "Be One" in *School Daze.* The first time I went out to L.A. to cast, I talked to Anita's manager, Sherwin Bass. Unless we offered Anita a speaking role in addition to the song, Bass said Anita would not be interested. I've always thought that if I'd been able to speak to Anita herself we could have worked things out. This is not to slight Phyllis Hyman, who was wonderful. In retrospect I think that we were better off with Phyllis. Anita won two Grammys in '86, and *Rapture* sold 4 million in the U.S., a four-time platinum. Phyllis needed the part in *School Daze* more than Anita, it's just that simple.

After I graduated from film school I tried to look for any film work I could while still working towards getting my first feature off the ground. I tried and tried to get music videos. I went to all the record companies. Eventually I did a video on spec for Grandmaster Flash, a song called "White Lines." Ernest and I received some grant money from my thesis film, *Joe's Bed-Stuy Barbershop* and I talked him into using it to do "White Lines." It's about this coke dealer who entices dancers to become coke addicts. Larry Fishburne is a lead actor. I cast Hajnas Moss, who is now his wife, as a dancer; that's how they met.

I took the video to Sugar Hill Records and they liked it. They claimed they were going to give me the money to finish it, but they never did. Instead those motherfuckers put the work print on the air. Not getting paid for it was one thing, but what made me really angry was the idea of them showing a work print; there were still splices in the piece, it was not broadcast quality.

I continued to go to record companies and ask to do music videos, and they continued to look at me like I was crazy. In fact, Robin Sloane, the head of the Video Department whom I dealt with at Elektra Records for "No One in the World," was one of the people who turned me down. It was only after the success of *She's Gotta Have It* that I started to get work doing music videos. First one I did was the *She's Gotta Have It* video, which Barry Brown and I edited. We had to fight tooth and nail to get $5,000 from Island to do it.

Shortly after, I got a call from Warner Brothers Records' Jo Bergman. She said, "Miles Davis has a new album coming out called *Tutu* and he wants you to do the music video." I was floored. Miles Davis. And he was asking me to do it. I said, "Bet." You hear a lot of stories about Miles, about how hard he is to work with. But we got along great. The number one reason why we got along, and why I was able to get Miles to do what I thought was best for the video, is because I'm Bill Lee's son. That made me legit in his eyes. I'm Bill Lee's son and he is an accomplished jazz musician. So Miles trusted me and had confidence that I knew something about the music.

Branford Marsalis approached me after I did *Tutu* to direct his "Royal Garden Blues." Now that turned out not to be the most happy of situations. I didn't see eye to eye with CBS. We shot the piece in the Bronx, at the Bronx Botanical Gardens. To me, it's a simple song and therefore required a simple approach. CBS wanted a MTV-rock approach. That was not the type of piece I wanted to do and not the type of piece that I told them I was going to do.

When we cut the video, Branford's manager, Ann-Marie Wilkins, started to have doubts. Ann-Marie didn't back me on this. She started to say she didn't like the video, then CBS didn't like it. Branford was caught in the middle. They wanted me to recut the whole thing. This was in November and I was really getting into the thick of preproduction for *School Daze.* We had a meeting with Joe Nardelli, my production manager for the video, and with Deborah Samuelson from CBS. I told her she could kiss my Black ass. Here I am getting ready to do a $6 million motherfucking film, and they're telling me how they want me to recut this video. I walked. I disowned it. They brought in an editor, recut it, did all kinds of stuff; I've never seen it.

When we came back from shooting *School Daze,* Doug Daniels, who used to work at Elektra, got in touch with me. I knew Doug from Atlanta—Monty, Pamm, and I were in school and Doug was working with WCLK, the Clark College radio station. Doug had been trying to get Robin Sloane to use me and other black directors to do videos for Elektra. Though they have many Black groups, they never use any Black production companies or directors for their videos. So Doug called me, and said, "Spike, it looks like you'll be doing Anita Baker's fourth single." Elektra called me in. I talked to Anita, and she was eager to work with me. While we were negotiating the deal I invited Anita to the office to show her some footage from *School Daze.* And each time she said, "No, I'm gonna be too upset." I really do think she regrets that she wasn't in the film.

Anita's first video, "Sweet Love," is funny. It's a direct steal from *She's Gotta Have It.* The whole video is candles, not only that, but candles on headboards, just like "Nola's" bed. I asked Anita about it and she laughed. I told her I considered it a compliment. I didn't see her next two videos, but I hear they didn't do her justice. One is a performance piece; in the other she goes back to Detroit, y'know, hometown girl makes good. The music video is a great form but rarely do you see great work. I liked both Anita's albums, and wanted to do her justice.

From going to a couple of amateur nights at the Apollo, I came up with the idea of making Anita a contestant in the video. It was her idea to put it in the past, to make it a period piece of sorts. She wanted to get all dressed up. When we discussed the idea, Anita was adamant about having a big budget. The budgets for her three previous videos probably didn't go any higher than $60,000. Anita complained that they had a grainy look and wanted "No One in the World" to be a better-quality piece. So I told her we'd have to shoot 35 millimeter, and she said, "Then let's shoot 35." She said, "Spike, don't worry about the cost. If we have to spend the money, let's do it." Anita Baker is Elektra's biggest act. And I know they spend more on music videos for these heavy-metal white boys than on Anita Baker, and she's won two Grammys and sold much records.

The video ended up costing almost $130,000. Anita's manager and the record company were worried at first about the length of the video, that we were gonna spend all this time and money on shooting a two-minute prologue before the song starts only for it to be cut. But once we began shooting and they saw the piece take shape and that I was going to be in it, they dropped their case. I actually make two appearances in the video, one as Slick Mahoney, "the funniest comic dead or alive," and as Mars Blackmon. It's the first time anyone has seen Mars, other than a brief spot on *Saturday Night Live* in the fall of '86, since *She's Gotta Have It*.

I've had many offers to re-create Mars. California Wine Cooler offered me $50,000 to build an entire ad campaign behind Mars Blackmon. John McClain, Janet Jackson's manager, tried to interest me in doing a rap record as Mars, please, baby, please, baby, please. I said that's definitely out.

MUSIC VIDEO SCRIPT ▸ **"No One in the World"**

Artist: Anita Baker
Album: *Rapture*
Written and directed by Spike Lee
Photographed by Ernest Dickerson

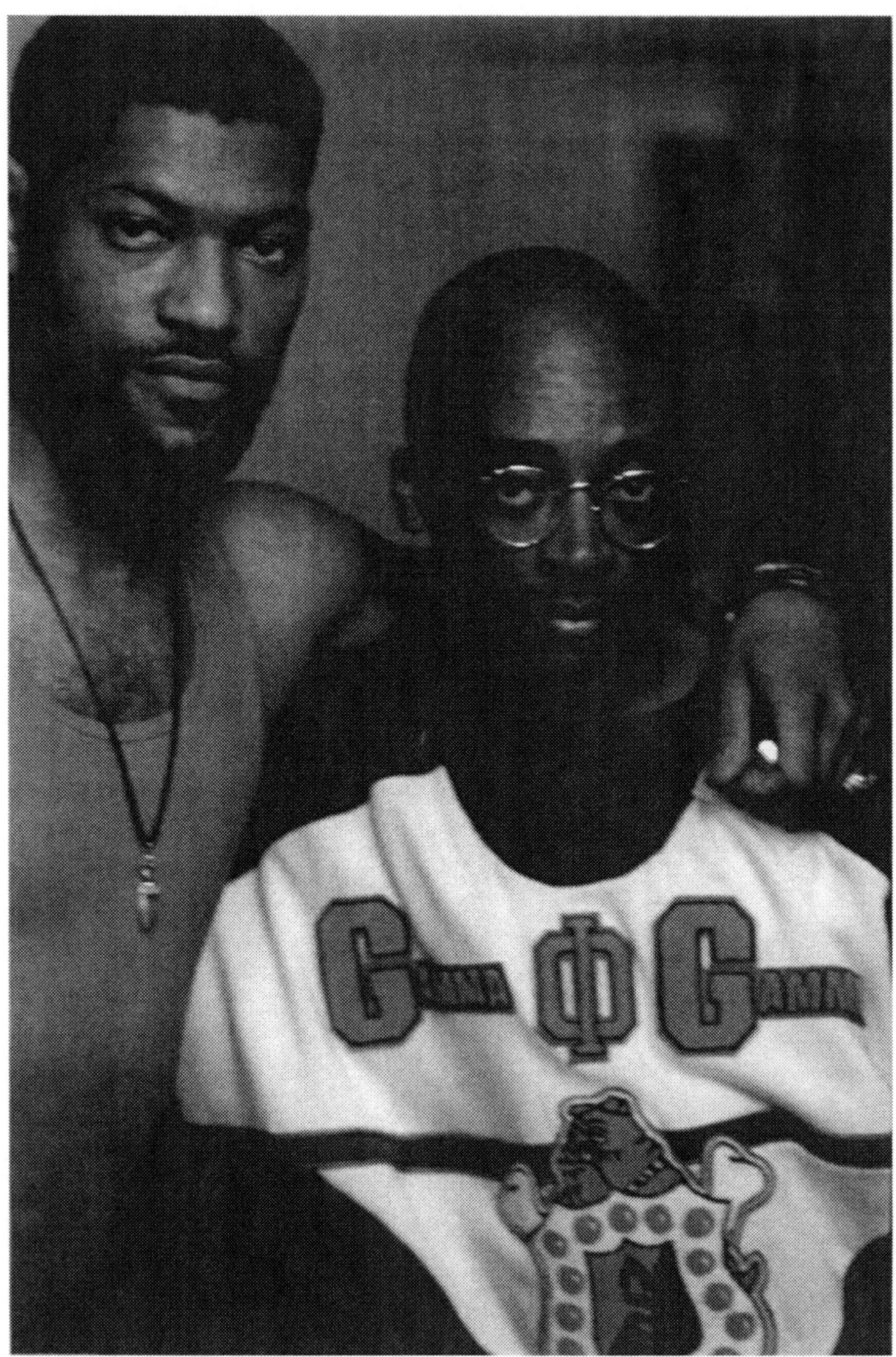

▲ Larry Fishburne and myself had a rocky working relationship. We're great friends but this was the first time we worked together. What enabled us to rise above the conflicts was both of us wanting what was best for the film.

▼ Monty nicknamed Ernest Dickerson "The Golden Eye" for his highly developed visual sense.

▼ Wake up!

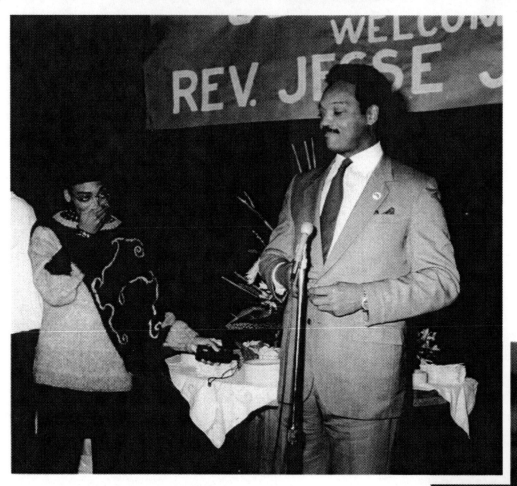

▲ The Rev. Jesse Jackson had me dying laughing when he told us he himself was a Q-dog—a member of the Omega Psi Phi fraternity.

This is what you call BEFORE and AFTER. We rehearsed "Straight and Nappy" on the Madame Re-Re set for one day before we came back to do the three-day shoot.

▼ Internal bickering amongst the ranks of Gamma Phi Gamma was a headache. There were six Gammas and every one of them had his own ideas. JESUS CHRIST ON THE CROSS!

▲ If "Be Alone Tonight" isn't a hit, I'll eat a rubber boot.

"NO ONE IN THE WORLD"

The TIME is 1945, the war is over, people are happy and want to have a good, good time. The place is HARLEM, U.S.A., and every Wednesday the inhabitants of Uptown pack the world-renowned APOLLO THEATRE for AMATEUR NIGHT. Amateur night is a tradition; many stars were discovered on the stage at the Apollo, before what is known as the world's toughest audience. If your act, your showmanship, isn't up to their high standards, they show no mercy on your soul. You'll be booed, hissed, cursed at, thrown at. Then the Executioner himself, with cap gun in hand, comes out, shoots you, and takes you off the hallowed stage. But if you're together, talented, there can be no better audience; they will let you know the deal, they appreciate your talent and their hearts go out to you. This is the backdrop for the music video, "No One in the World."

EXT: *STREET—APOLLO STAGE DOOR*

CLOSE HEADLINE—"V-J DAY—JAPAN QUITS"

We pull back and we see a young newspaper girl hawking an EXTRA edition of the *Daily News.*

GIRL

Extra! Extra! Read all about it, V-J Day! Japan quits.

The hand-held camera now is on a yellow cab that pulls up in front of the stage door. Emerging from it is Sol Weinstein, dragging his protégée LuLu McDuffie. The following dialogue is at breakneck speed.

WEINSTEIN

Let's go! You're ready for the Apollo.

LULU

No.

WEINSTEIN

You are. I got a lot invested in you.

LULU

I've heard about those audiences; they kill people.

WEINSTEIN

Relax. Trust me.

INT: *APOLLO*

The place is packed, filled with soldiers home from the war.

ANGLE—STAGE

The MC for the Apollo Amateur Night takes the stage and gets the crowd ready.

MC

Now for the first act straight from downtown, Ziggy Cuddles.

Ziggy Cuddles pushes his upright piano onstage and keeps the first note from drowning out his Tin Pan Alley tinker.

CLOSE—STAGE WING

The Executioner appears from the shadows and throws a knife.

CUT TO:

CLOSE—ZIGGY

He slumps over his piano; camera reveals knife in his back; he's dead.

ANGLE—AUDIENCE

They applaud.

CLOSE—LULU and WEINSTEIN

Weinstein has to restrain her from bolting out of there.

CLOSE—MC

MC

Next, one of the funniest men I know, dead or alive. Slick Mahoney.

CLOSE—SLICK

SLICK

Y'know, coming over here a bum
came up to me, said he hadn't a bite
in weeks so I bit him.

The crowd boos.

CLOSE—EXECUTIONER

He pulls back on a bow and arrow.

CUT TO:

CLOSE—SLICK

He has a funny look on his face; camera tilts to his chest, where an arrow protrudes. The crowd boos.

SLICK

OK. When I was young I used to take
an apple to my teacher. Now I take my
teacher to The Big Apple.

Slick gets another arrow for that one.

CLOSE—LULU and WEINSTEIN

She's doing everything to get out of the grip of her manager.

CLOSE—SLICK

SLICK

Ahhh. You got me.

The crowd applauds as he slumps to the stage floor.

CLOSE—MC

MC

This little lady sings like a bird.
LuLu McDuffie.

CLOSE—LULU and WEINSTEIN

He pushes her out onto the stage.

ANGLE—STAGE

LuLu walks out onto the enormous stage; one spotlight is on her. She stands there frozen. From the cheap seats we hear, "Sing, girl, we don't have all night."

CLOSE—LULU

She sings "No One in the World," and as if on cue, the audience becomes quiet.
Some vignettes to be interspersed throughout the song are:
1—Couples kissing.
2—The backup singers in a balcony box.
3—People throwing money onto the stage.
4—DIALOGUE:

SOLDIER

Now I know why I fought in the war.
Sing it, girl.

5—Weinstein smiling in the wings.
6—Weinstein flirts with another singer, then pulls out a contract for her to sign.
7—MC dancing in the wings.
8—LuLu's mother listening to her daughter sing on the radio.

ANGLE—STAGE

As LuLu finishes the song, she runs off the stage right past Weinstein. She doesn't hear the roar of the applauding audience.

EXT: *STAGE DOOR*

As LuLu exits the door we are in the present, but she is still in her 1945 attire. Her adoring public applauds and asks for autographs. However, they say she's Anita Baker. She answers, "I'm LuLu. LuLu McDuffie"—caught in a time warp. Mars Blackmon appears selling his tubesocks at three for $5 and says, "Please, baby, please, baby, please, baby, please, baby."

END

8

ON THE ROAD WITH *SCHOOL DAZE*

FIRST PUBLIC SCREENING: AUGUST 18, 1987, RITZ THEATRE, PHILADELPHIA, PA.

It was after the first screening for the big cheeses, David Puttnam and David Picker, that Columbia suggested the next one be for a recruited audience. I talked it over with Barry and we both agreed it was the thing to do. We couldn't edit the film any more, it was time to see how it played before an audience; then we could proceed after that. It couldn't be done in New York. No matter how hard we'd try, word would get out and there'd be a mob trying to rush the door. Plus who is to say a journalist wouldn't sneak in and write something? The film was still a work-in-progress and it wasn't ready to be reviewed.

I chose Philly for our first screening. It's only ninety minutes away from New York and has a sizable Black population. The theater would be the Ritz. *She's Gotta Have It* played there for something like twenty-six weeks. The date agreed upon was Tuesday, August 18, 1987. That morning Barry, Meredith, Monty, and myself

The Local Yokels:
You college motherfuckers think y'all are white. Y'all be niggers always, just like us.

The mighty men of the black-and-silver Gamma Phi Gamma. I rolled all the worst elements of the Qs, Alphas, Sigmas, Grooves, and Kappas into one. Pass da pussy, please.

The four beautiful, fine, serious, slammin', bumpin' sisters "Half-Pint" sees at the dorm when told to bring a "freak back to the Gamma house tonight. I don't care if she's blind, fat, no teeth, and has one leg with a kickstand." Though this does not apply to (left to right) Toni Ann Johnson, Kasi Lemmons, Paula Birth, and Tracey Robinson.

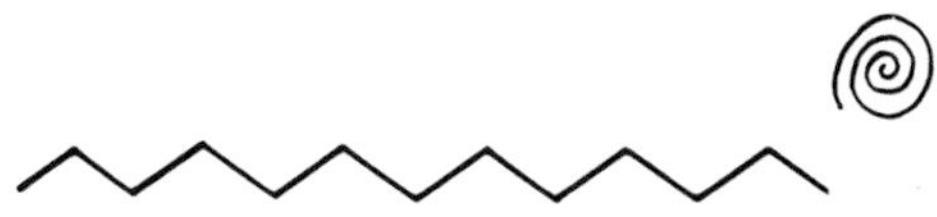

drove down to Philly. We got in around 10:39 A.M., checked in at the Sheraton-Society Hill. We walked over to the Ritz and had a run-through. Flying in for Columbia were Tom McCarthy, Dennis Green, Bob Dingilliam, Tom Rothman, and Lenore Cantor.

I had requested to Lenore that the demographics of the audience be 65 percent Black and 35 percent white. It became plain early on that we were not going to get that breakdown. The film was scheduled to run at 7:30 P.M. Folks began lining up at 5:30 outside the theater and many had to be turned away. In total, 335 showed; only 17 people were not Black.

The screening was a huge success. It's hard to explain what it feels like when you're sitting in the middle of the audience that is eating up your film. The people were into it, on every joke, and this wasn't even a finished work. However, two audience reactions did trouble me deeply. The audience began to howl when Tisha sang the first chorus of "Turn You Round," the song intended for the Death March. It was like someone was twisting a knife in my stomach. I looked over at Barry and he was feeling the same. Even though some people applauded at the end, it did me no good.

The other trouble spot was at the beginning of the Wake Up scene. Again, the audience was laughing and the end of the movie is definitely serious. That's why screenings like this can be a lifesaver. I'll look over the statistical reports and shit, but number one for me is being there with the people. That's what is most valuable to me, what works and what doesn't work.

After the screening, there was no doubt in anyone's mind that *School Daze* played very well before a predominantly Black audience. We decided to try for a larger percentage of whites for our next screening. The film was gonna play, period. I received a report from National Research Group, the people who recruited the surveyed audience, two days after the screening in Philly. What follows is the questionnaire and an excerpt from their results.

QUESTIONNAIRE FILLED OUT BY AUDIENCE AT RESEARCH SCREENINGS:

Please take a moment to let us know how you feel about the movie you just saw.

1. What was your reaction to the movie overall? ('X" ONE) (06(

EXCELLENT	( ) 1
EXTREMELY GOOD	( ) 2
VERY GOOD	( ) 3
GOOD	( ) 4
FAIR	( ) 5
POOR	( ) 6

2. Would you recommend this movie to your friends? ("X" ONE) (07(

YES, DEFINITELY	( ) 1
YES, PROBABLY	( ) 2
NOT SURE	( ) 3
NO, PROBABLY NOT	( ) 4
NO, DEFINITELY NOT	( ) 5

3. What would you tell your friends about this movie? Not just whether you liked it or not, but how would you describe it to them? (PLEASE BE AS COMPLETE AS POSSIBLE)

4. Please list what scenes you liked most and liked least, if any. (PLEASE BE AS SPECIFIC AS POSSIBLE IN YOUR DESCRIPTION OF THE SCENES.)

Scenes Liked Most	Scenes Liked Least
1.	1.
2.	2.
3.	3.
4.	4.
5.	5.

Scenes Liked Most	Scenes Liked Least
6. ______	6. ______
7. ______	7. ______
8. ______	8. ______
9. ______	9. ______
10. ______	10. ______

5. How would you rate each of the following characters or elements of the movie? Please mark one answer for each element.

	Excellent	Very Good	Good	Fair	Poor	Don't Remember	
Dap Dunlap, played by Larry Fishburne	( ) 1	( ) 2	( ) 3	( ) 4	( ) 5	( ) 6	(08-
Rachel Meadows, played by Kyme	( ) 1	( ) 2	( ) 3	( ) 4	( ) 5	( ) 6	23(
Julian Eaves, played by Giancarlo Esposito	( ) 1	( ) 2	( ) 3	( ) 4	( ) 5	( ) 6	
Jane Toussaint, played by Tisha Campbell	( ) 1	( ) 2	( ) 3	( ) 4	( ) 5	( ) 6	
Half-Pint, played by Spike Lee	( ) 1	( ) 2	( ) 3	( ) 4	( ) 5	( ) 6	
Jordan, played by Branford Marsalis	( ) 1	( ) 2	( ) 3	( ) 4	( ) 5	( ) 6	
Cedar Cloud, played by Art Evans	( ) 1	( ) 2	( ) 3	( ) 4	( ) 5	( ) 6	
President McPherson, played by Joe Seneca	( ) 1	( ) 2	( ) 3	( ) 4	( ) 5	( ) 6	
Virgil Cloyd, played by Gregg Burge	( ) 1	( ) 2	( ) 3	( ) 4	( ) 5	( ) 6	
The story	( ) 1	( ) 2	( ) 3	( ) 4	( ) 5	( ) 6	
The humor	( ) 1	( ) 2	( ) 3	( ) 4	( ) 5	( ) 6	
The settings	( ) 1	( ) 2	( ) 3	( ) 4	( ) 5	( ) 6	
The pace	( ) 1	( ) 2	( ) 3	( ) 4	( ) 5	( ) 6	
The music	( ) 1	( ) 2	( ) 3	( ) 4	( ) 5	( ) 6	
The dancing	( ) 1	( ) 2	( ) 3	( ) 4	( ) 5	( ) 6	
The ending	( ) 1	( ) 2	( ) 3	( ) 4	( ) 5	( ) 6	

6. Why did you rate the *ending* the way you did? (PLEASE BE SPECIFIC)

______

______

______

7. Which of the following words or phrases best describe the movie? (PLEASE MARK AS MANY AS APPLY) (19-21(

Entertaining	( ) 1	My kind of humor	( ) 1	Two slow in spots	( ) 1
Boring/dull	( ) 2	Fast paced	( ) 2	Moved just right	( ) 2
Interesting characters	( ) 3	Romantic	( ) 3	Thought provoking	( ) 3
Too unbelievable	( ) 4	Daring	( ) 4	Confusing	( ) 4
Sympathetic characters	( ) 5	Well acted	( ) 5	Too predictable	( ) 5
Nothing new/done before	( ) 6	Too long	( ) 6	Moving/emotional	( ) 6
Sensitive subject	( ) 7	Funny	( ) 7	Good and sexy	( ) 7
Not my kind of movie	( ) 8	Different/original	( ) 8	True to life	( ) 8
High quality	( ) 9	Exciting	( ) 9	Not scary enough	( ) 9
Action packed	( ) 0	Believable	( ) 0	Good and violent	( ) 0
Stylish	( ) x	Too silly	( ) x	Fun to watch	( ) x

8. What, if anything, did you find confusing about the movie that was not cleared up by the end? (PLEASE BE AS SPECIFIC AS POSSIBLE)

______

______

---

9. Which of the following movies have you seen at a theatre or drive-in? (MARK AS MANY AS APPLY)

She's Gotta Have It . . . . ( ) 1
Hollywood Shuffle . . . . ( ) 2
Jo Jo Dancer . . . . ( ) 3
A Soldier's Story . . . . ( ) 4 (27)
The Color Purple . . . . ( ) 5

10. Please indicate your sex:

Male . . . . ( ) 1 (28(
Female . . . . ( ) 2

11. Please indicate the last grade of school you completed.

Some high school or less . . . . ( ) 1 (29(
Completed high school . . . . ( ) 2
Some college . . . . ( ) 3
Completed college or more . . . . . . ( ) 4

12. Please indicate your age:

Under 15 ( ) 1 30 to 34 ( ) 6 (30(
15 to 17 ( ) 2 35 to 39 ( ) 7
18 to 20 ( ) 3 40 to 45 ( ) 8
21 to 24 ( ) 4 46 and over ( ) 9
25 to 29 ( ) 5

13. How many times have you been to movies at a theatre or drive-in during the past two (2) months?

(31(
(32(
____
(WRITE IN NUMBER)

14. What is your ethnic background?

Asian ( ) 1 White ( ) 4 (33(
Black ( ) 2 Other ( ) 5
Spanish-American ( ) 3

THANK YOU. PLEASE GIVE THE QUESTIONNAIRE TO THE PERSONS AT THE EXITS.

SUMMARY OF *SCHOOL DAZE* RECRUITED AUDIENCE SURVEY IN PHILADELPHIA (8/18/87)

I. *SCHOOL DAZE* PLAYED QUITE WELL TO THIS MOSTLY BLACK PHILADELPHIA AUDIENCE, GENERATING A 34% EXCELLENT RATING (NORM IS 20% "EXCELLENT"), A TOTAL HIGHLY FAVORABLE RATING OF 83% (NORM IS 60%), A 4.8 MEAN SCORE (NORM IS 3.5–3.9) AND A 76% "DEFINITELY" RECOMMEND SCORE (NORM IS 45%).

THE MOVIE PLAYED WELL ABOVE AVERAGELY WELL TO YOUNGER (UNDER 25) MOVIEGOERS AND ABOVE AVERAGELY WELL TO OLDER MOVIEGOERS. ALL OF THE SEX/AGE GROUPS PROVIDED WELL ABOVE AVERAGE "DEFINITELY" RECOMMEND SCORES.

II. THE MOVIE WAS MOST ENJOYED FOR ITS STORY ABOUT BLACK CAMPUS LIFE, ITS HUMOR, ITS MESSAGE ABOUT RACIAL PREJUDICE AND THE ENTERTAINING MANNER IN WHICH THESE COMPONENTS WERE COMBINED.

III. THE MAIN CHARACTERS WERE WELL LIKED, WITH LARRY FISHBURNE'S PERFORMANCE AS DAP DUNLAP BEING BEST LIKED, FOLLOWED BY SPIKE LEE'S PERFORMANCE AS HALF-PINT, GIANCARLO ESPOSITO'S PERFORMANCE AS JULIAN EAVES AND TISHA CAMPBELL'S PERFOR-

MANCE AS JANE TOUSSAINT. OF THE CO-LEADS, ONLY KYME AS RACHEL MEADOWS WAS RATED (SLIGHTLY) BELOW AVERAGE. MOST OF THE SUPPORTING PERFORMANCES WERE RATED ABOVE AVERAGE AS WELL.

IV. THE ELEMENTS ALSO TENDED TO BE WELL RATED, WITH THE HUMOR, THE MUSIC, THE STORY, THE ENDING AND THE DANCING ESPECIALLY WELL THOUGHT OF.

V. THE SCENES MENTIONED AS LIKED MOST WERE DANCING AND SINGING AT THE HAIRDRESSERS, THE STEP/GREEK, THE SPLASH JAM/BEACH PARTY, KENTUCKY FRIED CHICKEN, THE PLEDGES ON HELL NIGHT, THE ENDING, THE DANCING SCENES (UNSPECIFIED) AND THE HOMECOMING SCENES.

THE SCENES LIKED LEAST WERE THE ENDING (NEARLY AS MANY DISLIKES AS LIKES), THE LOVE/SEX SCENES, JANE WITH HALF-PINT AND DANCING AND SINGING AT THE HAIRDRESSERS (MORE LIKES THAN DISLIKES), WHICH WAS DISLIKED MAINLY BECAUSE IT WAS FELT THAT THIS SCENE (LIKE THE ENDING) WENT ON TOO LONG.

VI. WHILE THE MAJORITY LIKED THE ENDING, SOME FOUND ITS MESSAGE TO BE CONFUSING, WHILE OTHERS THOUGHT THAT IT WENT ON A BIT TOO LONG. SIMILARLY, ALTHOUGH THERE WERE NOT TOO MANY NEGATIVE COMMENTS, THE BULK OF THEM CENTERED ON THESE MINOR CONFUSIONS AND THE FILM'S EXCESSIVE LENGTH.

VII. THE RESULTS OF THIS SCREENING INDICATE THAT *SCHOOL DAZE* PLAYS QUITE WELL (AT LEAST TO A PREDOMINANTLY BLACK AUDIENCE). IT ALSO PLAYS WELL TO ALL SEX/AGE GROUPS AND PARTICULARLY WELL TO ALL YOUNGER AUDIENCE MEMBERS.

THE MOVIE'S MAIN PROBLEMS APPEAR TO BE THAT IT IS TOO LONG OVERALL AND TOO SLOW IN PARTICULAR SPOTS. SPECIFICALLY, VIEWERS MENTIONED THE DANCING AT THE HAIRDRESSERS AND (TO A SOMEWHAT LESSER EXTENT) THE SPLASH JAM/BEACH PARTY AND "WAKE UP" EXHORTATON AT THE END AS GOING ON TOO LONG.

WITH SOME TIGHTENING AND RECONSIDERATIONS OF A FEW SCENES, IT SEEMS LIKELY THAT PLAYABILITY WOULD IMPROVE FURTHER.

SECOND SCREENING: AUGUST 25, 1987, RKO, ROUTE 4, PARAMUS, N.J.

We had our second recruited screening in suburban New Jersey and, boy, do I hate malls. This place had ten screens. We drove out there at noon, had a run-through, ate, then came back for the eight o'clock screening. This was the first time that the Columbia people, apart from the bigwigs, were going to see *School Daze*.

The response to the screening was mixed. The recruited audience was much different from Philly's. It was younger and had a greater proportion of whites; this is what we wanted. This was one of the reasons we didn't get the same kind of response we had in Philly. I heard again and again the film was too long. The Philly cut was 2 hours and 25 minutes; this was 2:16. I felt it was too long also. How long? Too long! Too long! It was a sobering experience overall.

During this entire editing process, every time Barry and I thought we were almost there, something happened to remind us there was still work to do, and that we'd better light a fire under our asses. This was just what we needed—the more we held these screenings, the more I liked them. Over and over, we saw what worked and what didn't work.

What definitely didn't work was "Turn You Round." The audience laughter in Paramus, New Jersey, meant that was the last place that song played in *School Daze*. It's out. It was bad judgment on my part selecting that song for that particular moment. But I would have never found out without these screenings. I asked Barry to imagine people laughing at the number during the world premiere at the Ziegfield Theatre. We woulda died. Also cut after this screening was "Divest Now," the drum number at the beginning of the film.

After Paramus we started cutting at a feverish pitch to have a two-hour cut for the next screening. Now please understand, we weren't panicking. Barry and I had been buried under everybody's suggestions on what to cut. I would listen politely and that's it. We knew what we were doing, and when we found the length that the film played best, we'd know it. I wrote this letter to Barry when I got home from Paramus:

August 25, 1987

DEAR BARRY:

Hope you slept well. We have a lot of work to do. Fuck JIM CLARK. He's not touching one frame of this picture. [Jim Clark was the editor on some of Puttnam's pictures, among them *The Killing Fields* and *The Mission*. He was at the Paramus screening and had a conversation with Barry afterwards.] Monty and I had meetings with the Columbia people all day. Have Meredith put the reels together, here's my list of the stuff we need to fix:

1) CHANGE CRANE UP TO MCPHERSON AND CLOUD IN DIVEST NOW.
2) LENGTHEN REACTION SHOT—ODRIE MCPHERSON, CLOUD AT CORONATION.
3) PUT TAIL ON GRADY "WAKE UP" SHOT. LET HIM PUT THE COVERS ON HEAD.
4) PUT HEAD ON FIRST "WAKE UP." DAP RUNNING INTO CAMERA.

5) CUT DOWN SCENE BETWEEN CLOUD AND MCPHERSON IN MCPHERSON'S DEN.
6) EXTEND RACHEL AND DAP MAKING LOVE BY A FEW FRAMES—SHE NEEDS TO KISS HIM ON LIPS—THIS IS DURING CORONATION.
7) EXTEND INSERT SHOT OF NELSON MANDELA ON WALL—A CAR'S PASSING HEADLIGHTS GIVE PATTERNS ON WALLS SO I THINK WE COULD USE THE MOVING VENETIAN BLINDS.
8) PUT IN ON-SCREEN LINE FOR DAP "SO YOU THINK I HAVE BANK."
9) IN GREEK SHOW REPLACE STANDING OVATION AFTER ALPHAS.
10) JULIAN SCREAMING "GAMMA" AT BEGINNING OF DEATH MARCH.
11) CUT "TURN ROUND"—WE HAVE TO CUT THE DEATH MARCH DIFFERENTLY NOW THE SONG IS GONE, IT NEEDS TO BE TOTALLY RETHOUGHT.
12) IN "DA BUTT," PHILLY'S IS OUT OF SYNC.
13) CUT IN LATER, VICKY/GRADY WALKING DOWN HALL TO FELLAS.
14) CHANGE CLOUD'S "WAKE UP" SO IT'S LESS COMICAL.
15) TRIM "WAKE UP" SHOT BEFORE WE GET TO MONIQUE.
16) TIGHTEN "WAKE UP."
17) MORE "WAKE UP"; SEE IF THERE IS A TAKE WHERE TYRONE DOESN'T BUMP INTO THAT OTHER GUY BEFORE HALF-PINT COMES OUT OF DORM—FIXED.
18) CUT IN EARLIER—SCENE WHERE DAP IS BEING DRIED OFF BY RACHEL—OR CUT IN LATER AT HEAD OF SCENE.
19) LET'S THINK VERY SERIOUSLY ABOUT CUTTING DIVEST NOW. GO STRAIGHT TO GAMMAS COMING IN ON DAP'S SPEECH.
20) FOOTBALL SCENE NEEDS TO BE SHORTENED.
21) CUT VICKY SHOT IN SPLASH JAM.
22) DAP'S ROOM—CUT INTO IT MUCH LATER—"STAY OFF MY BED, IGNANT MOTHERFUCKERS."
23) CUT DOWN JANE CRYING ON RADIATOR.
24) CUT DOWN GAMMA CELEBRATION AT END OF DEATH MARCH.
25) REPLACE GRADY'S LINES THAT ARE COUGHED OVER.

Barry, in addition to all these changes, we have our sound editors starting Monday, plus we have to get five more dupes made. I want our next recruited screening to be in D.C. before a college audience only. The Black students from HOWARD UNIVERSITY and the white students from GEORGETOWN and AMERICAN universities. Hopefully we can do this next week.

I'll call you in the middle of the day. The film is gonna be great. I'm not even worried, last night was the best thing that could have happened to us. I'm grateful for the mixed response. It was a signal, we can't get SMUG. It's not there yet.

SPIKE

SUMMARY OF *SCHOOL DAZE* RECRUITED AUDIENCE SURVEY IN PARAMUS (8/25/87)

I. *SCHOOL DAZE* DID NOT PLAY VERY WELL TO THIS RACIALLY MIXED PARAMUS AUDIENCE, RECEIVING CONSIDERABLY LOWER RATINGS AND RECOMMENDATION SCORES THAN IT DID AT THE FIRST, PREDOMINANTLY BLACK SCREENING (8/18/87).

OVERALL, THE MOVE RECEIVED A 14% "EXCELLENT" RATING (NORM IS 20% "EXCELLENT") AND BELOW AVERAGE TOTAL HIGHLY FAVORABLE RATINGS OF 48% (NORM IS 60%), A 3.5 MEAN SCORE (NORM IS 3.5–3.9) AND A BELOW AVERAGE "DEFINITELY" RECOMMEND SCORE OF 35% (NORM IS 45%).

FROM BLACK AUDIENCE MEMBERS, THE MOVIE RECEIVED SLIGHTLY ABOVE AVERAGE "EXCELLENT" RATINGS OF 23% AND SOMEWHAT ABOVE AVERAGE HIGHLY FAVORABLE RATINGS OF 67%, AN AVERAGE MEAN SCORE OF 4.2 AND AN ABOVE AVERAGE "DEFINITELY" RECOMMEND SCORE OF 54%. IN CONTRAST, WHITES GAVE BELOW AVERAGE "EXCELLENT" RATINGS OF 27%, A LOW MEAN SCORE OF 2.7 AND AN EXTREMELY LOW 12% "DEFINITELY" RECOMMEND SCORE.

II. IN LINE WITH THE LOWER RATINGS AND RECOMMENDATION SCORES RECEIVED AT THIS SECOND SCREENING ALL OF THE PERFORMANCES AND ELEMENTS WERE RATED AT LOWER LEVELS OVERALL THAN AT THE FIRST SCREENING. AMONG THE PERFORMANCES, ONLY THOSE OF SPIKE LEE (WHO WAS RATED HIGHEST AT ABOVE AVERAGE LEVELS), AS HALF-PINT, AND LARRY FISHBURNE, AS DAP DUNLAP, RECEIVED AVERAGE OR ABOVE AVERAGE RATINGS. AMONG THE ELEMENTS, THE HUMOR WAS STILL RATED HIGHEST, BUT AT ONLY SLIGHTLY ABOVE AVERAGE LEVELS AS COMPARED TO THE SIGNIFICANTLY ABOVE AVERAGE RATINGS IT HAD RECEIVED AT THE FIRST SCREENING. THE DANCING, THE MUSIC AND THE STORY ALL RECEIVED SLIGHTLY ABOVE AVERAGE RATINGS AS WELL, WHILE THE ENDING AND THE PACE (WHICH WAS THE LOWEST RATED ELEMENT) OBTAINED BELOW AVERAGE AND WELL BELOW AVERAGE RATINGS, RESPECTIVELY.

ALTHOUGH BLACKS RATED ALL OF THE PERFORMANCES AND ELEMENTS MUCH HIGHER THAN WHITES, IN ALL CASES, THEIR RATINGS WERE STILL BELOW THOSE OBTAINED AT THE PREVIOUS, MOSTLY BLACK AUDIENCE SCREENING. BOTH BLACKS AND WHITES WERE MOST FAVORABLE TOWARD SPIKE LEE AMONG THE PERFORMERS. BLACKS RATED THE HUMOR THE HIGHEST AMONG THE ELEMENTS, AND WHITES RATED THE DANCING THE HIGHEST.

III. AS BEFORE, THE MOVIE WAS MOST ENJOYED FOR ITS STORY ABOUT BLACK CAMPUS LIFE (MAINLY BY BLACK AUDIENCE MEMBERS), ITS HUMOR, ITS MESSAGE ABOUT PREJUDICE AND THE ENTERTAINING MANNER IN WHICH THESE ELEMENTS WERE COMBINED. HOWEVER, MANY MORE AUDIENCE MEMBERS AT THIS SCREENING (BOTH BLACKS AND WHITES) CRITICIZED THE MOVIE THAN AT THE PREVIOUS SCREENING, MAINLY FOR BEING TOO LONG AND SLOW (BOTH

The Singing Rays—"Boy, y'know I love ya." In the film, check out their vicious butt rolls, good Jesus. Also, it's their voices you hear singing "Be Alone Tonight." No dub shit here, Holmes. Left to right: Jasmine Guy, Tisha Campbell, Paula Brown (she has the butt of life), and, kneeling, Angela Ali.

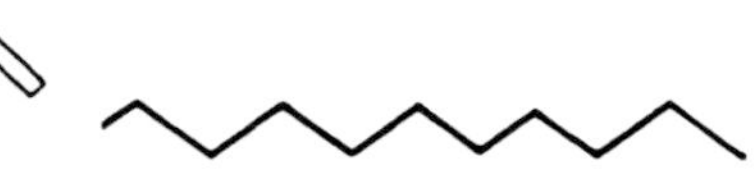

Cinque Lee as the spokesperson for the delicacies of microwave cuisine—Pop-Tarts and Pizza Deluxe. His scenes as the character "Buckwheat"—MC of the coronation, Greek Show, and Splash Jam—were cut from the film.

The entire film is jammed with conflict and confrontations. This one between the Fellas and the local yokels is the most poignant. I remember many of my classmates looking down at and avoiding the Black lower class that lives in and around the Atlanta University Center. Their community is called "The Bottom."

BLACKS AND WHITES) AND AT TIMES, CONFUSING (MORE WHITES THAN BLACKS). IN ADDITION, SOME WHITES DESCRIBED THE MOVIE AS BEING DIFFICULT FOR THEM TO RELATE TO BECAUSE IT WAS "TOO BLACK."

IV. IN CONTRAST TO THE FIRST SCREENING, THE MAJORITY OF AUDIENCE MEMBERS FELT NEGATIVELY ABOUT THE ENDING, FINDING IT CONFUSING, TOO ABRUPT AND UNRESOLVED. SIMILARLY, SOME AUDIENCE MEMBERS (BOTH BLACKS AND WHITES) COMPLAINED THAT THE STORY AND THE MESSAGE WERE CONFUSING.

V. THE SCENES MENTIONED AS LIKED MOST WERE KENTUCKY FRIED CHICKEN, THE PLEDGES ON HELL NIGHT, DANCING AND SINGING AT THE HAIRDRESSERS, THE STEP SHOW/GREEK AND THE DANCING IN GENERAL.

THE SCENES LIKED LEAST WERE THE ENDING (MENTIONED ALREADY AS TOO LONG AND CONFUSING), THE DANCING AND SINGING AT THE HAIRDRESSERS (ALSO FELT TO BE TOO LONG), THE SINGING/MUSIC (UNSPECIFIED), THE LOVE/SEX (UNSPECIFIED) AND THE SPLASH JAM/BEACH PARTY.

THIRD SCREENING: SEPTEMBER 3, 1987, TENTLEY CIRCLE THEATRE, CHOCOLATE CITY

Washington, D.C., was the best screening so far. *School Daze* was shown at the length of 2 hours and 7 minutes. Little by little, step by step, inch by inch, frame by frame, this bad boy was being shaped, molded, and pressed into its final form. At first, you say, "No, we can't cut that scene, the whole movie will be fucked," but then you realize that things must go for the sake of the entire picture. What I thought was so crucial wasn't, after all. Once we cut a scene, it was hard to remember it, let alone why we wanted it in the first place.

Of the three recruited audiences to date, Chocolate City was the most vocal—comprised entirely of college students. The intended mix of 75 percent Black, Howard, and 25 percent white, Georgetown and American universities, didn't happen. Word got out at Howard and the students started lining up two hours beforehand, shutting the late-coming white students out. It was fun seeing how Black college students reacted to a film about themselves. It's the first time it's ever been done. They were eating up *School Daze*. The film rang true and I knew I had done my job.

Before the screening, I introduced myself and explained that the reason we didn't shoot *School Daze* at Howard was because I needed REAL Black colleges like Morehouse and Spelman. On cue the students began to boo and hiss, and not a second too late the lights dimmed and the film began. It was good to be back on track after Paramus.

FOURTH SCREENING: OCTOBER 1, 1987, GATEWAY THEATRE, SAN FRANCISCO, CALIF. RICE-A-RONI, DA SAN FRANCISCO TREAT—DINGDONG

Tonight was our last recruited screening and the film played well. The audience was an ethnically mixed one from the Bay Area. *SGHI* did well at this theater. There was no doubt that this was the best cut we'd had so far on *School Daze*. It ran a fast-paced 1 hour 58 minutes, without end credits.

For the second time in a row, I spoke to a focus group after the screening. There were these six ignorant guys, members of Black Greeks, talking shit. I blasted them into oblivion. I have no problems with folks not liking my shit. If I was that sensitive, I wouldn't be a filmmaker. But goddamn, at least dislike the film for some intelligent reasons. The guys' ignorance was glaring. They were so small-minded. They didn't like the way the frats were depicted, they saw nothing else, and were turned off. The frat shit is just a small part of the film. This film is about something bigger, more important. It's about our existence as a people in white America. WAKE UP.

Afterwards Monty and I took two sisters, Michelle Hill and Pam George, out to eat. They went to school with us, attended Spelman. After the first three screenings, we all went to the hotel and ate a huge spread. The Columbia people and we would sit around the table and say how great the screening went. I never liked these sessions; they felt stupid and awkward. "Spike, it was great." "Spike, I like the changes you made." All that polite stuff really isn't necessary.

On the road with *School Daze* was finally over. Barry Brown and I had labored over this film for the past twenty-three weeks, molded it, and shaped it to its present form. We weren't finished yet, the picture was not locked yet, but we were closer now than at that first screening in Philadelphia. I felt good about it, had always from the start. David Picker was present along with some other execs from Columbia and most of them hadn't seen the film since the Paramus, New Jersey, screening. I hadn't seen the film myself for two and a half weeks; I wanted to get some distance from it. Films can get stale as shit. Directors and editors must see their films thousands of times before they're completed. Regardless, it becomes a new film each time I see it with an audience. I've got to give it to David Picker for suggesting these recruited screenings. They've given me a way to work things out—like a workshop. We're making *School Daze* the best film it can be. It won't be all things to everybody, but only the best it can be.

The morning after, I fly to L.A. to spend the whole day at Columbia. Picker asked me to drop by his office so he could offer his comments and criticisms. Sometime around the middle of October I'll be back out to L.A. to screen our final cut to the two Davids. Whoa, let me rephrase that, what Barry and I feel is the final cut. It's to be expected that Columbia people will have their own ideas. I hope it does not get ugly. It's been pleasant working with Columbia up to now. But don't fuck with our final cut. We shall see what we shall see. Back to Brooklyn, back to the editing room in the kitchen of Forty Acres and a Mule to complete the editing. The February 12 opening date is getting closer and closer. OH YEAH.

OCTOBER 2, BURBANK STUDIOS

I flew back to Burbank along with the rest of the people from Columbia. Upon reaching the studio I had a thirty-minute meeting with David Picker, to hear his comments and criticisms about the screening the previous night in 'Frisco. I shook David's hand, plopped onto the sofa, took out my notebook, and listened. First off, he said the film is tremendously better, and for the first time he can see it in it's final form. I sat there quietly waiting for the really real. He said that "Straight and Nappy" is still too long, specifically the instrumental part. He urged me to cut it down or possibly, for the next screening, take it out altogether just to see how it plays. We had already cut it down. I felt that once the number was finished, meaning when all the sound work—footsteps—and dialogue were complete, it would play much better. One interesting thing he said to me is that I make my point and then end it. It's no "America" (from *West Side Story*). Well, that comment would have suited my father fine. That's why Otis and him had static. My father didn't want it to be an imitation of a Hollywood-MGM musical number. For that matter, neither did I. What Jerome Robbins and Leonard Bernstein did was great, but that doesn't have to be the standard that has to be attained. For instance, if you're a Black student who happens to be an English Lit major, you'll hear about Hemingway, Shakespeare, etc., etc. It's like Langston Hughes, James Baldwin, Toni Morrison, Ralph Ellison, Richard Wright, and Zora Neale Hurston don't exist, and if they do, only in a Black Lit class. They're not included with the literary giants. This is the kind of cultural arrogance I had to deal with at NYU. But getting back to Picker, he thought the scene where "Julian" tells "Jane" he never told her to bone "Half-Pint" should also be jettisoned. It is too cruel an act and it weakens the ending. The 360° turn that "Julian" makes at the end of the picture is too severe. And with the last major point, he suggested using flashbacks at the end to help the audience understand why "Dap" goes off at the end of the finale. It isn't just because of "Half-Pint" boning "Jane," but everything that has happened up to that point. Now my reactions: What "Julian" does is despicable and the four audiences to date haven't liked it. It's not to be liked. "Julian" is a monster and we all have some parts of "Julian" in us —some more than others. It's not my job to make people like him. I do hope they understand him and see the transformation he makes at the end. The last suggestion about the flashbacks, I think, would make it infantile. The audiences are sophisticated enough to get it. To include flashbacks for a very small percentage of the audience would be a mistake.

After he finished, I said, "David, what happens if it comes down to your saying 'Straight and Nappy' has to go and I say it has to stay?" He looked me in the eye and said, "Spike, I'm not that type of person." I believe him. I've dealt with David Picker from that first initial meeting in January and he has been a decent and honest man throughout. He let me make the film I've wanted to make.

9

THE SCRIPT

SPIKE ▸ The film *School Daze,* unlike *SGHI,* is a lot different from the script. Nothing is wrong with this. Scripts, for the most part, are like blueprints. I encouraged a lot of ad-libs. Plus, actors change what you write in the script, anyway. Larry Fishburne hardly ever said the dialogue the way it was written. More often than not, his words were better. When you write a script, you think you need every scene and every word of dialogue. Once you get into production, you throw shit out the window left and right. It never fails. If I could get that clarity when I write—boy oh boy oh boy! The dynamics of making a film are . . . dynamic. HA HA! The internal and external forces in this galaxy change your ideas, change your words, your scenes, even ya characters' names. When you read the script, you'll see that "Dap" in the movie is "Slice" in the script. Ya see, Coca-Cola owned Columbia, and Slice is a Pepsi product, and the powers that be let me know "Slice" had to go. The powers being what they be, I said, "I see, I see," and presto chango, hocus-pocus, "Slice" became "Dap." It wasn't a big deal to me. Now, if they had said, "Spike, ya gotta change the title of the movie," that's different. Even if the powers are being, I wasn't seeing. So dat's an example of what can happen. To help you read this bad boy an [X] in the left side of the margin means the scene was never shot. Why wasn't it shot? you ask. Well, let me tell ya. It wasn't shot because:

1. It was terrible writing anyway.
2. We didn't have the time to shoot it.
3. We never got the location.
4. A light went off in my noggin and I realized we didn't need that shit.

A [C] means the scene was shot but cut from the film during the editing process. You'll see a lot of scenes like this. The first rough cut was 2 hours and 36 minutes; as of this moment, as I write, it's now 1 hour and 58 minutes.

To the potential screenwriters out there, please read the script after you see the film. That practice helped me in my development as a writer-director. For everybody else, it's still good reading.

The Wake Up scene. It was Lisa Jones who suggested that "Dap" turn to the camera to say the final two words of the film, "Wake Up!" Larry Fishburne and Giancarlo Esposito had their own secret thing going on between them throughout the film. But it was most pronounced in this scene.

SCHOOL DAZE

BY SPIKE LEE

Third Draft
January 1, 1987

Forty Acres and a Mule Filmworks, Inc.
Ya-Dig Sho-Nuff
By Any Means Necessary
WGS EAST, INC. #39658

A NOTE

This script takes place at a fictitious, predominantly Black college in the South. The student body is divided into two factions: the Haves and the Have-Nots. This division is based upon class and color. The Haves, the affluent students at Mission, are all with light skin, "good hair," blue or green eyes, and so forth. While across the tracks are the Have-Nots. They are dark, have kinky nappy hair, and many of them are the first members of their families to ever get a college education; in other words, the black underclass. Each faction has a name for the other. It's the WANNABEES VS. THE JIGS!!! Wanna Be White and Jigaboos. Remember, it's about class and color.

Spike Lee
September 14, 1986

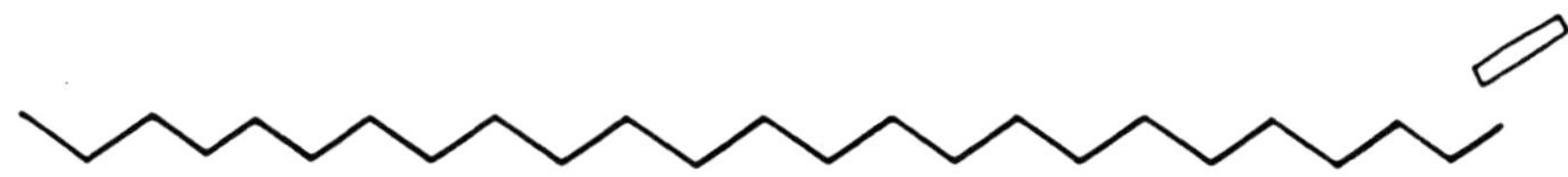

TITLE ON BLACK

MISSION COLLEGE
Founded 1883
UPLIFT THE RACE

OPENING MONTAGE

The music, an old Negro spiritual, "I'm Building Me a Home," accompanies a MONTAGE of still photographs of Mission College, a predominantly Black college in the deep South. WE SEE photos from its basement beginnings to one building to many. WE SEE various ground-breaking ceremonies, dignitaries on campus, commencement exercises. Also student-led sit-ins, demonstrations, voter registration drives, which took place during the civil rights movement. These images are in chronological order, giving us a sense of the history of this institution up to the present. As the last note of the song is sung we

DISSOLVE TO:

TITLE—FRIDAY

1 **EXT:** *ADMINISTRATION BUILDING—DAY*

From high in the sky, WE SWOOP DOWN to the steps of the Administration Building. Banners hang from the windows: "END APARTHEID—DIVEST NOW." Students hold signs and listen intently to a young man who is addressing them with microphone in hand. This is our "main man"—SLICE DUNLAP. His voice rises and lowers to emphasize his remarks, his conviction. Behind Slice are houses made of cardboard and wood, a shantytown; spray-painted on the houses are slogans.

SLICE

Yo! This is it. Once again we, as a people, are late, late, and mo' late. But let us move on. How is it Columbia, Harvard, Yale, all those supposed greater institutions of higher learning, can beat us, Mission College, to the punch? Again I ask, how is this? Can anybody answer this little question for me?

VOICE (OS)

What question?

SLICE

This question. How is it those schools that I mentioned and a lot more, I might add, how is it they have divested their money in South Africa and we backward Negroes here at the so-called finest Black school in the land, Mission College, are holding on to it like how a wino clutches his last bottle?

There is a small patter of applause.

SLICE (contd)

To me, this is indefensible. Our Black sisters and brothers are dying in South Africa every day and here we are assisting the racist regime of Botha and the South African government.

VOICE (OS)

So what do you want us to do?

CLOSE—SLICE

CAMERA IS CLOSE ON Slice, then MOVES UP to a window in the Administration Building where two figures, the president of Mission College and a visitor, watch intently the proceedings.

SLICE

We gotta move on this. This is a moral dilemma. I propose continued pressure on the administration and faculty till it's dealt with. Till we have completely divested. We should march, protest, disrupt classes, shut the school down if need be. Stay all in their ass.

The students seem to be divided, half applaud, the others voice their disapproval. In the BG we can hear the distant thunder of drums. As the drums get nearer, Slice continues.

SLICE (contd)

Homecoming is the perfect
opportunity to mount this
attack on apartheid. The
time is now. I ask you,
the student body, to make a
stand. We need a strong showing
starting right now, this homecoming weekend. To kick it off,
we got our own Marching Tigers
to fire it up.

[C] Those thundering drums are the Marching Tiger Band that is now here at the rally. The crowd moves back to give it some room.

[X] A tall, handsome man walks up to Slice and steps in front of the microphone. He has a saxophone strapped around his neck. This is JORDAN RIGGS, one of the Fellas. The Fellas are a close-knit group of brothers who are "down for the cause." We shall meet them all soon.

[X] Jordan counts it off and we hear his song, "Divest Now," an up-tempo funk number that has a chanting chorus of "Divest now, divest now." This is at first sung by the band, but quickly the students pick it up.

[X] CLOSE—JORDAN

He is wailing away on his sax solo when

[X] ANGLE—BAND

the band starts to break into dance.

[C] 2 WIDE SHOT—SCHOOL LAWN

The students soon follow and now it's a spontaneous party. However, a choreographed spontaneous.

[X] The flag girls wave their maroon-and-white banners in time to the music, the drummers drum, the horns blow, and the educated "feet" step. This is a big production number.

3 CLOSE—WINDOW

The two figures in the window are still there.

[C] 1A CLOSE—JORDAN

Jordan runs back up to the mike and the band stops, but the students still shout "Divest now." He raises his hand and the band comes right back in. The crowd goes wild. The song is over. OS we hear booming male voices.

VOICES (OS)

G-Phi-G. G-Phi-G.
Bad as we want to be.

4 ANGLE—CROWD

The crowd parts and WE SEE a strange sight. In a straight line march eight students, all dressed exactly the same, in black, from their wraparound Ray-Bans to their black-and-silver hi-top Nikes, elbow pads, catcher's shin guards. Their newly shaven heads glisten in the sun; a silver G is painted on their foreheads. These eight men are pledging Gamma Phi Gamma, the elite of several fraternities on campus. Gamma is also the leading element of the Wannabees. They are led by JULIAN EAVES, a.k.a. Big Brother Almighty. At his side are his frat brothers; all wear the same black Gamma jackets or sweaters. In one hand each Gamma holds a leash which is attached to a dog collar that is around each Gammite's neck.

JULIAN

Gammites halt.

The eight Gammites stop on a dime.

A crowd gathers around them. Pressing up next to Julian is JANE TOUSSAINT, a very attractive female (Creole) from New Orleans. Jane has blond hair down to the middle of her back; she also has green eyes. Jane is president of the Gamma Rays, a club of women who are like the groupies of Gamma Phi Gamma, and queen of the female Wannabees. They too are dressed in black, but in Gamma Ray sweatshirts with their names on the backs.

ANGLE—SLICE

Slice moves towards the Gammas.

CLOSE—JULIAN

Julian, seeing Slice, steps over to Gammite #8, SLIM DADDY, and whispers in his ear.

ANGLE—GAMMITES

Slim Daddy in turn whispers to the next Gammite. This whispered command is quickly passed down until it's reached Gammite #1, HALF-PINT. We hear . . .

SLIM DADDY

Gammites, speak.

GAMMITES

It takes a real man to be a
Gamma Man because only a
Gamma Man is a real man.

SLICE

That's enough, Julian, so take
your Gamma Dogs somewhere else.

JULIAN

We don't approve of this African
mumbo jumbo and we're here to
let you know about it.

Next to Slice move his boys—the Fellas, who are Jordan, BOOKER T. WASHINGTON, GRADY McKISSICK, and EDGE HARDISON. They have his back.

SLICE

You need to wake up.

EDGE

That's right, goddamnit.

Julian and the Gammas stare at Slice and the Fellas, daring them to do something. After a beat, both begin to move towards one another when in squirts—

VIRGIL CLOYD. Virgil is a Joe Neckbone in every sense of the word. He also happens to be president of the Student Government Association. How he ever got elected is still the biggest mystery on campus. He enunciates like an Oxford scholar.

VIRGIL

We will have none of this. As
president of the SGA and a key-
wearing member of Phi Beta Kappa,
I abhor and will not tolerate

violence or the threat of violence
on this sacred campus.

The Gammas, Fellas, and students all groan and mumble. We can hear OS . . .

VOICE (OS)

Scrotum Face.

Virgil continues on like he hasn't heard their comments.

VIRGIL

It's safe to say President
McPherson agrees with me
one hundred percent.

Virgil gives a knowing glance up to the president's window where he and his visitor are all eyes and ears.

VIRGIL (contd)

So let's break this up.

SLICE

Virgil, shut the fuck up.

Everyone laughs.

VIRGIL

You heard what I said.

Nobody moves. Slice and Julian stare at each other. Neither flinches.

VIRGIL (contd)
(pleading)

Please, will you leave?

JULIAN
(shouts)

Dog walk!

The Gammites start barking like dogs and jump down on all fours. The Gammas walk them on leashes. Before leaving, Gammite #8 lifts his leg up on Slice's sneaker like it's a fire hydrant and pretends to piss on it.

Slice is about to go after him when he is held back. He spins around, furious, and sees RACHEL MEADOWS, a fine, dark-chocolate Black sister who is Slice's lady.

RACHEL

Let it go, Slice. Don't pay them no mind. Julian is bugged out.

SLICE

Plus ignorant.

Slice turns once again but Rachel pulls him back.

RACHEL

Walk me to my class.

SLICE

Can't.

RACHEL

I'll see you later.

She is joined by her girlfriends, DORIS WITHERSPOON and LIZZIE LIFE. Rachel tiptoes and kisses him on the mouth. The girls leave for class.

The crowd, disappointed that there wasn't a fight, disperses with the encouragement of Virgil.

The Fellas all pat Slice on the back.

ANGLE—GAMMAS

Jane takes Julian's hand as WE SEE the Gammas leave with the Gammites on leashes. They are followed by the ever-so-loyal Gamma Rays. The dog barks grow faint as we

FADE OUT.

FADE IN:

5 **INT:** *PRESIDENT McPHERSON'S OFFICE—DAY*

PRESIDENT McPHERSON, an elderly, distinguished man, moves away from the window. He turns and sees CEDAR CLOUD shaking his head. Cloud is a short, stubby man whose body doesn't know what to do with the expensive suit he's wearing. McPherson goes to his desk and slumps into his chair. They both look at each other.

[X] 6 **INT:** *CLASSROOM—DAY*

PROFESSOR MAMABAZO stands at the head of the class. He takes a long, hard puff from his unfiltered, funny-smelling cigarette. He is an exile from South Africa who's now teaching history.

DR. MAMABAZO

In just a few months you are going to be gone from Mission College. Believe it or not, these last four years you have been living the high life. While your parents slaved to put you through school, all that was asked of you was to study and get good grades. There will be a rude awakening in May . . . for those of you who do graduate.

The class laughs.

MAMABAZO (contd)

Ladies and gentlemen, it's a very crucial time. Please do not joke. It's too serious to laugh. How many of you were at the rally?

ANGLE—CLASS

A quarter of the class raises their hands. WE CAN SEE Rachel, Doris, and Lizzie in the last row.

MAMABAZO

Thank you. You can put your hands down. Can I have some comments? Anybody have something to say?

No one moves.

MAMABAZO (contd)

Come, come, now.

The students look at one another.

MAMABAZO (contd)

Then I'll have to call on someone. You. Yes, you. Mr. Leaves.

He has called on MONROE LEAVES, also one of the Fellas. Monroe is short and shy and barely speaks above a whisper. It is precisely because of this that he was adopted by the Fellas. He slowly rises from his seat.

MAMABAZO (contd)

We are waiting.

MONROE

Slice is my . . .

MAMABAZO

Speak up, man!

MONROE
(almost shouting)

Slice is my friend. I like him a lot, but I don't know if he's approaching this in the right manner. Protests and demonstrations. I just don't know.

Rachel shoots back.

RACHEL

Monroe, who cares what you think.

Now, as if on cue, the entire class joins in at once, for and against divestment. Professor Mamabazo listens in amusement; a minute ago he was pulling teeth, now he has a raging debate going on in his classroom.

MAMABAZO

So you are alive. Quiet, quiet, please. Settle down. What took you so long? This is what I wanted, but in an orderly fashion.

ANGLE—LIZZIE

LIZZIE

Professor Mamabazo, your family is still in South Africa.

MAMABAZO

Yes.

LIZZIE

I want to ask you: Let's say,
for instance, what we do here
directly affects your family.
I mean to say, because of what
we do here, the government makes
it harder on Blacks in South
Africa, including your family.
Would you still want us to act?

MAMABAZO

A lot of them have been killed
already. To answer your question,
I say yes.

LIZZIE

Even if it gets more people you
love killed.

Mambazo nods his head.

LIZZIE (contd)

Will you ever see them again?

MAMABAZO

One day I will.
(he looks at his watch)
That will be all for today.
Enjoy your last homecoming
weekend as a student here at
Mission. Time is running out.

The class gets up to leave. Rachel, Lizzie, and Doris walk by Monroe, bumping his desk and throwing mean looks. He waits till they leave the classroom before he moves.

7 **INT:** *GAMMA HOUSE—DAY*

We are in the lounge. The Gammas sit on chairs and sofas surrounding the eight blocks of Gammite, the eight pledgees. The Gammites stand at attention in a straight line facing the Big Brothers. Julian "Big Brother Almighty," president and dean of pledgees, paces up and down in front of the line.

JULIAN

Roll call . . .

[C] Each Gammite, as he says his line name, steps forward, kneels, places his hand over his heart, talks, then drops back into line.

HALF-PINT

Big Brothers, I humbly kneel
before you. I am the first
Gammite, Number One, Half-Pint.
Good things come in small packages.

BIG BROTHER GENERAL GEORGE PATTON

Like ya dick.

The Gammas laugh.

DOO-DOO BREATH

Big Brothers, I humbly kneel
before you. I am Gammite Number
Two, Doo-Doo Breath. No medical
cure has been found for my breath.

BIG BROTHER LANCE

You ain't lying.

The Gammas hold their noses.

DOUBLE RUBBER

Big Brothers, I humbly kneel
before you. I'm Gammite Number
Three, Double Rubber. I can be
counted on to cry, whine, and
complain.

YODA

Big Brothers, I humbly kneel
before you. I'm Gammite Number
Four, I am called Yoda. Try
not-do. Do or do not. There is
no try.

The Gammas applaud.

MUSSOLINI

Big Brothers, I humbly kneel
before you. I am Mussolini,
"Il Duce." Gammite Number Five.
I dine on pigs' titties served
on a silver platter topped with
Cool Whip.

BIG BROTHER CHUCKY

What did I tell you about eating that swine?

MUSTAFA

Big Brothers, I humbly kneel before you. I am Gammite Number Six, Mustafa. I love the smell of moist panties in the morning. It . . . it smells like victory.

BIG BROTHER LANCE

That'll work.

SIR NOSE

Big Brothers, I humbly kneel before you. I am Gammite Number Seven, Sir Nose, atomic dog descendent of the Mothership from the planet Lovetron, in funk we trust.

The Gammas yell.

SLIM DADDY

Big Brothers, I humbly kneel before you. I am the last Gammite, Number Eight, Slim Daddy, Dark Gable, the ladies' man.

BIG BROTHER X-RAY VISION

Slim Daddy, you're a skinny motherfucker.

BIG BROTHER DR. FEELGOOD

Put some meat on them bones.

BIG BROTHER GENERAL GEORGE PATTON

Julian, this is a pitiful lot. Next semester it has got to be better.

BIG BROTHER CHUCKY

How long have they been on line?

The rest of the Gammas echo these sentiments.

JULIAN

Gammites, do you hear this?
Here it is, six weeks on line
and you still do not meet the
approval of your Big Brothers.
This deeply grieves my heart.
When you began there were ten
Gammites, now only eight remain.
I don't know how many of you
will cross the burning sands to
the oasis of Gamma Phi Gamma.
There is no room for any
pretenders, a weak link amongst
the ranks. Which one of you
is it?

The Gammites stare straight ahead as Julian walks back and forth eyeing them. Each one is praying to the heavens above that Big Brother Almighty does not stop in front of him. Fate is not so kind to Half-Pint. Julian is all in his mug.

JULIAN (contd)

Half-Pint!

HALF-PINT

Yes, Big Brother Almighty.

JULIAN

How tall are you?

HALF-PINT

Five feet three-quarter inch.

JULIAN

You're a five foot three-quarter
inch of shit.

HALF-PINT

Yes, Big Brother Almighty.

JULIAN

I don't even know why you
pledged. This isn't for you.
Gamma men are real men.

HALF-PINT

I am a real man. A Gamma man.

JULIAN

Were you asked to speak? Brothers, I suspect this sawed-off human being hasn't even had a girl.

HALF-PINT

That's not true.

JULIAN

Isn't that right? I bet you're still a virgin, aren't you?

HALF-PINT

No, Big Brother Almighty.

JULIAN

Are you calling me a liar?

HALF-PINT

No, Big Brother Almighty. I haven't been a virgin since ninth grade.

JULIAN

Bullshit! You're a goddamn virgin, you ain't seen no parts of the *Pussssssy*.

The Gammas roar with laughter. Half-Pint is becoming visibly shaken.

HALF-PINT

I'm not no virgin.

JULIAN

You'll become a Gamma over my dead body. How in the hell did you get this far? You're weak, a pussy just like your cousin.

HALF-PINT

I'll be a good Gamma man, you'll see, you'll see.

JULIAN

The hell I will. You better get a freak over here tonight, no Gamma Rays either. I don't care if she's blind, fat, no teeth, and has one leg with a kick stand. I ain't pledging no virgins. . . . Wipe your nose and stop crying. Get out of here, all of you.

The Gammites run out of the lounge. The Gammas scream with laughter.

8 **EXT:** *ADMINISTRATION BUILDING—DAY*

[C] Slice is talking to a group of students when he is tapped on the shoulder by DINA, one of the Gamma Rays. Slice excuses himself.

SLICE

A Gamma Ray?

DINA

That's me.

SLICE

May I help you?

Dina hands Slice a note. Before he can thank her, she is gone. He unfolds it, then reads.

9 **EXT:** *BROWNER DORM—DUSK*

Slice is walking around behind the dorm looking for someone or something. He's about to go into the rear door of the building when he hears his name. He looks and sees Half-Pint in the shadows of a corner; Slice goes to him.

HALF-PINT

Sorry, but I can't let my Big Brothers see me talking to you.

SLICE

Thanks a lot. Whaddup?

HALF-PINT

Big Brother Almighty went off on me.

SLICE
(joking)

I told you not to pledge. What else is new?

HALF-PINT

This is no joke. I got to bring a girl back to the Gamma house tonight. He thinks I'm a virgin.

SLICE

For once he's right.

HALF-PINT

C'mon, Slice.

SLICE

What do you want me to do?

HALF-PINT

You gotta help me. I'm your first cousin, family. We're blood. You've helped me before. The grapevine says we'll be going over tomorrow night and any fault they can find will X me.

SLICE

When you needed money I gave it, when you needed me to do your laundry I did it, but I don't have any females lying around, and if I did, I wouldn't help, not for that.

HALF-PINT

Can't you forget about your differences with Big Brother Almighty?

SLICE

Y'mean Julian.

HALF-PINT

Big Brother Almighty.

SLICE

Julian.

HALF-PINT

To me he's Big Brother Almighty.

SLICE

All right already.

HALF-PINT

Think about me. This is going to be my funeral. Can't ya talk to Rachel? She has a lot of girlfriends.

SLICE

You must be on crack.

Half-Pint slumps to his knees; he sees his six weeks of pledging going up in smoke. Slice looks at his pitiful cousin and has a change of heart.

SLICE (contd)

Don't you know any women?

Half-Pint shakes his head.

SLICE (contd)

Just go ask them.

HALF-PINT

What will I say?

SLICE

Lie ya butt off. Tell them what they want to hear.
(Slice helps his cousin up)
Get up! You'll be a Gamma man tomorrow night.

A confident Half-Pint takes Slice's hand and raises himself.

SLICE (contd)

You go first. We wouldn't want Big Brother Almighty to see us.

HALF-PINT

Thanks, cous'. I won't forget this.

Half-Pint peeks around the corner of the dorm, the coast is clear, he disappears.

[C]10 **EXT:** *PRESIDENT'S HOUSE—DUSK*

LONG SHOT—PRESIDENT McPHERSON AND CLOUD

walk up to the old white-columned plantation-style mansion.

ANGLE—DOOR

[C] ODRIE McPHERSON, the president's wife, an elegant elderly woman, is there to open the door. She kisses her husband and shakes Cloud's hand.

ODRIE

Cedar, how are you?

CLOUD

I'm doing nicely. Yourself?

ODRIE

Fine, dinner is ready. I don't want to be late for the coronation.

11 **INT:** *DEN—DUSK*

CAMERA PULLS BACK from painting of John Flemister, a stoic white male, TO REVEAL Cloud admiring it.

CLOUD

He had a vision and that vision was passed down to his son, Haywood.

Cloud points to the other portraits.

CLOUD (contd)

And Haywood Flemister the Third still believes in it.

McPHERSON

And it's he who sent you down here.

CLOUD

First things first.

He looks at McPherson, it's a "do not interrupt me again" look. When he feels that McPherson has gotten the message, he continues.

CLOUD (contd)

Mission was founded to educate the sons and daughters of slaves. Flemister did it because he thought it was just, and I'm proud to say his legacy has been continued.

McPHERSON

You don't have to recite our history to me. We have been and will continue to be thankful for the support of the Flemister family.

Odrie knocks, then enters.

ODRIE

The food is getting cold.

McPHERSON

We're coming.

ODRIE

You know I don't like to warm over my food.

She closes the door. Cloud is getting tired of being interrupted.

CLOUD

These are the eighties and Black Americans have made great strides and progress.

McPHERSON

And a lot more has to be made.

CLOUD

Mission, which began in a church basement, is now spread over two hundred acres. It's grown and the family is concerned.

(annoyed)

I'm getting there.

(he continues)

Be patient. There is a feeling that the predominantly Black college for all intents and purposes has outlived its usefulness. Over the years it has been vital to our elevation in this great country, but the need no longer exists in an integrated society.

McPHERSON

That's absurd. The need *does* exist. It exists at Notre Dame, at Yeshiva and Brandeis, at Brigham Young. Tell me what is the difference?

Cloud fires back.

CLOUD

The difference is Catholics alone support the Notre Dames, Jews alone support the Yeshivas, Mormons support Brigham Youngs. Who supports the Black schools? I'll tell you who. The federal government and philanthropists like the Flemisters. Harold, Mission has produced some of our greatest minds; why don't or why can't we support our own? Why don't Blacks support Tuskegee, Morehouse, Spelman, Howard?

McPherson does not have an answer.

CLOUD (contd)

Look, as chairman of the board of directors, I was sent to talk to you. Flemister does not like this divestment mess that's going on here and I don't like it either. You have to nip this right here and now or I will. If not, you'll be in danger of losing the Flemisters.

McPHERSON

There it is.

CLOUD

That's it. The whole ball of wax. People like them get very touchy when they get told what to do with their money; old, old money.

(Cloud moves to the door)

The food is getting cold.

12 **INT:** *SLICE'S ROOM—NIGHT*

Slice enters the room; his roommate, Grady, is stretched out on his bed trying to read. Sitting next to him is Edge. Standing on the other side of the room is Jordan, practicing scales on his sax. On Slice's bed, Booker T. has Monroe in a headlock.

JORDAN

Yo! Yo!

SLICE

All you motherfuckers in my room again.

EDGE

That's right, goddamnit.

Slice goes to his bed.

SLICE

Get up. Get up, I said. Leave da boy alone.

Booker T. releases Monroe from the half nelson.

SLICE (contd)

Go get yourself a woman and
stop picking on the kid.

BOOKER T.

I keeps me some women.

GRADY

Here we go.

BOOKER T.

I got so many I'm gonna need
a dick transplant.

SLICE

Then you'll have two and a half inches
instead of one.

Jordan plays some mocking notes.

BOOKER T.

Play this.

He grabs his crotch and Jordan threatens to bang him upside the head with a Bruce Lee roundhouse kick.

SLICE

Get off my bed.

He picks Monroe up and tosses him.

MONROE

Take it easy, Slice.

SLICE

Don't sit here again. I told
you 'bout this, stay in your
own room.

GRADY

I thought that's ya main man.

SLICE

Not mine. Yo! Who's going back
to the Administration Building
with me tonight?

GRADY

Not me.

JORDAN

No. No.

MONROE

Don't look at me.

BOOKER T.

Are you crazy? We're going to the coronation. Mo' butts and mo' titties.

EDGE

That's right, goddamnit.

SLICE

I thought y'all were down for the cause.

GRADY

You're my brother, but goddamn.

EDGE

That's right, goddamnit.

The Fellas are dying.

BOOKER T.

You need to lighten up on that shit, Malcolm!

JORDAN

He's right, Nat Turner!

MONROE

Frederick Douglass!

GRADY

Marcus Garvey!

The Fellas are having a scream at Slice's expense.

SLICE

Y'all can kiss my black ass twice.

BOOKER T.

Preach, Jesse, preach.

EDGE

Don't be so sensitive . . .
Farrakhan.

The Fellas once again are dying. Grady has rolled off his bed onto the floor.

SLICE

Funny, funny. . . . OK, what about
the parade?

GRADY

I'm down, but not tonight. I
gots to see me some butt shaking.

EDGE

Word.

SLICE

What about the rest of you?

They nod.

SLICE (contd)

Enjoy yourselves. See you in
the morning, nine sharp.

JORDAN

We'll be there.

13 **EXT:** *FLEMISTER HALL—NIGHT*

Half-Pint stands outside Flemister Hall, one of the women's dorms. There is heavy traffic in and out of it. Several women lean out of their windows, seeing who's seeing who. He talks to himself under his breath, claps his hands, and enters the dorm.

[C] 14 **INT:** *OFFICE—NIGHT*

He sees MISS WIGGINS, the dorm mother, behind the desk. Miss Wiggins has been in this dorm for the past thirty years; she's old as Moses and famous for being overprotective. She acts like each female is her only daughter.

MISS WIGGINS

May I help you?

Half-Pint is paralyzed.

MISS WIGGINS (contd)

Would you like to see someone?

HALF-PINT

Yes, ma'am.

MISS WIGGINS

Young man, you'll have to tell me her name.

HALF-PINT

I forgot.

MISS WIGGINS

How am I going to know if you don't? I can't help you.

HALF-PINT

Do you have a list? If I saw her name I'd remember.

Miss Wiggins reluctantly hands him the dorm roster. Half-Pint looks while she eyeballs him. He can't decide which name to choose.

MISS WIGGINS

Son, why don't you come back when you get it together?

HALF-PINT

Got it. Perry Sardner, that's her.

MISS WIGGINS

You wouldn't remember what she looks like?

HALF-PINT

She's about yay big, black hair . . .

She cuts in.

MISS WIGGINS

Perry has red hair and freckles.

HALF-PINT

It was dark. I met her at a party.

Miss Wiggins does not believe a word he's saying. She's been around the corner a couple of times and has heard eight million similar bullshit stories like Half-Pint's. Half-Pint knows she knows and tries to play it off. Nonetheless, she speaks into the intercom, giving him the benefit of the doubt. He has the uncanny gift of making people feel sorry for him. Sometimes looking pathetic can get you a few things.

MISS WIGGINS

Perry Sardner, Perry Sardner, you have a caller.

Half-Pint smiles at her.

PERRY (OS)

Thank you. Be right down.

MISS WIGGINS

Please wait in the lounge.

HALF-PINT

Thank you, ma'am.

Miss Wiggins shakes her head as Half-Pint exits.

15 **INT:** *LOUNGE—NIGHT*

As Half-Pint enters the lounge he views couples talking. He finds an unoccupied sofa in the corner. He sits down, then stands again to take off his jacket.

ANGLE—PERRY SARDNER

She strides into the lounge wearing a T-shirt and cutoff jeans. What Miss Wiggins forgot to tell Half-Pint is that Perry is also fine, one of those reddest of the red bone babes.

PERRY

Somebody call me . . . Perry?

HALF-PINT

It was me.

PERRY

Hey! Hey!

She sits on the sofa with him.

HALF-PINT
(surprised)

Do you know me?

PERRY

Yeah, I've seen you on line.
Aren't you Number One?

Half-Pint is happy now.

HALF-PINT

That's me. Half-Pint, Gammite
Number One.

PERRY

Pleased to meet you. It's
almost that time.

HALF-PINT

Yeah, it will be any day now.

PERRY

Are you excited?

HALF-PINT

A little.

He messes with his cuticles, not knowing what to say.

PERRY

Half-Pint, so what can I do
for you?

He laughs, trying to buy time.

HALF-PINT

I'll be a Gamma any day now and
I would like to know if we could
maybe see each other. Go out
to a movie, a restaurant, pop
some Jiffy Pop popcorn together,
y'know, enjoy each other's
company.

PERRY

That sounds nice. I would like
that. Come by after you go over.
I'm usually in at night.

Perry motions as if she's getting up. Half-Pint puts his hand on her.

HALF-PINT

I was really thinking soon.

PERRY

How soon?

He hesitates.

HALF-PINT

Like now, over at the Gamma
house.

PERRY

Sorry, I can't.

DIFFERENT ANGLE—HALF-PINT

who is begging.

HALF-PINT

We would have fun, big fun.
Just give me one reason why
not? Just one.

ANGLE—MURIEL

MURIEL is sitting where Perry was. The following sequence will be JUMP CUTS.

MURIEL

First of all I don't know you from Adam. You just pop out of thin air and I'm supposed to say yes. Be for real.

ANGLE—HALF-PINT

HALF-PINT

I've always been attracted to you. I couldn't tell you, I was shy. But now since I've been pledging I'm a different person for the better.

ANGLE—CARLA

CARLA

I'm not attracted to you, besides I don't want a physical relationship. All you guys are dogs. I heard 'bout you Gammas.

ANGLE—HALF-PINT

HALF-PINT

I'm being sincere. I'm not trying to dog you. Look at my face. I wouldn't dog a fly. Can't a *real* man be attracted to you? Huh? Because I am. This is from the heart.

ANGLE—ROZ

ROZ is the healthiest of all the girls.

ROZ

Is this some kind of joke? Did your Big Brothers send you over here? I don't have time for children's games. You're so small I'd break you in two.

Roz rises from the sofa and walks.

ANGLE—HALF-PINT

His face is buried in his hands.

[C] 16 **INT:** *JANE'S APARTMENT—NIGHT*

OS we hear an up-tempo song. The CAMERA PANS around the apartment. An apartment that looks like it's been designed and furnished by an interior decorator. The two dominant colors being of course black and silver. It is hard to imagine that this is the "crib" of a college student. But it is, as WE SEE Jane lying on her black leather sofa. She holds a remote control in her hand and aims it at her big-screen television.

CLOSE—SCREEN

Channels flash by.

ANGLE—JANE

Jane looks at her watch and clicks off TV.

CLOSE—SCREEN

Screen goes black.

As Jane gets up, we get a good look-see. No doubt about it, she is stunning. But our eyes are drawn magnetically to her behind. Jane has a butt that won't stop.

[C] 17 **INT:** *BATHROOM—NIGHT*

CLOSE ON—FEET

as she steps out of her clothes and into the shower. Hey, wait a minute. Are her toenails painted black? Holy shit, Batman, they are *black*.

CLOSE—SHOWER

Jane's hand turns on the water.

ANGLE—BATHROOM

The bathroom is steam-filled. WE CAN FAINTLY MAKE OUT Jane behind the shower curtain.

[C] 18 **INT:** *BEDROOM—NIGHT*

CLOSE—BED

Her clothes are laid out, hand COMES INTO FRAME snatching Gamma Ray sweatshirt.

[C] 18A CLOSE—MIRROR

Jane paints on fire-truck-red lipstick.

[C] 19 **EXT:** *CONDOMINIUM—NIGHT*

Jane, carrying a garment bag, gets into her silver Mercedes-Benz convertible.

[C] 19A CLOSE—LICENSE PLATE (REAR)

Her license plate reads "DIVA-1." We hear the ignition turned on and she speeds away.

[C] 20 **EXT:** *MERCEDES-BENZ—NIGHT*

Jane turns on the radio and the same song we heard in her apartment we hear again. The wind flows through her blond, long, long, long "good hair." Is that a weave or the real thing? Only her hairdresser and Diana Ross know for sure.

21 **EXT:** *CAMPUS GATE—NIGHT*

Jane slows down at the gate, just long enough to let the campus guard wave her on through. The campus is alive with students running everywhere getting ready for the homecoming festivities.

22 **INT:** *LOUNGE—NIGHT*

Jane quickly walks into a room of Gamma Rays. All wear the black-and-silver Gamma Ray sweatshirt. All are light skinned except for one, TASHA, who is black as they come. They move chairs into a circle and sit.

JANE

Let's not make it long. We have
to get dressed. What have we
decided?

DINA

I talked to the brothers and the Gammites will definitely be going over tomorrow night. We should give them a party.

KIM

They haven't had fun in a long while. A jam will be on.

JANE

Where? The frat house?

DINA

Yeah, the Gamma house. The brothers said it was cool, but that we have to clean it up first.

MIRIAM

Clean it up? We've been cleaning up after those sorry, tired, trifling, shiftless Negroes from day one.

JANE

Miriam, why are you always complaining? It's for G-Phi-G.

MIRIAM

Yet and still, I'm no maid.

TASHA

Who's paying for it this time?

JANE

We're giving it, we should pay for it. Dina, how much did we make from the bake sale?

DINA

Enough!

23 **EXT:** *LAUNDRY ROOM—NIGHT*

The laundry room is located in the basement of the infirmary. Half-Pint knocks on the window and gives the Gammite whistle. The lights from inside flicker on and off.

24 **INT:** *LAUNDRY ROOM—NIGHT*

The Gammites appear from behind the washers and dryers. This is their hideout from their Big Brothers.

SIR NOSE

Where's the freak?

HALF-PINT

I couldn't get one.

DOUBLE RUBBER

Fuck, we're done for.

MUSSOLINI

Half-Pint, you've been jamming us up all along.

HALF-PINT

I tried.

SLIM DADDY

Shoulda went instead. I got more rap than Reynolds.

The Gammites laugh and everybody is speaking at once, getting on Half-Pint's case.

YODA

Chill. It's no thang! Big Brother Almighty was just messing with him. Give da boy some slack.

The Gammites chill.

[C] 25 **INT:** *LOUNGE—NIGHT*

JANE

We intend to turn it out tonight. As for the party, we have to look our best for the Gammites. It will be the biggest night of their lives.

VELDA

Just keep that animal Mussolini away from me.

The Gamma Rays laugh.

TASHA

That Sir Nose is so fine.

KIM

He can't hang with Mustafa.

DEIRDRE

Slim Daddy's for me. Girl, I don't need nuthin' else.

JANE

We have to make all of them feel good, not only the "fly" guys.

VIVIAN

Even Doo-Doo Breath?

JANE

Even Doo-Doo Breath.

MIRIAM

Those Gammites are gonna drop us like we have AIDS after they go over. You watch.

KIM

You never could keep a man, could you?

DEIRDRE

She has to get one first.

MIRIAM

Don't try it. I'll read you from A to Z.

JANE

All right. All right. Let's go.

26 **INT:** *DORM CORRIDOR—NIGHT*

The Gamma Rays come out of the lounge into a corridor where Rachel, Doris, Lizzie, and some other female Jigs are sitting. Everyone becomes quiet as the two factions, Wannabee and Jig, meet. Jane takes the lead and the Gamma Rays step over the Jigs, who are still sitting down. Jane accidentally, or maybe not, steps on Rachel's hand.

RACHEL

The word is "excuse me."

JANE

Nobody told you to sit here in
the hall either. "Excuse me."

RACHEL

That's better, Miss Thing.

Jane gives Rachel a long, hard look. She then flips her hair at Rachel and the Gamma Rays follow suit.

DORIS

It's not real.

DINA

Say what?

LIZZIE

You heard.

The Jigs stand up and the battle lines are drawn.

RACHEL

It ain't *even* real.

JANE

You wish you had hair like this.

DORIS

Girl, y'know you weren't born
with green eyes.

LIZZIE

Green contact lenses.

DINA

They're just jealous.

RACHEL

Jealous?

JANE

Rachel, I've been watching you look at Julian. You're not slick.

RACHEL

If that was true he's not much to look at.

JANE

Pickaninny.

DORIS

Barbie doll.

RACHEL

High-yellow heifer.

DINA

Tar Baby!

VIVIAN

Wanna Be White!

KIM

Jigaboo!

RACHEL

Don't start.

JANE

We're gonna finish it.

27 PRODUCTION NUMBER

We begin the production number—"STRAIGHT AND NAPPY." We

CUT TO:

A SET

where each group dances and sings about the beauty and virtues of their hair. Jane and Rachel trade lyrics about having straight hair versus nappy hair. As the song is finished we

CUT BACK TO:

28 INT: *CORRIDOR—NIGHT*

Members of each group are running their fingers through their hair.

CLOSE—RACHEL AND JANE

JANE

Watch it.

RACHEL

I will.

CUT TO BLACK.

[C] 29 INT: *LAUNDRY ROOM—NIGHT*

The Gammites are lying all over the laundry room.

SIR NOSE

When it's over I know what's
the first thing I'm gonna do.

MUSSOLINI

Yep, my nuts ache.

DOO-DOO BREATH

Same here.

HALF-PINT

What?

SIR NOSE

You don't know?

HALF-PINT

Why do you think I asked?

SLIM DADDY

Guess.

SIR NOSE

He doesn't know.

MUSTAFA

Tell him.

DOUBLE RUBBER

Yeah, tell him.

SIR NOSE

My unenlightened Gammite, it's affectionately known as hootchie, snatch . . .

CLOSE—SLIM DADDY

SLIM DADDY

trim, poontang . . .

CLOSE—MUSTAFA

MUSTAFA

nookie, pencil sharpener . . .

CLOSE—YODA

YODA

coodleberries . . .

CLOSE—SIR NOSE

SIR NOSE

bush pudding . . .

CLOSE—MUSSOLINI

MUSSOLINI

Snatch.

CLOSE—DOO-DOO BREATH

DOO-DOO BREATH

ya know—hide da salami.

The Gammites are dying.

HALF-PINT

Oh, that. Now that you've mentioned it, I've been feeling kinda doggish myself.

The Gammites jump on top of Half-Pint.

30 **INT:** ***RACHEL'S ROOM—NIGHT***

Rachel is going over her English notes at her desk. There are no posters on the walls, but instead a lot of plants.

DORIS

Ms. Jane Diva is gonna get it.

RACHEL

Isn't she on the Gamma Court?

DORIS

She's the queen. Are you ready? We won't get a seat if we don't leave now.

RACHEL

I'm not going.

DORIS

I suppose Slice isn't going either.

RACHEL

That has nothing to do with it.

DORIS

Please, spare me.

Rachel laughs.

DORIS (contd)

Y'know you haven't seen anybody else since freshman year. Don't you ever feel like having other relationships, seeing other guys?

RACHEL

No.

DORIS

Slice is a nice guy, probably one of the few positive brothers on campus, but I betcha he's snaking. He can't help it. He's a man, it's their nature. . . . Are you coming or not?

RACHEL

See ya.

Rachel goes back to her work. The seed has been planted.

31 INT: *LAUNDRY ROOM—NIGHT*

WE CAN BARELY MAKE OUT the figures of the Gammites as they take a well-deserved nap. OS we hear voices whispering. Double Rubber, the light sleeper, the watchdog, peers up, looks. It was nothing, and he goes back to sleep when—

Screams pierce the quiet. The lights come on and the Big Brothers storm into the laundry room. The Gammites are caught surprised and scurry around like trapped rats.

JULIAN

You can't run and you can't hide.

BIG BROTHER GENERAL GEORGE PATTON

Gamma is too high to go over,
too low to go under.

BIG BROTHER X-RAY VISION

Don't y'know we see your every
move, read your every thought?

JULIAN

Line up!

The Gammites fall in.

YODA

Most honorable Big Brothers of
Gamma Phi Gamma, we beg for your
forgiveness. Have mercy on our
souls.

JULIAN

Enough!

BIG BROTHER DR. FEELGOOD

What we have here is a menace to
Gamma. I motion for the death
penalty.

BIG BROTHER GENERAL GEORGE PATTON

I second it.

BIG BROTHER X-RAY VISION

I triple it.

BIG BROTHER LANCE

Death would be too good for these offenders of the law. Let's make the streets safe to walk again.

BIG BROTHER CHUCKY

We have to decide on the gas chamber, electric chair, or death by injection.

BIG BROTHER DR. FEELGOOD

Let's make an example out of them.

The Gammas huddle in a circle, just barely speaking above a whisper and occasionally glancing at the accused. The Gammites strain to pick up any bits and parts of the powwow. The Gammas nod in agreement and face the Gammites as beads of perspiration roll off the latters' foreheads.

JULIAN

After much deliberation, we have reached a verdict. Guilty on eight counts of treason. Guilty on eight counts of conspiracy. Having been found guilty as charged, you are sentenced to meet Bertha Butt.

The Gammites bite their lips. Big Brother General George Patton pulls out a big, wide black-and-silver paddle inscribed "Bertha Butt."

BIG BROTHER LANCE (VO)
(like baseball announcer)

Ladies and gentlemen, boys and girls, leading off, playing second base, Big Brother General George Patton, number two. Patton.

ANGLE—BIG BROTHER GENERAL GEORGE PATTON

He acts like he's a baseball player. He knocks the dirt from his cleats, and takes some practice swings to loosen up.

JULIAN

Gammites, about-face.

They turn around.

JULIAN (contd)

Unbuckle, unzip, drop, bend over.

The Gammites follow their commands.

BIG BROTHER DR. FEELGOOD

Knock it outta here.

JULIAN

Keep those buttocks in the air.
Play ball!

WE TRACK down the line, CLOSE ON each controted Gammite face waiting to be hit.

Whack.

HALF-PINT

I'm coo-coo for Cocoa Puffs.
I'm coo-coo for Cocoa Puffs.

Pow.

DOO-DOO BREATH

Yabbadaba-doo!

Whack.

DOUBLE RUBBER
(singing)

The Addams Family started when Uncle Fester farted they all became retarded, the Addams Family.

Whack.

YODA

Fathers, forgive us for we have sinned.

Smack.

MUSSOLINI
(singing)

I'm singing in the rain,
I'm singing in the rain,
What a glorious feeling,
I'm happy again.

Crack.

MUSTAFA

There's no need to fear
Gammite Dog is here.

Pow.

SIR NOSE

Engine, engine number nine,
coming down the Chicago line,
if the train falls off the track
do you want your money back?

Kapow.

SLIM DADDY

Is there a doctor in the house?

BIG BROTHER LANCE
(like baseball announcer)

Look out, it's way back, way
back, it's going, going, gone.
Kiss dat baby goodbye.

Big Brother General George Patton trots the bases like he's just hit a home run. The entire Gamma team is there to greet him at home plate.

ANGLE—GAMMITES

The Gammites rub their bare, sore asses.

32 **EXT:** *ADMINISTRATION BUILDING—NIGHT*

Slice sits in one of the cardboard shacks with his comrades. Rachel walks to Slice, who's at his post. Unlike this afternoon, only the few faithful remain.

He, however, is delighted to see her smiling face.

RACHEL

Where is everybody?

SLICE

Where do you think?

RACHEL

I know, dumb question. Doris tried to get me to go too.

SLICE

I'm happy to see you.

RACHEL

You look like you could use the company. How long are you going to stay out here?

SLICE

All night.

RACHEL

Not me.

SLICE

Leave when you're ready.

RACHEL

Don't rush me.

[X] 33 **EXT:** *MARTIN LUTHER KING, JR., CHAPEL—NIGHT*

A large, orderly crowd is in front of the chapel waiting for the doors to be opened. The moment they're opened, the crowd becomes a throng, a mob. People are pushing and shoving, trying to file into the entrances.

CLOSE—DORIS AND LIZZIE

Doris and Lizzie are trying not to get crushed.

CLOSE—THE FELLAS

The Fellas seem to be enjoying this madness.

CLOSE—THE GAMMA PHI GAMMA CONTINGENT

Led by Big Brother Almighty, the Gammites and the Gammas have formed a shield of protection around the Gamma Rays.

[C] 34 **INT:** *CHAPEL—NIGHT*

Three seats are roped off in the front row, dead center. An usher removes the rope and seats President McPherson, Odrie, and Cloud.

McPherson waves to various members of the administration and faculty.

ANGLE—CHAPEL

There is a mad scramble for seats and as quick as you can say "That's right, goddamnit" the joint is packed.

The lights go dim.

[C] 35 ANGLE—STAGE

Onto the stage walks BUCKWHEAT. He's the master of ceremonies for all the homecoming events.

CLOSE—GRADY

He stands and shouts.

GRADY

It's Buckwheat.

ANGLE—AUDIENCE

STUDENTS

Hi, Buckwheat.

ANGLE—BUCKWHEAT

BUCKWHEAT
(somewhat annoyed)

My name's not Buckwheat, it's Roosevelt.

STUDENTS (OS)

Buckwheat! Buckwheat!

BUCKWHEAT

We welcome you back to Mission College for homecoming.

The audience applauds.

BUCKWHEAT (contd)

I want everyone to stand up, that's right, stand up, c'mon. Turn to the right and face your neighbor, give him a hug and say, "Happy homecoming."

CUT TO:

VARIOUS SHOTS—STUDENTS, ALUMNI, AND FACULTY

hugging each other.

STUDENTS

Happy homecoming.

ANGLE—BUCKWHEAT

BUCKWHEAT

Didn't that feel good? Now turn to the left and do the same.

CUT TO:

THE FELLAS AND GAMMA CONTINGENT

FELLAS AND GAMMAS

Happy homecoming.

CLOSE—BUCKWHEAT

BUCKWHEAT

Sit your butts down!

The students laugh.

BUCKWHEAT (contd)

The theme of this year's coronation is REENERGIZE. LET HOMECOMING BEGIN.

We hear music, the curtains part, the stage lights come up, and WE SEE the Mission College dance troupe perform.

[C] 36 **EXT:** *ADMINISTRATION BUILDING—NIGHT*

SLICE

It's getting kind of cool.

RACHEL

I'm fine.

SLICE

You sure?

RACHEL

Yes.

SLICE

It's getting chilly. How long
are you gonna be out here?

RACHEL

Are you trying to get rid of me?

SLICE

It's not like that. I don't
want you catching a cold.

RACHEL

And?

SLICE

And what?

RACHEL

And?

SLICE

And it's warmer in my room.

RACHEL

Slice, you ain't no good.

He starts to laugh.

RACHEL (contd)

What about this?

SLICE

I'll come back after you and
I get warmed up.
(he takes Rachel by the hand)
Let's go.

She smiles.

RACHEL

Warmed up, huh.

Slice tells the group he'll be back shortly.

[X] 37 **INT:** *CHAPEL—NIGHT*

The Senior Court is on the stage. The five ladies dance in full-length blue-sequined gowns.

CLOSE—McPHERSON, ODRIE, AND CLOUD

They applaud as the Senior Court leaves the stage.

We hear a tremendous roar; Cloud looks puzzled.

ODRIE

It's just the Gammas.

[C] 38 ANGLE—GAMMA SECTION

The Gammas, Gammites, and Gamma Rays are all standing on their seats, making much noise. The men are barking like dogs (their trademark) while the ladies meow like cats.

39 ANGLE—STAGE

The stage goes BLACK. Fog starts to rise from the orchestra pit. WE SEE five women move onto the stage.

There is a buzz throughout the audience as they wait in anticipation for the Gamma Court.

MONTY ROSS'S VOICE (OS)

On this planet only a few are
chosen, you do or you don't,
you will or you won't, Black
and Silver does. . . . Ladies and
gentlemen, friend and foe, I
present Miss Gamma Phi Gamma,
Jane Toussaint, and her court.

With a clap of thunder and a ball of fire, the lights come up and the Gamma Court—Jane, Dina, Kim, Vivian, Velda—breaks into an up-tempo song. Jane has the lead. With the court backing vocals, their choreography would give the Supremes a battle. They look lavish in silver dresses adorned with black ostrich feathers.

38A ANGLE—GAMMA SECTION

The entire section is going wild.

[X] 40 ANGLE—THE FELLAS

They are clapping and whistling, so is the rest of the audience.

GRADY

Lawd have mercy.

39A ANGLE—STAGE

The Gamma Court struts to the front of the stage and does several bumps and grinds (serious pelvic thrusts), syncopated to the big beat.

37A CLOSE—PRESIDENT McPHERSON

An embarrassed McPherson covers his face.

CLOSE—CLOUD AND ODRIE

They both are enjoying this.

39B ANGLE—STAGE

The music ends, the Gamma Court freezes, the lights go black.

ANGLE—GAMMA SECTION

The entire section is on its feet, screaming.

GAMMA SECTION

G-Phi-G, G-Phi-G.

ANGLE—DORIS AND LIZZIE

They are not moved at all.

[C] 39C ANGLE—STAGE

The lights come back on and the Gamma Court, led by Jane, takes a curtain call. Jane throws kisses to the crowd.

JANE

I love you too! I love you too!

41 **INT:** *SLICE'S ROOM—NIGHT*

Slice is straightening up. All the work is being done on Grady's side of the room. He kicks Grady's dirty clothes under the bed. From the closet, Slice pulls out a can of air freshener and gives the room a long, hard blast. The fumes make him and Rachel cough. She opens the windows.

RACHEL

Didya have to use the whole can?

SLICE

Grady doesn't feel at home unless it smells like a locker room.

Slice pulls Rachel towards him and kisses her. Before he can develop this any further, she pushes him away.

RACHEL

We had static with Jane and the Wannabees.

SLICE

Yeah, what happened?

RACHEL

The usual.

SLICE

Fuck 'em! I dont' give two motherfucks 'bout dem.

RACHEL

Here we go.

SLICE

I don't care.

RACHEL

Don't start. I have my problems with them, but with you, it's a crusade. I'm beginning to think you're color struck. Slice, you definitely have a thing against light-skin Blacks.

SLICE

Rachel, come off it. They are the ones who are color struck. It's them, not me, not me.

(he adds sarcastically)

I love octoroons, quadroons, mulattoes.

(he laughs)

So, so, so unpure.

RACHEL

Like you're one hundred percent pure. Massa was in your ancestors' slave quarters like everybody else.

SLICE

No! No! No! No white blood in me. My stock is one hundred percent real pure Nubian stock.

RACHEL

You're so silly.

SLICE

On the serious tip. Some of the Wannabees are all right. The rest suck.

(he laughs again)

OK, OK. Seriously, if a person is cool with me, I'm cool with them.

RACHEL

You're fulla shit. Anyway, you need to check yourself on that tip.

Rachel sits up and pulls her T-shirt over head. She turns around and lets Slice unsnap her bra. Slice kisses the nape of her neck and slowly works his way (I mean works) down to the base of her spine. Suddenly Slice jumps up.

RACHEL (contd)

What's the matter?

SLICE

Stay put.

Rachel watches him go to the stereo.

RACHEL

Oh, no, not again. Last time
it was John Coltrane.

Slice removes an album from the rack, puts it on the turntable, and jumps into the bed. We hear the intro to the song "Ballad Black." One of those vicious slow jams, the kind that you wanted played when you were in one of those basement, house-party, grind-against-the-wall jammies. This song will continue into the next scene.

SLICE

I, I, I, I loooves ya.

RACHEL

You don't have a bit of sense.

They make whoopee, "gotta make da donuts."

DISSOLVE TO:

42 **INT:** *STAGE—NIGHT*

CLOSE ON—TWO HANDS

Placing a silver crown on a head.

ANGLE—PRESIDENT McPHERSON AND
MISS MISSION COLLEGE

In SLOW MOTION, McPherson has just crowned Miss Mission College. Over her Snow White dress she wears a maroon cape which flows five feet behind her. In her arms she cradles two dozen red roses. Flashbulbs are going off like mad.

42A **INT:** *STAGE—NIGHT*

Still in SLOW MOTION, Miss Mission College walks to the front of the stage as tears stream down her face. Her court, the First and Second Attendants, applaud in the BG. The houselights come up and all the courts come out from the wings to hug her. The show is over.

[X] 43 **EXT:** *CHAPEL—NIGHT*

The fired-up crowd leaves the chapel.

[X] 44 **EXT:** *CAMPUS—NIGHT*

Julian takes Jane by the hand as they walk. She is still dressed in her Miss Gamma gown and fur wrap. The campus is packed now; off in the distance we hear chants. As Julian and Jane walk, she is congratulated on her performance.

WE SEE a pep rally/bonfire in progress. They stop to watch as the flames warm the cool autumn evening, throwing a golden glow on the students.

[X] ANGLE—STUDENTS

The students surround the bonfire, led by the cheerleaders in the chants.

STUDENTS

Huckleberry, blackberry,
blueberry pie
V-I-C-T-O-R-Y
You can hit us on our head,
You can knock us off our feet,
But the Mission Tigers can't be beat.
Oh, you can't stop the TIGER machine.
No, you can't stop the TIGER machine.
NO! NO! NO! NO!

[X] 45 **EXT:** *GAMMA HOUSE—NIGHT*

CLOSE—HAMMERS

Hammers are pounding nails in time to the above cheer.

ANGLE—FLOAT

A half-finished float sits in front of the Gamma house. The Gammas give instructions to the Gammites as they build and decorate the float for tomorrow's parade. They are also helped by the Gamma Rays.

CLOSE—JULIAN AND JANE

as they approach the float.

JULIAN

It looks good, real good. Make sure you glue the tissue paper on tight.

GAMMITES

Yes, Big Brother Almighty.

JULIAN
(to Jane)

Where's the car parked?

Jane smiles and he puts his arms around her. He turns his head and winks at Half-Pint.

CLOSE—HALF-PINT

He smiles.

[C] 46 **EXT:** *MERCEDES-BENZ—NIGHT*

Julian is driving on the highway; Jane is snuggled up next to him.

JULIAN

I can't drive with you all over me.

Jane moves closer.

JULIAN (contd)

Did you hear what I said? Do you want me to drive us both to our graves?

JANE

You are no fun.

Jane moves back to her side of the car.

JANE (contd)

My parents sent me some more money. Do you need to borrow any?

JULIAN

No, I don't. And as soon as I get my check I'll pay you back the amount I already owe you.

JANE

I already said you could have it. Keep it, I want to give it to you.

JULIAN
(explodes)

I'm sick of this shit. I don't need your welfare. I got my own money. You keep yours. Keep your money. Keep your charity.

JANE

I was just trying to help.

JULIAN

Help? Help? Who needs your fucking help? I got my own money.

JANE

Forget you then.

JULIAN

Keep ya money.
(he thinks)
And another thing, take your car keys back too!

46A **EXT:** *HIGHWAY—NIGHT*

[C] The Mercedes accelerates into the night.

47 **INT:** *SLICE'S ROOM—NIGHT*

Slice has his arm around Rachel, her head rests upon his shoulder.

SLICE

Watch out.
(he removes his arm from around Rachel)
It was going asleep.

RACHEL

It's getting late. Don't you have to go back?

SLICE

Spend the night.

RACHEL

What about Grady?

SLICE

Don't worry about him.

RACHEL

I have something to tell you.

SLICE

Good or bad?

RACHEL

Good.

(she sits up)

Take a guess.

SLICE

Go on. I have no idea whatsoever.

RACHEL

Not even a wild guess? You're hopeless. I'm pledging Delta next semester.

Slice jumps up!

SLICE

You're what?

RACHEL

I'm going to pledge Delta next semester. I've been to a couple of rushes and if they accept me I'm gonna do it.

SLICE

First Half-Pint, now you. You're kidding. I can't believe it.

RACHEL

Believe it. Believe it. You really know how to spoil a pleasant evening.

SLICE

Me! I didn't bring up pledging.

RACHEL

I must have been sick in the head to think I would have your support.

SLICE

You don't need my support.

RACHEL

I thought I did.

SLICE

Sororities are just as bad as the fraternities.

RACHEL

Slice, this is something that I want to do. You have every right not to like Greeks. But this is another matter.

SLICE

The hell it is. They do something to people. You won't be the same. People change for the worse after they pledge. If I've seen it once, I've seen it a million times.

RACHEL

I'll be the same Rachel and I will still love you.

SLICE

Uh huh!

Rachel gets out of the bed and quickly puts on her clothes.

SLICE (contd)

You might as well join the Gamma Rays while you're at it.

Rachel, dressed now, looks at him.

RACHEL

Wait a minute, honey. This has nothing to do with the Gamma Rays, all right? Y'know, I've often wondered if you're with me because I'm the darkest thing on campus, good for your all-the-way-down pro-Black image.

She closes the door behind her.

CUT TO:

48 **INT:** *JANE'S APARTMENT—NIGHT*

Jane opens the door and Julian follows her. He closes the door and jumps all over her. Before Jane knows it, he has half of her clothes off. She laughs as he rolls her panties down her legs. They make love; no, that's not it. They are boning, oops, I forgot, boning on da thick plush carpet.

[C] 49 **INT:** *PRESIDENT McPHERSON'S BEDROOM—NIGHT*

McPherson and Odrie are in bed.

ODRIE

What does Cedar Cloud want?

McPHERSON

He's an errand boy for the Flemisters. Just an errand boy.

ODRIE

It's this divestment issue, isn't it?

McPHERSON

I believe it is.

ODRIE

Maybe . . . Cloud has had his eyes on your job for years. I don't trust that man as far as I can throw him, don't trust him a lick.

McPHERSON

This is tearing the students apart.

ODRIE

It'll work out.

McPHERSON

Something good and wonderful has been happening here at Mission for over a century . . .

ODRIE

. . . and it will continue.

Odrie hugs him.

McPHERSON

I'm old and tired and my faith is wavering.

[C] 50 **EXT:** *ADMINISTRATION BUILDING—NIGHT*

LOW ANGLE—SLICE

walks in front of the Administration Building and looks up at the banners hung from it. He's the lone person there. He sits down; on the steps at his feet is a placard that has been stepped on and trampled. It reads . . .

CLOSE—PLACARD

"AFRICA WILL BE FREE!!!"

FADE OUT.

FADE IN:

TITLE—SATURDAY

[C] 51 **INT:** *JANE'S APARTMENT—MORNING*

ANGLE—JULIAN AND JANE

Julian and Jane are in the bed. She turns over to see if he is still asleep and nudges him gently. He moans. Jane kisses him gently.

JANE

Wake up.

He pulls the sheet over his head.

JANE (contd)

Honey, wake up.

Jane pulls the sheet away and kisses him again.

JULIAN
(still sleepy)

What time is it?

JANE

Eight. Are you hungry? I'll make you breakfast.

JULIAN

No thanks. Let me lie here for a couple more minutes.

JANE

I'm a great cook.

JULIAN

I need sleep, not food.

JANE

I'll let you sleep then. . . . Julian, I want you to come visit me in New Orleans. You'll like it and my parents want to meet you. Especially my father. Daddy is glad you're a Gamma like him.

JULIAN

Don't tell me, ya moms was Miss Gamma.

JANE

How did you know? Did I mention that before?

JULIAN

I took a wild guess.

JANE

I've told them all about you. How you're president of the chapter, also dean of pledgees. They wanted to visit for homecoming, but I told them not to come. I wanted to spend it alone with you. You sure you don't want me to cook you something? It won't take but a hot minute.

He's trying hard not to explode.

JULIAN

Jane, I thank you very much for your hospitality, but I'm not hungry.

JANE

I want to make sure, because it's no bother. . . . You're not mad at me, are you?

JULIAN

I am not mad.

JANE

Good! Because I don't like it when you're mad. . . . When do you like me?

JULIAN

What kind of question is that?

JANE

When do you like me?

JULIAN

When you shut up!

JANE

That's not funny, Julian. I'm being serious and you're playing. You never let me in. I want to know what you're thinking, what you're feeling.

JULIAN

Have you ever considered I don't want you to know?

JANE

What are you scared of? . . . Do you love me?

JULIAN

Jesus Christ on the cross, can I get twenty more minutes of sleep?

JANE

Do you love me?

JULIAN

Will you stop pumping me?

JANE

Answer me then.

JULIAN

What do you want me to say? I'm attracted to you, you're attracted to me, boom, we have a good time together.

JANE

That's a start. Let me ask you this. When we first met, started seeing each other and we made sweet love for the first time, did you ever ask yourself, "Why did she let me?"

He shrugs.

JULIAN

No, I never thought about it.

JANE

I know what I'm doing.

JULIAN

You do?

JANE

I do.

JULIAN

If I eat something will you stop asking me all these questions?

JANE

How do you like your eggs?

Jane smothers his face with kisses.

52–52A OMIT

53 **EXT:** *MAIN STREET—MORNING*

It is a bright and sunny morning. Neighborhood residents along with the students and alumni of Mission College line both sides of Main Street five feet deep awaiting the homecoming parade. Off in the distance we hear drums.

Over the hilly street appear two motorcycle cops with lights flashing, leading the parade. The music, louder now, is played by a high-school band.

ANGLE—PRESIDENT McPHERSON'S CAR

Odrie sits between her husband and Cloud. They are riding in a Lincoln Continental convertible. Signs on both sides of it read "PRESIDENT McPHERSON, ODRIE McPHERSON, and CHAIRMAN OF THE BOARD, MISSION COLLEGE, MR. CEDAR CLOUD." The crowd applauds respectfully and in return they wave.

53A ANGLE—PARADE

The parade continues with a long line of floats and cars. Each organization on campus is represented. WE CATCH GLIMPSES of ROTC, the Math Club, Detroit Alumni Association, Miss Glee Club, etc., etc. Pretty women and handsome men dressed nicely sit on cars and on floats. The floats for the most part belong to the frats. Each one is elaborately decorated in its own colors. Interspersed throughout the parade are various drill teams and marching bands from the local high schools.

53B ANGLE—GAMMA FLOAT

The Gamma Phi Gamma float approaches. It's huge, all done up in black and silver. The Gamma Court (Jane, Dina, Kim, Vivian, and

Velda) sits majestically on thrones, waving to the crowd and throwing black licorice. On each side of the float walk the Gammites. The Gamma Rays and Gammas ride in the back of a pickup truck that pulls the float.

GAMMAS AND GAMMA RAYS

G-Phi-G bad as we want to be.
G-Phi-G is the only one for me.

CLOSE—JULIAN AND JANE

Julian and Jane are singing with the others.

53C ANGLE—FELLAS

Behind the Gamma float are Slice, Jordan, Booker T., Monroe, Edge, Rachel, Doris, Lizzie, plus other people. They carry a banner that goes from one side of the street to the other. It reads: "McPHERSON DIVEST NOW, SOUTH AFRICA MUST BE FREE." They chant slogans, etc.

ANGLE—SLICE AND RACHEL

He looks at her.

SLICE

I apologize.

RACHEL

It's not important.

She turns away.

[X] 53D ANGLE—CROWD

Some of the crowd start to heckle Slice and his group.

VOICE (OS)

Go back to Africa.

VOICE (OS)

You're all a bunch of communists.

ANGLE—PROTESTERS

Slice and the group continue to march.

53BB ANGLE—GAMMA PICKUP TRUCK

Julian motions to his frat brothers and they jump out of the truck and walk back to protesters. They are joined by the Gammites. They form a wall of black and silver that impedes Slice from marching forward. It's a stalemate, when in flies Virgil Cloyd. He's wearing an armband that reads "PARADE MARSHAL."

VIRGIL

Slice, you are in direct violation. You need a permit from my office to participate in this parade and you don't have one.

SLICE

We don't need no stinking permits.

JULIAN

You heard what Virgil said. No permit, no parade.

VIRGIL

Julian, I can handle this myself. Give me the banner.

SLICE

We ain't giving you shit.

EDGE

That's right, goddamnit.

SLICE

Look, we pay tuition here like everybody else. You Wannabees make me sick.

VIRGIL

Give me the banner.

The Gammas snatch the banner from them. It's a tug-of-war when we hear it tear. The Gammas cheer and wave the shreds in the air. Slice and Edge try to go after Julian, but are restrained by Jordan, Booker T., Monroe, and Rachel. Slice is red-hot and is pulled to the ground.

ANGLE—GAMMAS AND GAMMITES

They run triumphantly down the street to catch up with their float.

CLOSE—VIRGIL

VIRGIL

Niggers and flies
I do despise.

54 **INT:** *LOCKER ROOM—DAY*

The Mission College football team, with bowed heads, kneels, surrounding its beloved coach. COACH ODOM (who back in his day starred at Mission) is a good head coach who actually missed his calling. Coach Odom would have been a great preacher. He leads his squad in the Lord's Prayer.

COACH ODOM

Our Father which art in heaven,
Hallowed be thy name.
Thy Kingdom come. Thy will be
done in earth, as it is in heaven.
Give us this day our daily bread.
And forgive us our trespasses, as
we forgive those who trespass
against us. And lead us not into
temptation, but deliver us from evil.
For thine is the kingdom and the
power and the glory, forever.
AMEN!

The team rises and begins to clap, shouting:

TIGERS

FIRED UP! FIRED UP! FIRED UP!

Coach Odom moves to the front of the cramped, dingy, and dusty locker room. A heavenly light shines through the windows. He raises his hands and a hush falls over the locker room. Service has begun.

COACH ODOM

Men, we have gathered here today
to do a job. God explained to
Jonah that the essence of love
is to labor for something and to
make something grow, that love
and labor are inseparable. One
loves that for which one labors
and one labors for that which
one loves. When we step out on

that gridiron, it's what we've labored for all week. I want every man to think about his responsibilities, his role. This is a team made up of sixty-five players and it will take a total effort by a committed, dedicated, never-say-die, never-give-up group of sixty-five individuals who have come together as one to win this battle. I don't have to tell you that the stands are packed with your friends, classmates, your family. Alumni have traveled from near and far. I won't even mention that your lady friends will be watching.

TIGERS

Yes, Jesus.

Coach Odom has caught the "spirit" and he begins to strut like he's on the pulpit. The team is his congregation. It's call and response.

COACH ODOM

Do you want to let them down?

TIGERS

Hell no!

COACH ODOM

Do you want to make a bad representation of Mission College?

TIGERS

Hell no!

COACH ODOM

Do you want to lose homecoming for the fourth year in a row?

TIGERS

Hell no!

COACH ODOM

Do you want me to lose my job?

TIGERS

Hell no!

COACH ODOM

Do you like Satan?

TIGERS

Hell no!

COACH ODOM

Well, Satan is in the other locker room. Today Satan is in the white jerseys. Can I get a witness?

TIGERS

Thank you, Jesus! Amen!

COACH ODOM

I want intensity!

TIGERS

Oh, yeah!

COACH ODOM

I want reckless abandon!

TIGERS

Oh, yeah!

COACH ODOM

Remember this is Mission College. Now go out there and kick some butt.

The players butt helmets, shoulder pads, practically kill each other.

The Tigers, worked up to a frenzy, charge out of the locker room, sweeping Coach Odom up along with them.

55 **INT:** *RUNWAY—DAY*

The Tigers fire down the runway (screaming like banshees) in the bowels of the stadium to the playing field.

56 **EXT:** *PLAYERS' ENTRANCE—DAY*

The cute and leggy cheerleaders hold up a large banner that reads: "TO BEAT US IS MISSION IMPOSSIBLE." POW!!! The Tigers tear through it out to the field.

57 ANGLE—MISSION COLLEGE BAND

The Mission College Marching Band strikes up the school fight song.

58 ANGLE—STANDS

They are jam-packed and everyone rises to sing.

59 ANGLE—McPHERSON, ODRIE, AND CLOUD

President McPherson stands at his seat and turns to lead the homecoming crowd in the fight song. Cloud and Odrie watch, amused at his show of exuberance.

60 CLOSE—RACHEL, DORIS, AND LIZZIE

They too are singing.

61 ANGLE—SLICE, JORDAN, BOOKER T., MONROE, AND EDGE

[C] A canteen filled with wine is passed down. Each one takes a nip. Jordan gives it to Booker T., who raises it to his lips and takes a long swallow. All four watch him. Jordan nudges him, then grabs the canteen.

JORDAN

This has to last until kickoff.

BOOKER T.

Fired up Mission.

62 CLOSE—FOOTBALL ON KICKING TEE

[X] A foot COMES INTO FRAME in SLOW MOTION.

63 ANGLE—FOOTBALL FIELD

[C] Mission College has won the coin toss; the visiting team in the white jerseys has just kicked off. Mission's return man catches the ball at the 20, follows his wall of blockers up the middle, then veers outside to the sideline, eluding the onrushing tacklers. The kicker is the last man between him and the end zone. He gives him a head and shoulder fake, the kicker goes for it, diving at air. He races into the end zone.

TOUCHDOWN!!!

[X] 64 ANGLE—MISSION BENCH

The entire Mission team leaves the bench to dance in the end zone.

58A ANGLE—STANDS

The crowd is in an uproar.

60A ANGLE—RACHEL, DORIS, AND LIZZIE

Doris hugs Rachel and Lizzie.

61A ANGLE—SLICE AND HIS BOYS

Slice gives Monroe, Booker T., Edge, and Jordan low, medium, and high fives.

59A ANGLE—PRESIDENT McPHERSON, ODRIE AND CLOUD

Cloud shakes McPherson's hand; the president is beaming. Odrie is reserved; she's seen this before.

ODRIE

It's just the first quarter.

[X] 63A ANGLE—UP FIELD-GOAL UPRIGHTS

The football is kicked straight and true through the uprights. The extra point is good.

65 CLOSE—SCOREBOARD

It reads: HOME 7—VISITORS 0

[X] 63B ANGLE—FOOTBALL FIELD

The visitors have turned on their bruising ground game. Play after play, the ball is handed off to their 240-pound fullback.

The fullback takes it up the middle seven, eight yards a clip. It takes four, five, six Mission defenders to bring him to the ground.

66 CLOSE—GRADY

on sideline.

GRADY

Big D. Big D.

61B CLOSE—SLICE

SLICE

Somebody stop that guy.

[X] 63C ANGLE—FOOTBALL FIELD

The ball is handed off to the fullback once again. He barrels into the end zone with people hanging all over him.

[C] 63AA CLOSE—REFEREE

The ref raises his arms.

TOUCHDOWN!

65A CLOSE—SCOREBOARD

It reads: HOME 7—VISITORS 7

PA ANNOUNCER (OS)

That's the end of the first quarter.

[C] 58B/C ANGLE—CROWD

A group of students jumps up and yells.

SECTION #1

This is Section Number One, Number One, Number One, Number One,
This is Section Number One,
Where the hell is Number Two?

Another group of students stands up and responds.

SECTION #2

This is Section Number Two, Number Two, Number Two, Number Two,
This is Section Number Two,
Where the hell is Number Three?

No one stands to answer and everyone laughs.

[X] 56A ANGLE—CHEERLEADERS

The cheerleaders, all endowed with long, lean legs and healthy breasts, pick up their pom-poms.

CHEERLEADERS

Peanuts, Popcorn,
Sis, Boom, Bah,
Mission, Mission,
Rah, Rah, Rah!

They end it with splits, handstands, cartwheels, etc.

[X]63D ANGLE—FOOTBALL FIELD

A wide receiver for the visiting team catches a pass over the middle. He's hit instantly by two linebackers and slumps to the ground like a fifty-pound bag of potatoes.

66A CLOSE—GRADY

on sideline.

GRADY

Way to stick, way to stick.

58D ANGLE—STANDS

The crowd cheers.

CROWD

I said whoops upside da head,
Said whoops upside da head.
I said whoops upside da head,
Said whoops upside da head.

63E OMIT

63F OMIT

61C OMIT

63G OMIT

[X] 63H ANGLE—FOOTBALL FIELD

The tide has turned. The visitors have the momentum; Mission starts to fall apart at the seams like a 14th Street suit. They drop passes, miss tackles, incur stupid penalties, and fumble the ball.

A split end for the visitors catches a sixty-yard bomb.

TOUCHDOWN!

65B CLOSE—SCOREBOARD

It reads: HOME 7—VISITORS 14

[X]61A CLOSE—SLICE

SLICE

It don't mean a thing. It's
early, don't mean a thing.

59B CLOSE—McPHERSON

McPHERSON

It's still early.

56B ANGLE—CHEERLEADERS

CHEERLEADERS

Push 'em back, push 'em back,
Harder, harder.
Push 'em back, push 'em back,
Harder, harder.

[X] 63I ANGLE—FOOTBALL FIELD

Mission's quarterback is back to pass when he's hit from behind, jarring the ball loose. A huge lineman scoops up the pigskin and rambles into the end zone and spikes it.

TOUCHDOWN!

65C CLOSE—SCOREBOARD

It reads: HOME 7—VISITORS 21

60C ANGLE—RACHEL AND DORIS

DORIS

Where's the blocking? Who let the monster breeze in so he could clobber Jimmy? I can pass block better than that.

RACHEL

Me too!

[C] 61E ANGLE—SLICE

SLICE

What's going on? Pass the wine.

57A ANGLE—BAND

The drum major has the band strike up the fight song.

59C ANGLE—McPHERSON, ODRIE, AND CLOUD

CLOUD

Doesn't look good.

McPHERSON

Mission never says die.

[C] 61F ANGLE—SLICE

Slice stands up and begins to hand out leaflets about divestment.

[X] 63J ANGLE—FOOTBALL FIELD

The Mission punter is back in the end zone when the ball is snapped. Before he can get the kick away, the visitors come surging in and block the punt. The ball goes straight into the air and they fall on it in the end zone.

61G ANGLE—SLICE AND HIS BOYS

SLICE
(he yells)

Son of a bitch. What the fuck is going on? I've been here for four years and we've lost every homecoming. You're playing like a bunch of . . .

SMACK!

Someone has hit Slice upside the head with a balled-up leaflet. He turns around to see who did it.

VOICE (OS)

Down in front.

ANOTHER VOICE (OS)

Go back to Niger, nigger.

SLICE

Whoever threw that ain't got
no mother.

The Fellas laugh.

Slice turns back around. SMACK! SMACK! He's hit twice upside the head again. Slice takes a leaflet, crumples it up, and fires it in the general direction of where he thinks the culprit is. Monroe, Jordan, Booker T., and Edge pick up the cue. In a flash the stands are engaged in a free-for-all. What football game?

[X] 59D ANGLE—McPHERSON, ODRIE, AND CLOUD

McPHERSON

I think it's time for us to
leave.

CUT TO:

67 **INT:** *McPHERSON'S OFFFICE—DAY*

Cloud stands by the window as McPherson walks to Slice, who is seated.

McPHERSON

Vaughn Dunlap.

SLICE

Yes, President McPherson?

MCPHERSON

Where did you get the name
Slice?

SLICE

Just a nickname, that's all.

McPHERSON

Anyway, Vaughn, you have been
a good student for four years;
you've grown into a fine young
man.

SLICE

Thank you.

McPHERSON

That's why I'm surprised about
your recent activities.

SLICE

Oh, that.

McPHERSON

You've become a disruptive force
on this campus. You're hinder-
ing people from getting an
education.

Cloud walks from the window to Slice's chair.

CLOUD

Let me make it plain.
(he leans over Slice for emphasis)
Young man, you don't really have
a choice. If you continue your
antics you'll be expelled, plain
and simple, short and sweet.

Cloud looks at McPherson. The president is peeved; he feels that Cloud has overstepped his boundaries.

McPHERSON

This is Cedar Cloud. Chairman
of the board of trustees. . . .
What he says is true.

Slice stands up.

SLICE

True! He doesn't even know the
meaning of the word. People
like you kill me. So you marched
with King. So what? That was

more than twenty years ago.
Black people are still catching
hell the world over in 1987.

McPHERSON

There has been progress.

SLICE

Says who? There is no way in
hell you can defend not divesting
totally. No ifs, ands, or buts.

CLOUD

It's your tactics, methods that
are being questioned.

McPHERSON

You can't hinder the student
body receiving their education.
An education that they paid for.

SLICE

I'll do what I have to do.

CLOUD

So will I. Y'know, you have a
lot of living to do. You are
young. I had classmates here
at Mission just like you. Now
they're old and bitter people.

SLICE

You still don't understand, do
you?

McPHERSON

Make us understand.

Slice looks at the president and sees that it is a sincere request.

SLICE

The struggle for equality is an
ongoing thing. It shouldn't stop,
no matter how successful, famous,
or rich you become. What the two
of you, or better yet, what anybody has done in the past is

great. They are to be commended.
But what I'm talking 'bout is
don't let it stop there. Keep
going.

President McPherson looks at Slice; he's actually quite proud of him.

McPHERSON

You're a good speaker.

CLOUD

And what he says doesn't make a
bit of sense.

Slice shakes his head in disbelief.

SLICE

Anything else?

President McPherson looks at Cloud, who says nothing.

McPHERSON

You may go.

CLOUD

We'll be watching.

SLICE

So will I.

Slice leaves the room.

[X] ANGLE—McPHERSON AND CLOUD

CLOUD

I've seen his kind before.
He'll knuckle.

McPHERSON

I don't know; his father was
a militant too. He raised
sand here back in the sixties.

68 **INT:** *SLICE'S ROOM—DAY*

Slice enters the room and Grady is on his bed.

GRADY
(almost apologetic)

I'm sorry 'bout the game.

SLICE

We gave it the old Mission College try.

GRADY

No we didn't.

SLICE

So I lied.

They both laugh. Grady moves to his own bed, props two pillows under his leg and lies down. Slice grabs the phone and dials.

SLICE (contd)

Did Rachel call?

GRADY

Not since I been here.

The phone rings but no one answers. Slice hangs up and calls again. He presses the receiver against his ear; it rings, rings, and rings some mo'. He lies down and looks at Grady with his leg propped up.

69 **INT:** *RACHEL'S ROOM—DAY*

The phone is ringing and we can hear the jingling of keys in the door. The lock turns and Rachel runs for the phone. As she grasps it, the ringing stops.

RACHEL

Shoot!

Doris and Lizzie follow her.

RACHEL (contd)

I bet that was Slice.

DORIS

If it was, he'll call back.

RACHEL

Let him call.

DORIS

That doesn't sound like the president of the Slice Dunlap Fan Club.

LIZZIE

Yeah.

RACHEL

I handed in my resignation. Girl, it's like what you said, four years I've been tagging behind him like a puppy.

DORIS

Forget what I said.

RACHEL

Naw, naw, you were right. I told about me pledging and he went off.

DORIS

So that's what happened.

LIZZIE

You pledge? That's a surprise.

RACHEL

It shouldn't be. I've always wanted to.

DORIS

Since when?

RACHEL

Since I got here. I have a sense of who I am. I'm not joining for status. I honestly feel I can do some good. Not all Greeks are like the Gammas.

DORIS

Why wait until your senior year?

RACHEL

I was afraid of what Slice would think of me.

DORIS

What we do for men.

LIZZIE

Which brings us to Louis.

RACHEL

Your lover man.

[C] **LIZZIE**

I god rid of that boy. He was getting on my last nerve.

RACHEL

What?

LIZZIE

Shaky as they come. He would tell me A, B, C, then go turn around and do X, Y, Z.

DORIS

I thought you kiss the ground he walks on.

LIZZIE

Told him the deal and he's still sniffing around.

RACHEL

Can we have *one* conversation that doesn't include men?

DORIS

For real.

They laugh.

70 **INT:** *SLICE'S ROOM—DAY*

The Fellas are parked in Slice's room as usual.

MONROE

Can we go?

SLICE

I'm starving like Marvin.

GRADY

Me too.

MONROE

I have to be back in time for rehearsal.

JORDAN

Wait a minute, wait a minute. Slice, I hear McPherson called you in on the carpet.

SLICE

Dag. Who told ya?

JORDAN

You know you can't hide anything from your boys.

BOOKER T.

Holding out on us. So what that be about?

SLICE

McPherson is on me about this South Africa thing.

BOOKER T.

I knew it. I knew it.

MONROE

What else?

SLICE

He also tried to scare me by threatening me with expulsion, kicking me out.

GRADY

What did I tell ya.

BOOKER T.

Scare. That isn't no threat. That's a promise.

SLICE

I doubt it. Look, y'all are supposed to be my boys, right?

FELLAS

Right.

SLICE

We all agree that Mission has to divest, right?

The Fellas don't answer so quickly this time.

SLICE (contd)

Right?

FELLAS

Right.

SLICE

Then that's it. We have to do something big. I don't know what it is yet, but something to let McPherson, the administration, and the world know that we won't be part of it. I need you. The rest of these okey-dokey Negroes are too worried about graduating and getting a gig. But you, I need your back. If you ain't down you're all a bunch of foot-shufflin', wanna-be-white Uncle Toms.

The tension in the air could only be sliced with a "Texas chain saw."

BOOKER T.

Slice, I love you like my brother, but shit. What's wrong with wanting to get a nice job? My daddy and moms slaved all their damn life to send my black ass to school.

SLICE

Do you think I got bank?

BOOKER T.

I'm not finished. I'm the first one ever in my family to go to college. Do you realize what that means? The first ever. All my family has always been sharecroppers, since slavery.

SLICE

And apartheid is slavery.

BOOKER T.

You can do what you want to do. I ain't throwing it away for nobody, not you, not Bishop Tutu, not even Jesus Christ himself.

Slice looks for sympathy elsewhere. The Fellas turn away. They do not look him in the eyes.

SLICE

Don't leave me hanging.

This falls upon deaf ears.

SLICE (contd)

McPherson is bluffing y'all.

Grady gets up off his bed.

GRADY

Slice, in life there are times to be quiet, to shut up. This is one of them.

All of the Fellas walk.

SLICE
(yelling)

So that's the way it is, huh? Bet. That's a bet. Later for you cheese-eating niggers. Fuck y'all.

Slice slams the door.

ANGLE—DOOR

Grady opens the door and the Fellas stand behind him. Slice looks up.

SLICE

What do you two-faced back-stabbing bastards want?

GRADY

We want to know if revolutionaries eat Church's Fried Chicken?

[C] 71 **EXT:** *CAMPUS PARKING LOT—DAY*

WE TRACK with the Fellas in the parking lot past the Wannabees and their Volvos, BMWs, Porsches, and Mercedes-Benzes.

[C] ANGLE—1972 FORD

The Fellas pile into Booker T.'s Ford. They are taunted by the Wannabees, some words are exchanged. Booker T. floors the pedal, then steps on the brakes, coming within inches of hitting a new BMW. The Wannabees quiet down after that. As the Fellas pull off, they give the Wannabees the finger.

INT: *1972 FORD—DAY*

Booker T. is behind the steering wheel of his beat-up car, which is also badly in need of a wash. Detroit didn't build this car to ride six comfortably, they're jammed into it. Slice and Grady sit up front with Jordan, Monroe, and Edge in the rear. Slice turns on the radio and the knob comes off in his hand.

SLICE

Booker T., when are you going to fix this raggedy-ass car?

BOOKER T.

What's wrong with it? It runs like a stocking.

He pats the dashboard like a person would pat his dog on the head.

BOOKER T. (contd)

And furthermore, you wouldn't believe how many females I done boned in that there back seat.

JORDAN

Hold up. Get a new word, you're running boning.

BOOKER T.

Like what?

JORDAN

Blend, no more bone, blend.

BOOKER T.

Bet. You wouldn't believe how many females I done blended in that there back seat.

JORDAN

You're right. We wouldn't believe it.

BOOKER T.

It can never be said that Booker T. Washington didn't satisfy a woman. I lay much pipe.

JORDAN

If that's so, how come I haven't seen you with a female this semester?

BOOKER T.

I'm taking a rest.

They laugh.

MONROE

That's all you guys think about.

JORDAN

Yeah, right.

They all turn to look at Monroe. Rarely does he ever voice his opinion.

EDGE

What do you want us to think about?

SLICE

World affairs?

JORDAN

The economy?

GRADY

Who's gonna win the Super Bowl?

MONROE

I just get tired of you talking about women.

BOOKER T.

You ought to try it sometime.

SLICE

Beats singing.

EDGE

That's right, goddamnit.

MONROE

And that's another thing.

SLICE, GRADY, JORDAN, BOOKER T., AND EDGE
(in unison)

Shut up.

[C] 72 **EXT:** *CHURCH'S FRIED CHICKEN—DAY*

The battered Ford drives into the parking lot. One by one the crammed bodies emerge.

73 **INT:** *CHURCH'S FRIED CHICKEN—DAY*

Heads turn as Slice leads the way up to the counter.

COUNTER GIRL

Welcome to Church's Fried Chicken, may I help you?

They order.

73A ANGLE—TABLE

In the corner sits a group of local yokels. These six guys appear to be in their twenties. LEEDS, the smallest one, is the leader. They stare in the direction of Slice and company. All six wear Jerri curls, some have those plastic caps on their heads to keep their curls moist. (Look like shower caps but in loud, bright colors.)

ANGLE—COUNTER

Monroe notices them.

MONROE

I think we better eat somewhere else.

GRADY

Bye!

They sit down at a table.

ANGLE—TABLE

JORDAN

You see any salt?

BOOKER T.

Over there.

Jordan gets up from his seat and looks for the salt. He tries several shakers, but they are empty. He sees one on the table where the locals sit.

ANGLE—LOCALS' TABLE

JORDAN

Can I borrow the salt, please?

LEEDS

We ain't finished.

JORDAN

When will you be finished?

LEEDS

What time is it?

Jordan shakes his head and goes back to his seat.

ANGLE—SLICE'S TABLE

GRADY

Where's the salt?

JORDAN

Bad for you, gives you high
blood pressure.

ANGLE—LOCALS' TABLE

LEEDS
(effeminate voice)

Yoo-hoo!

He holds up the saltshaker.

ANGLE—SLICE'S TABLE

They all look at Leeds.

JORDAN

Let's not get into any static.

They continue eating, trying to ignore the taunts.

BOOKER T.

Slice, how's Rachel?

SLICE

She's doin' fine.

LEEDS (OS)

Yoo-hoo! Over here.

GRADY

What do you want?

ANGLE—LOCALS' TABLE

LEEDS
(effeminate voice)

Do you boys go to Mission?

GRADY (OS)

Yeah.

LEEDS
(effeminate voice)

Is it true what they say about
Mission men?

The locals scream.

ANGLE—SLICE'S TABLE

Grady begins to rise. Slice holds him back.

SLICE

Let's go.

They get up and leave, the locals are close behind.

74 **EXT:** *CHURCH'S PARKING LOT—DAY*

As they all leave Church's, Slice turns around and confronts the locals.

SLICE

Brother, what do you want?

SPOON

We ain't kin.

LEEDS

And we're not your brothers. How come you college mother-fuckers think you run every-thing?

BOOKER T.

Is there a problem here?

SPOON

Big problems.

MOSES

I heard that.

LEEDS

You come into our town year after year and take over. We were born here, been here, will be here all of our lives, and can't find work 'cuz of you.

MONROE

Slice, let's go.

LEEDS

We may not have your ed-u-ca-tion, but we ain't dirt either.

SLICE

Nobody said all that.

LEEDS

You Mission punks are always talking down to us.

SLICE

I'm sorry you feel that way, I really am.

They walk towards the Ford, Grady watches over his shoulder just in case.

LEEDS

Are you Black?

Those three words stop Slice in his tracks.

ERIC

Take a look in the mirror.

Slice walks up to Leeds, he's right in his face. The Fellas follow.

SLICE

You got a legitimate beef, but it's not with us.

LEEDS

Who then?

SLICE

Don't *ever* question whether I'm Black. In fact, I was gonna ask your country, BAMA ass, why do you put those Jerri-curl, drip-drip chemicals in your black nappy hair?

EDGE

That's right, goddamnit.

SLICE

And on top of that, come out in public with those plastic shower caps on your heads.

JORDAN

Just like a bitch.

MOSES

Who you calling a bitch?

BOOKER T.

If the shoe fits.

Leeds steps back, trying to take back the upper hand that the local yokels have obviously lost.

LEEDS

I betcha you niggers think
y'all are white. College
don't mean shit, you'll always
be niggers, always, just like
us.

SLICE

You're not niggers.

The Fellas leave, walking backwards, though; you never turn your back.

75 **INT:** *1972 FORD—DAY*

There is an uneasy silence as they ride back to campus. Those verbal attacks by the locals really burned their ears. Monroe breaks the ice.

MONROE

Do we really act like that?

JORDAN

My name is Bennett. I'm not
in it.

MONROE

You know, what that guy was
saying about us.

SLICE

We're not Wannabees.

BOOKER T.

They were ignorant.

MONROE

I don't think so.

GRADY

Look, motherfuckers got to try and start to better themselves. Just like we're trying to do.

MONROE

Maybe they've tried and given up.

JORDAN

Grady, you think everything is always so simple.

GRADY

Hell, yeah. You work or you starve. I want to eat sirloin.

SLICE

The guy was right.

Monroe looks at Grady.

MONROE

Told you.

GRADY

What does he know?

MONROE

Can't you drive any faster? I'm going to be late for Glee Club practice.

BOOKER T.

Hold your horses.

MONROE

You guys have made me late three times already.

BOOKER T.

Monroe, do you sing solo?

MONROE

Yes.

BOOKER T.

So low we can't hear you?

The Fellas scream.

BOOKER T. (contd)

Do you sing tenor?

MONROE

Yes.

BOOKER T.

Good, go sing ten or fifteen
miles away from here.

The Fellas have tears in their eyes.

76 **EXT:** *STREET—DAY*

The Ford passes by and disappears around a curve.

77 **INT:** *FORD—DAY*

SLICE

Slow up. It's Julian.

77A ANGLE—JULIAN AND JANE

WE SEE MOVING POV of them walking.

INT: *FORD—DAY*

SLICE

I'm getting out.

MONROE

Me too. You guys have made
me late again. Darn it.

Slice and Monroe jump out. Monroe runs by Julian and Jane in a sprint.

GRADY

We'll wait.

ANGLE—SLICE, JULIAN, AND JANE

SLICE

I got a few things you should know.

Slice glances at Jane, who is stuck to Julian's side as if she'll be the one to protect him if there is any trouble.

SLICE (contd)

Jane, can you excuse us?

She looks at Julian.

JULIAN

I'll be with you in a second. Go on.

Jane reluctantly walks over to the side. They both look at her until she's out of hearing distance.

JULIAN (contd)

Yeah, what is it?

SLICE

You're dean of pledgees, you have juice. My cousin will be a Gamma man in the morning. You will see to this.

JULIAN

I've heard better threats before.

SLICE

Julian, you are a simple, weak motherfucker, but that's beside the point. Don't mess over Half-Pint.

JULIAN

I'll look out for him all right. Y'know, me and you are gonna come to blows.

SLICE

C'mon with it.

JANE (OS)

Julian, let's go. He's not
worth it.

JULIAN

You talk more shit than a
little bit. Back to Mother
Africa, that's bullshit.
We're all Black Americans.
You don't know a goddamn thing
'bout Africa. I'm from Chi-
town. So go Watusi ya monkeyass
back to Africa if you want to.

Julian and Jane leave.

CLOSE—SLICE

Slice shakes his head.

SLICE
(mutters)

Wake up.

[X] 78 **INT:** *CHAPEL—DAY*

Monroe runs down the aisle up to the stage.

ANGLE—STAGE

The Mission College Glee Club is in place, warming up. Monroe tries to slink to his spot, but no. He's caught by the director of the Glee Club, DR. BAGLEY. He's on Monroe like white on rice, stink on shit, yeah, I know you get the picture.

DR. BAGLEY

Young man, why are you late
again?

MONROE

I . . .

Dr. Bagley doesn't even let him start.

DR. BAGLEY

See me in my office immediately after rehearsal. . . . Now that Mr. Leaves is here we can begin. First number.

The Glee Club performs the song "Betelehemu" along with special guest star OLATUNJI.

79 **EXT:** *CAFETERIA—DAY*

This space outside the cafeteria is jam-packed. The students, most of them women, are here to see the Greek show. A Greek show is an event where each fraternity does its steps, its marches. Each step is accompanied by a song or a rap boasting about the uniqueness of the particular fraternity. Almost all in particular are about sexual prowess. This is what attracts the females. Even though the gestures and language are "nasty," every time there is a Greek show the females will be there.

ANGLE—BUCKWHEAT

BUCKWHEAT

Here's the event we've all been waiting for. The highlight of every homecoming . . . the Greek show.

The students applaud.

BUCKWHEAT (contd)

First off I present those gentlemen of black and gold. You know who I'm talkin' 'bout. The one and only Alpha Phi Alpha.

WE SEE Alpha Phi Alpha do the "Alpha Train." Kappa Alpha Psi does "He Was a Gladiator, He Was Glad He Ate Her." They also do a number with red-and-white candy-striped canes, and WE SEE the men of blood and thunder, Omega Psi Phi. This frat has a nationwide rep as the nastiest of the nasty. Their classics are "Ah Tit-Tit" (they run into the audience at the end of the song, squeezing young, plump, firm breasts) and the ultimate showstopper, "Pass da Pussy Please." You've got to see this one to believe it.

Finally the Gammas take the stage. They all wear black capes and masks à la Zorro.

ANGLE—CROWD

WE SEE Slice and the Fellas move in and out of the crowd. Something is going on.

ANGLE—GAMMAS

The Gammas are stepping, Julian is getting off. They finish and the crowd applauds. When we hear . . .

FELLAS

Brothers, march.

The crowd makes an opening for Slice, Grady, Jordan, Booker T., Monroe, Grady, and Edge. They step into the circle doing a very exaggerated mockery of a frat step. The Gammas are furious as the crowd roars with laughter. The Fellas are shouting.

FELLAS (contd)

Daddy Long Stroke, ooo, ooo.
Daddy Long Stroke, ooo, ooo.
Daddy Long Stroke, ooo, ooo.

SLICE

Brothers, halt.

FELLAS

Shoot the juice, shoot the juice,
shoot, shoot, shoot the juice.

By now the crowd is screaming. The Fellas have succeeded in making total fools out of the Greeks, especially the Gammas, who stand there completely embarrassed. Big Brother Almighty can no longer take it. He moves towards Slice.

SLICE

Brothers, halt. Ladies and gentlemen, we, the brothers of Fella Phi Fella, are the baddest motherfuckers on this campus. Not the Alphas, not the Qs or the Kappas, and definitely not the Gammas.

The crowd starts to bark.

SLICE (contd)

And to prove it, I challenge the Gamma Dogs.

JULIAN

The Gamma Dogs accept.

SLICE

Good. I knew you would. I expected no less.

JULIAN

We're down for anything.

SLICE

Everybody knows the greatest lovers are the frats. And we Fella Phi Fellas are it.

JULIAN

Then why are your women so black and ugly?

The Gammas laugh.

SLICE

This is the big-dick Olympics.

Now the crowd is in a delirium. Slice tries to quiet them down.

SLICE (contd)

You heard right. We challenge you. Whip it out.

The Gammas are on the spot and don't know what to do.

JULIAN

We'll give you the honor of going first.

SLICE

No heart, huh? Brothers, whip it out.

ANGLE—FELLAS

The Fellas unzip their pants and pull out foot-long knockwursts and run around.

The crowd completely loses it, and Julian and the Gammas have lost face. To save it, Julian takes a wild swing at Slice, fights break out, and Edge pulls out a stink bomb and, boy, does it smell. Everybody makes a mad dash, beats it. In a matter of seconds the area is cleared.

[C] 80 **EXT:** *ROOFTOP—DUSK*

The Gammites are on the roof of the library. Behind them the sun sets in an orange-and-purple haze. It's the magic hour. They sit and stare at the sunset, tense and silent, for they know the moment is fast approaching. The moment when the Gammas will come for them to commence the Death March.

DOUBLE RUBBER

This is it. I hope we make it. We should, shouldn't we?

SLIM DADDY

Of course, stop thinking negative.

DOUBLE RUBBER

I've done everything I've been told. There should be no reason for *me* not to make it.

SIR NOSE

We all have.

DOO-DOO BREATH

I'm scared.

Yoda rises.

YODA

We're all scared. But remember these past weeks. We have dressed alike, eaten, slept, lived together. We have become one, that's the true meaning of fraternity. I know what we had to go through is bullshit, but it's just a test, hurdles put in our path only to be leaped.

The rest of the Gammites rise in a circle and touch hands lifted to the sky.

GAMMITES

We act as one
brother to brother
together or never
Gamma Phi Gamma.
From the nipple
to the bottle.

81 **INT:** *GAMMA HOUSE—NIGHT*

Julian is leading the Gammas in a meeting.

JULIAN

They are gonna pay.

BIG BROTHER GENERAL GEORGE PATTON

The payback is a mutha!

BIG BROTHER LANCE

When?

BIG BROTHER X-RAY VISION

Fire 'em up.

JULIAN

We'll get 'em, and leave Slice
for me. Everybody cool out.
(he continues)
Tonight is the Death March and,
please, let's try to adhere to
the rules and regulations as so
stated in your Gamma good book.

Julian winks at his brothers.

BIG BROTHER GENERAL GEORGE PATTON

Aw shit, I was just getting
accustomed to whipping some ass.

He swings "Bertha Butt."

BIG BROTHER X-RAY VISION

Till next semester is a long
time to wait.

JULIAN

I understand, y'all want to
strike blows in the name of

Gamma, but use some discretion.
All we need is to be put on
probation again.

The Gammas grumble.

JULIAN (contd)

Is this understood?

BIG BROTHER GENERAL GEORGE PATTON

Yes.

JULIAN

Good. The Gamma Rays will be
giving a set after the Gammites
go over. Your attendance is
mandatory.

BIG BROTHER LANCE

I'll be there, but it's time
for some new Gamma Rays.

BIG BROTHER DR. FEELGOOD

Let's clean house, put their
tired, sorry butts on waivers.

JULIAN

What's wrong with the Gamma Rays?

BIG BROTHER DR. FEELGOOD

These babes are too sometimey,
no gusto.

BIG BROTHER CHUCKY

We need babes who will bleed
black and silver.

BIG BROTHER GENERAL GEORGE PATTON

They don't make 'em like they
used to. Now Sheila, that was
a true Gamma Ray, do anything
I'd ask, anything.

BIG BROTHER LANCE

Anything?

BIG BROTHER GENERAL GEORGE PATTON

Any-thing.

The Gammas bark.

BIG BROTHER DR. FEELGOOD

Julian, you aren't complaining
'cuz you got the best one.

JULIAN

Me?

BIG BROTHER DR. FEELGOOD

Yeah, you! Jane is good to go.

BIG BROTHER LANCE

The finest too.

BIG BROTHER X-RAY VISION

What I wouldn't do to get some
of that. I'd run my hands through
her long, long hair all night long.

He sings.

BIG BROTHER CHUCKY

Why must you be like that? Always
chase the cat.

THE GAMMAS

Must be the dog in you.

The Gammas laugh.

JULIAN

I'm getting ready to cut her
loose. Jane is wearing on me.

BIG BROTHER LANCE

You're illing.

BIG BROTHER X-RAY VISION

You dog, you. I hear she looooves
you . . .

BIG BROTHER CHUCKY

Already picked your kid's name.

BIG BROTHER X-RAY VISION

Bad, bad crib, cold crushin'
Mercedes joint . . .

BIG BROTHER LANCE

Cash dollar bills . . .

BIG BROTHER GENERAL GEORGE PATTON

Green eyes. Me and her would make some pretty babies.

JULIAN

OK. OK. After tonight anyone who wants her can have her, I'm giving her away.

The Gammas argue over who will be the one.

JULIAN

Hold up. Hold up. Start putting the word out for new Gamma Rays.

[C] 82 **INT:** *PRESIDENT'S DEN—NIGHT*

McPherson and Cloud are sitting next to each other, drinking coffee. Suddenly the president gets up and comes back, smiling, holding a bottle of expensive Scotch. McPherson breaks the seal and pours a nip into each cup.

CLOUD

Breaking out the good stuff.

President McPherson pulls his chair up closer to Cloud.

McPHERSON

This is as good a time as any.

CLOUD

This Slice character is going to be a problem.

McPHERSON

I don't think so. He's a very intelligent man. He knows the score.

CLOUD

Good, I hope you do. Mission has had seven presidents, do you want to go down in history as the last?

McPHERSON

Some more?

Cloud nods and McPherson replenishes both cups.

McPHERSON (contd)

I wouldn't be the last, no, not at all. Not as long as you're on the board.

CLOUD

You are old, your day has come and passed. Mission means so much more to me.

McPHERSON

How so?

CLOUD

Old man Flemister was one of the state's largest slave owners. His initial wealth was amassed in the cotton, sugar, and tobacco industries. When the Emancipation Proclamation came, he started Mission to keep the peace and the abolitionists off his back. All his slaves stayed on as workers. They got a roof over their heads and food in their stomachs. He kept the land and the money. Stay with me now.

McPHERSON

I'm with you.

CLOUD

You see, they can't give us anything. They owe it to us. That's why I'm against this old Marcus-Garvey-Back-to-Africa-divest mess. We are owed. I want to collect.

McPherson nods.

CLOUD (contd)

Old man Flemister was also my great-great-great-grandfather.

McPHERSON

Well I'd be damned.

CLOUD

That's why this school means more to me, and nobody is going to jeopardize its existence.

On that note the president pours himself a stiff one.

83 **EXT:** *SOJOURNER TRUTH HALL—NIGHT*

Slice stands outside Sojourner Truth Hall. He looks up at Rachel's window on the second floor.

ANGLE—SLICE'S POV

The window shade is down but the lights are on.

CLOSE—SLICE

A smile comes to his face and he runs up the steps to the dorm.

84 **INT:** *OFFICE—NIGHT*

[C] Slice walks into the office and CANDY, the RA (Resident Assistant) on duty, sits behind her desk.

CANDY

Hi, Slice.

SLICE

Sweet as candy. How are you with your pretty smile?

CANDY

Bored. I suppose you're here to see Rachel.

SLICE
(laughing)

Why do you say that? I only live to see your smile. That

twinkle in ya eyes. That hole
in ya dimple.

CANDY

Slice, don't even try it.
Anyway, you are in luck.
She's in.

Candy presses the button on the intercom.

CANDY (contd)

Rachel Meadows, Rachel Meadows,
you have a caller.

85 **INT:** *RACHEL'S ROOM—NIGHT*

[C] Rachel, Doris, and Lizzie are reading magazines.

CANDY (VO)

Rachel, you have a caller.

RACHEL

Slice?

LIZZIE

Ask and find out.

Rachel gives Doris a sad look. Doris gets up from the floor and goes to the intercom.

DORIS

Who's calling?

CANDY (VO)

Slice!

Rachel doesn't respond.

DORIS

Are you going to make the man
wait forever?

RACHEL

I'm not in.

86 **INT:** *OFFICE—NIGHT*

[C] **SLICE**

Can you try again?

CANDY
(into intercom)

Rachel, if you're in, please
come down to the lobby, Slice
is here.

DORIS (VO)

Hi, Slice, this is Doris.
Rachel is out. Do you want
to leave a message?

Slice shakes his head.

CANDY

No message, Doris.

87 **INT:** *RACHEL'S ROOM—NIGHT*

Rachel turns out the lights.

DORIS

Girl, are you tripping?

LIZZIE

Serious changes.

88 **EXT:** *SOJOURNER TRUTH HALL—NIGHT*

SLICE
(yelling)

Yo, Rachel! Yo, Rachel! I
know you're in there. C'mon,
come down, please.

Slice waits for an answer. There is none.

SLICE (contd)

Rachel!

Slice's yelling has the women looking out their windows to see what the deal is.

SLICE (contd)

Rachel!

ANGLE—WINDOW

CECELIA
(imitating Slice)

Rachel! Rachel!

PAULA

That's right, beg for it, on your knees.

ANGLE—SLICE

He tries to ignore them.

SLICE

I'm sorry, Rachel.

ANGLE—WINDOW

TINA

Now you're sorry. What about before? It's gonna cost you this time.

This exchange has attracted a crowd in front of the dorm. Slice is being ridiculed by the hecklers, but he stands pat.

ANGLE—SLICE

SLICE

You can pledge, if that's what you want. I'm behind you. I'm behind you all the way.

ANGLE—WINDOW

PAULA

If I was Rachel, you'd be in the doghouse.

ANGLE—SLICE

SLICE

What a coincidence, with ya face you should be in a kennel. So be quiet!

ANGLE—WINDOW

PAULA

Be quiet? Who's screaming at the top of his lungs in front of my window?

CECELIA

You look *too* pitiful.

ANGLE—SLICE

SLICE

Rachel, I wouldn't be here taking this abuse if I didn't care.

TINA (OS)

Don't believe a word. He's lying through his teeth.

ANGLE—WINDOW

PAULA

Girlfriend, he'll say anything to get back in.

ANGLE—SLICE

SLICE

Shut the fuck up.

Why did Slice say that? Now he's really in trouble, as he's bombarded by the women.

ANGLE—WINDOW

TINA

Don't get nasty . . .

PAULA

He just wants one thing . . .

CECELIA

They all do . . .

DANA

The panties . . .

PAULA

He's no different . . .

TINA

That's right.

CLOSE—SLICE

SLICE

Why don't you please be quiet! Rachel, I'm not gonna stand here and take this abuse forever. I need—

SPLASH!!!

Some of the girls have dumped a bucket of water on him from above. The girls and the crowd are in stitches. Slice is soaking wet. He smiles at the girls in the window.

ANGLE—WINDOW

The girls wave back.

ANGLE—SLICE

SLICE

Fuck it. You win, I'm leaving.

The girls applaud as Slice walks away. A defeated and wet man. Before he can get too far, Rachel, who has come down from her room, runs and catches up with him.

RACHEL

Slice.

Slice turns around and she begins to laugh. Slice looks like a wet fool.

RACHEL (contd)

You're soaked.

She is still laughing.

SLICE

You have a great bunch of friends. I apologize.

RACHEL

Slice, you have to stop being so judgmental.

SLICE

I don't have to do nuthin'.

RACHEL

You are too hard on folks, give us mere mortals a chance. Don't be so quick to judge.

SLICE

I don't judge . . . well, not exactly. There's right and wrong.

RACHEL

Right and wrong.

SLICE

Right.

Rachel closes his mouth.

RACHEL

Shhh!!! Let's get you in some dry clothes.

She takes Slice by the hand.

ANGLE—WINDOW

TINA

He'll act right now.

The girls have a final laugh and stick their heads back into their rooms.

[X] 89 **EXT:** *CAMPUS—NIGHT*

Slice and Rachel walk hand in hand. Every time he takes a step we can hear the squish-squish of his wet sneakers.

90 **INT:** *SLICE'S ROOM—NIGHT*

A sliver of light cuts into the dark room as Rachel and Slice enter. Slice closes the door and turns on his desk lamp.

RACHEL

Get out of those clothes
before you catch pneumonia.

She goes to his closet and pulls out several towels while Slice peels off his wet clothes. A puddle has formed around his feet. Rachel walks toward him as he stands naked as a jaybird in the middle of the room. Slice tries to snatch the towels but Rachel holds on.

RACHEL (contd)

Be still.

She starts toweling him off without his cooperation.

RACHEL (contd)

Be still, I said.

Slice relents and lets her dry his body. Rachel is doing this with great care as she works down from his shoulders. Periodically Slice flinches and giggles. When she starts to dry his privates, he covers up with both hands.

RACHEL (contd)

Don't get new on me.

Slice removes his hands. She finishes, goes to his bureau, and throws Slice his pajamas. Slice hurriedly puts them on and pulls Rachel to the bed. She stops him as he covers her face with kisses.

RACHEL (contd)
(jokingly)

The sisters were right.

Slice backs off.

SLICE

No, no. I'm cool.

RACHEL

Good. Just hold me.

Slice puts a pleading look on his face, but it will take more than that, because Rachel isn't *even* about to budge, not tonight, buddy.

RACHEL (contd)

I just need to be held.

He does as asked.

SLICE

McPherson read me the riot act. If I don't chill, he's giving me da "boot."

CLOSE—SLICE AND RACHEL

They hold each other.

91 **INT:** *McPHERSON'S BEDROOM—NIGHT*

[C] President McPherson and Odrie are in bed.

McPHERSON

I've been feeling my age. I'm feeling old, old.

Odrie kisses him.

McPHERSON (contd)

What would you say if we retired after this year?

ODRIE

Are we ready? With you as president and me head librarian I thought we'd be here forever.

McPHERSON

Honey, forever is a long time.

ODRIE

Being around these young people has kept me youthful.

McPHERSON

It seems they get younger every year while I'm getting older.

ODRIE

What is Cloud doing to you?

McPHERSON

It's him, divestment, everything. I don't want to expel Vaughn Dunlap.

ODRIE

Show me the strength you've
demonstrated time and time again.
Don't let Cloud bowl you over
into early retirement.

DISSOLVE TO:

TITLE—SUNDAY

92 **EXT:** *GAMMA HOUSE—NIGHT*

The school bell rings from the chapel, it is 12:00 midnight. The Gamma Rays, fashionably attired in black leather, stand in front of the Gamma house. They become quiet as the Gammas emerge from the frat house. We hear a gong that is being beaten by Big Brother Chucky. The bare-chested, blindfolded Gammites follow him, each holding a silver torch in one hand with arm fully extended; a silver circle has been painted on their foreheads; they also sport metal-spike wristbands, belts, black leather pants and boots. When the entire line is out of the house, they stop in front of the Gammas. Julian comes out from the frat house holding the big torch. He glides to the head of the line and addresses them.

JULIAN

When the gong calls, the quest
begins to the land of Gamma Phi
Gamma. Keep your beacons from
touching the ground or you shall
perish . . . May I have the
source.

Big Brother General George Patton steps forward with a small lantern. Julian lights the big torch and holds it high above his head.

JULIAN (contd)

The eternal lantern, follow it
and you shall be free.

Big Brother Chucky beats the gong and the Gammites take the first step. The Gamma Rays are on both sides to offer assistance and moral support.

[X] ANGLE—FRAT HOUSES

Members of the other fraternities stand outside their houses watching the procession go by.

ANGLE—ENTRANCE TO FRAT ROW

Julian walks through the gate at the entrance to Fraternity Row. The Gammites follow, taking one step at a time, answering the gong of Big Brother Chucky.

93 **EXT:** *CAMPUS—NIGHT*

The distance between Julian and the Gammites has lengthened considerably. WE CAN JUST MAKE OUT the flame from Julian's big torch. Big Brother Chucky, seeing this, picks up the beat. Now that the procession has left Frat Row and is out on the campus grounds, it has attracted quite a few spectators.

ANGLE—LINE

The faces of the Gammites are beginning to show strain. Although the torches are not that heavy, when held with arm fully extended for any length of time, they begin to weigh a ton.

CLOSE—HALF-PINT

Half-Pint is biting his lip. WE SEE his arm quivering from muscle spasms. As his arm is about to drop, Gamma Rays Jane and Dina hold it up.

JANE

Half-Pint, just rest,
we got it.

CUT TO:

94 **INT:** *GAMMA HOUSE—NIGHT*

The Gammites are on all fours. In front of each one is a doggie dish with a can of Alpo dog food.

BIG BROTHER GENERAL GEORGE PATTON

Eat.

The Gammites attack the Alpo as if it's a New York sirloin steak.

CUT TO:

94A ANGLE—LINE

Big Brother Chucky beats the gong and the Death March continues. Jane and Dina still support Half-Pint's arm until Big Brother Dr. Feelgood sees this and breaks it up.

BIG BROTHER DR. FEELGOOD

Ladies, let his arm go. They
got to make it on their own.

Jane and Dina reluctantly turn his arm loose.

ANGLE—JULIAN

Julian turns around and sees how far behind the line is. He stops, giving them a chance to get closer.

CLOSE—BIG BROTHER X-RAY VISION

BIG BROTHER X-RAY VISION

Watch the eternal lantern,
never let it out of your
sight.

CUT TO:

95 **INT:** *BATHROOM—NIGHT*

The blindfolded Gammites are rushed into the bathroom and pushed to the toilet bowl.

JULIAN

Kneel.

The Gammites kneel around the toilet bowl.

JULIAN (contd)

Put your hands in the bowl.

HIGH ANGLE—TOILET BOWL

JULIAN

What did I say?

The Gammites stick their hands in it. What they think is human feces is actually bananas.

JULIAN (contd)

Squish it. Squish it.

CUT TO:

96 **EXT:** *CAMPUS—NIGHT*

The line finally catches up with Julian only to have him walk away again. The Gammites are eager to follow but they wait for the gong. The Gammites cry out in pain.

ANGLE—LINE

KIM

Hit the gong.

VELDA

Chucky, we're ready.

VIVIAN

Chucky, let's go. Julian is
getting a big lead.

BIG BROTHER LANCE

Gamma Rays, be quiet.

The Gammites are straining.

BIG BROTHER CHUCKY

I have to feel it to hit it
and I don't feel it.

The Gammas laugh. Tasha picks up a stick, hits the gong, and the Gammites move. The Gammas pull Deirdre away. The spectators applaud.

CUT TO:

97 **INT:** *HALLWAY—NIGHT*

The Gammas line both sides of the dark hallway. At the farthest end stand the Gammites. One by one, the Gammites run through the line. They cover their heads as the Big Brothers hit them, whack, beat the shit out of them. This is called going through the Gamma Mill.

98 **EXT:** *CAMPUS—NIGHT*

The line has once again almost caught up with Julian, who's about twenty yards ahead. All of the Gammites are near complete exhaustion.

ANGLE—LINE

Big Brothers Dr. Feelgood and Lance corner Slim Daddy.

BIG BROTHER DR. FEELGOOD

How are you making out, Slim Daddy?

SLIM DADDY

Fine, Big Brother Dr. Feelgood.

BIG BROTHER DR. FEELGOOD

Hmmm, that looks heavy.

BIG BROTHER LANCE

Why don't you do yourself a
favor and put that torch down?

SLIM DADDY

No thank you.

Big Brothers X-Ray Vision and General George Patton start working on Half-Pint

BIG BROTHER X-RAY VISION

Are you in pain?

HALF-PINT

I've never felt better, Big
Brother X-Ray Vision.

BIG BROTHER GENERAL GEORGE PATTON

Half-Pint, isn't the pain leaving
your arm and spreading over your
entire body? There is still hope,
if only you would drop the torch,
we won't have to amputate.

BIG BROTHER X-RAY VISION

Lay your burden down.

HALF-PINT

Never.

Big Brother General George Patton tries to wrestle the torch from Half-Pint, who is holding on for dear life. All of the Gamma Rays surround him and pull him off Half-Pint.

JANE

You ain't no good.

VELDA

That's not fair. Leave Half-
Pint alone.

The Gammas begin to taunt, punch, and pull on the Gammites' arms, just fucking with them. The Gamma Rays once again come to their defense.

[C] **JANE**

Don't listen. Don't listen.
We're almost there.
(she starts to sing)
Don't let nobody turn you 'round,
Turn you 'round, turn you 'round.
Don't let nobody turn you 'round,
Keep on walkin', keep on talkin'
Till you get to Gamma land.

The other Gamma Rays start to clap and sing also. It isn't long before they are joined by the spectators. The Gammas try to muzzle the girls, but it's no use; they are all singing at the top of their lungs. This song, which kept people going during slavery and the civil rights movement, has the same effect on the Gammites. Despite the pain, they have found inspiration and strength. Big Brother Chucky gives in and hits the gong. The Death March marches.

99 **EXT:** *FOUNTAIN CIRCLE—NIGHT*

Julian stands by the fountain, which is in the middle of the campus. The Gammites have finally reached their goal. The crowd becomes solemn as the ritual of passage commences.

JULIAN

Will the Gammites form a circle
around me.

The Gammites form the circle.

JULIAN (contd)

Lift your torches to the heavens.

The Gammites raise their torches. Julian lights each one. As he does this, Big Brother Lance removes their blindfolds.

JULIAN (contd)

Congratulations, you have become the men you've strived to be. Welcome to the brotherhood.

GAMMITES

It's good to be home.

JULIAN

Brothers, the changing of the light.

Each Gamma holds a torch with one of the new Gammas.

GAMMAS

We of the eternal lantern guiding us through the misty mist and the dusty dust on the straight and narrow path. Righter of the wronged, protector of the weak, we who so proudly wear the black and silver, from the nipple to the bottle, Gamma Phi Gamma.

The new Gammas fall to the ground from fatigue. The Gamma Rays jump on top of them, huggin' and kissin', and the spectators cheer.

[X] 100 **EXT:** *GYMNASIUM—NIGHT*

A banner hangs above the gymnasium: "HOMECOMING SPLASH JAM." A mob is at the entrance trying to get in.

ANGLE—DOOR

At the door are Grady, Jordan, Booker T., Monroe, and Edge. All are wearing trench coats. A person in front of them is arguing, which is holding up the line.

BOOKER T.

Yo, in or out, what's it gonna be?

STUDENT AT DOOR

I don't care what you say.

The student walks away, grumbling. The Fellas flash open their trench coats and the student looks them over and waves them on through.

101 **INT:** *GYM—NIGHT*

Grady, Jordan, Booker T., Monroe, and Edge very majestically take off their trench coats. Each is wearing bikini trunks and sneakers. They begin to flex their oiled, well-defined muscles for the benefit of the ladies. All of them, you can tell, lift weights, with the exception of Monroe (who's a skinny melink).

ANGLE—VICKY

Vicky, a six-foot stallion, glides by; all of the Fellas' mouths drop. They not only see Vicky, but a whole gym packed with Vickys geared in one- and two-piece bathing suits. They smack their lips and start to snake.

102 **INT:** *STAGE—NIGHT*

Buckwheat runs on stage and grabs the mike from the stand.

BUCKWHEAT

The Splash Jam, all right. We're gonna turn this mutha out.

ANGLE—JORDAN AND EDGE

JORDAN

Buckwheat, what's up with your hair?

EDGE

Take that man to a barber.

The students laugh.

CLOSE—BUCKWHEAT

BUCKWHEAT

My name's not Buckwheat. . . . Anyway, I'm gonna bring on the hottest go-go band in the land, that D.C. funk. Here to introduce the dance sensation across the nation—DA BUTT. Put your hands together for EU!!! EU, y'all!!!

The live band kicks off a jam and the gym rocks.

ANGLE—STUDENTS

Students dancing up a storm.

103 **INT:** *GAMMA HOUSE—DEN—NIGHT*

The same song we heard in the gym is blasting from the stereo. The new Gammas give each other the high five, kiss the Gamma Rays, and embrace their Big Brothers. Hands reach into an ice-filled garbage can for beer. Dina has a black plate in her hand filled with joints. She goes around the room like a good hostess offering the goods.

[C] CLOSE—JULIAN

Julian raises his hand and gets everyone's attention. The music is turned down in the BG.

JULIAN

I'd like to propose a toast. Did everyone get the Gamma ganja?

They cheer and hold up the joints . . .

JULIAN (contd)

To our eight new brothers. G-men always and forever. Cheers.

. . . and take long, hard drags.

104 **INT:** *GYM—NIGHT*

Grady, Booker T., and Monroe are standing off to the side watching the people dance.

BOOKER T.

Anybody who doesn't get some tonight just doesn't want any.

GRADY

That's what I'm talking 'bout.

CLOSE—GRADY

Grady is checking out the scene when someone catches his eye. He winks.

ANGLE—GRADY'S POV

Grady is winking at Vicky. She looks away, then sneaks to see if he is still watching her.

CLOSE—GRADY

Grady raises his eyebrow and smiles.

GRADY

Later.

ANGLE—GRADY AND VICKY

GRADY

Would you like to dance?

Vicky smiles and they go to the middle of the floor and dance.

ANGLE—BOOKER T.

Booker T. is dancing close to a girl and she backs away.

ANGLE—GRADY

105 **INT:** *GAMMA DEN—NIGHT*

People are dancing (again to the same song we hear in the gym), drinking beer, and smoking that Gamma ganja. Yoda embraces Half-Pint, who then stumbles to a sofa. Julian sits down beside him.

JULIAN

You did it.

HALF-PINT

I want to thank you for everything. I know I messed up a lot, you coulda X'd me more than once.

JULIAN

Big Brother Half-Pint, you deserved it.

Jane comes by and pulls Julian up to dance; Half-Pint sits there enjoying it all.

106 **INT:** *STAGE—NIGHT*

[X] The band finishes up the song and the students go wild. Buckwheat jumps on stage with mike in hand.

BUCKWHEAT

EU. EU. Hey! How is everybody feelin'?

STUDENTS

All right.

BUCKWHEAT

I said, how is everybody feelin'?

STUDENTS
(much louder)

All right!!!

BUCKWHEAT

Yeah, that's what I like. Can we dim the lights some?

Nothing happens.

BUCKWHEAT (contd)

Yo, Joe, dim the lights.

The lights go dim and the students cheer.

BUCKWHEAT (contd)

Thank you, Joe. . . . We're gonna slow it down a bit for all the lovers in the house.

As soon as the first note is played, the men make a mad dash for the finest women.

[X] ANGLE—MONROE

As Monroe is about to ask someone to dance, Doris muscles him; he is in her clutches.

[X] ANGLE—JORDAN

He dances with two women at the same time.

ANGLE—BOOKER T. AND EDGE

Booker T. and Edge are slow-dancing with girls. Booker T. sees Doris engulfing Monroe and points it out to Edge. They both start laughing.

[X] CLOSE—MONROE AND DORIS

Monroe shrugs his shoulders and continues to dance.

CLOSE—GRADY AND VICKY

Grady's and Vicky's bodies are intertwined. She rests her head on his shoulder and closes her eyes.

GRADY

I couldn't help but notice you in this bathing suit. You look really nice.

Vicky doesn't respond.

GRADY (contd)

Do you go swimming often? I can't swim a lick and I'm a Pisces. Ain't that a trip? What's your sign?

No response.

GRADY (contd)

Don't tell me, let me guess. Virgo. No, that's not it. I'm getting Capricorn vibes from you.

No response.

Grady tries again.

GRADY (contd)

Your bathing suit is serious. May I inquire where you purchased it?

Vicky lifts her head ever so softly and looks in his eyes.

VICKY

Is your roommate in?

Grady practically falls to the floor.

107 **INT:** *GAMMA DEN—NIGHT*

Couples are dancing to the same slow jam we heard in the gym. The Gammas who are not dancing, watch, waiting to cut in on their brothers.

[C] CLOSE—JULIAN AND JANE

Jane has her arms around Julian's neck as they dance.

JANE

It's been a long weekend.

JULIAN

Tired?

Jane nods her head, then looks at the new Gammas.

JANE

The new brothers look so happy. I remember when they were ready to quit. I kept telling them, "The sun will shine."

108 **INT:** *SLICE'S ROOM—NIGHT*

Slice and Rachel are silhouettes against a window of his room as they slow-dance also to the same song.

CLOSE—RACHEL

She stops dancing and looks at Slice, says nothing, and puts her head back on his shoulder.

DISSOLVE TO:

[X] 109 **EXT:** *GAMMA HOUSE—NIGHT*

Julian and Jane stand on the steps of the house saying good-byes to the Gammas and Gamma Rays.

[C] 110 **INT:** *GAMMA HOUSE—DEN—NIGHT*

The new Gammas are still here; they lie all over the den, high and drunk. Sir Nose gets up from the sofa and goes to the stereo.

SIR NOSE

This is 'pose to be a party,
not a wake.

He puts on a record and starts dancing by himself.

[C] ANGLE—JULIAN AND JANE

JANE

I think you deserve the credit.
It was you who made them Gamma
men.

JULIAN

I don't know about that.

JANE

It's you. And I got a present
for you, back at the apartment.

JULIAN

Jane . . .

JANE

I hope you like it. You
earned . . .

JULIAN

Jane . . .

JANE

Let's go back to my place.

JULIAN

Will you shut up?

JANE

I'm sorry. I'll be quiet.

JULIAN

Do you love me?

JANE

Yes.

JULIAN

Do you love Gamma Phi Gamma?

JANE

Yes.

JULIAN

You're gonna have to prove it.

CLOSE—JANE

JANE

I love you.

ANGLE—JULIAN AND JANE

They both walk into the meeting room.

JULIAN

Brothers, listen up.

The MUSIC is turned down.

JULIAN (contd)

Tonight is Half-Pint's night.

CLOSE—HALF-PINT

Half-Pint (very unsteady) rises out of his seat to stand up next to Julian.

ANGLE—JULIAN, JANE, AND HALF-PINT

JULIAN

I told your cousin I would take care of you and that's what I'm goin' to do.

HALF-PINT

Big Brother Almighty, what are you talking about?

JULIAN

Julian. Julian. Tonight I'm giving you a gift, from me to you.

Julian takes Jane by the hand.

CLOSE—JANE

HALF-PINT (OS)

I can't.

Jane looks as if somebody has just slit her throat. All the color is out of her face and the tears soon follow.

JULIAN (OS)

What do you mean? I know, we all know, you're still a virgin. Go.

ANGLE—GAMMAS

They begin chanting.

GAMMAS

Go! Go! Go!

Half-Pint has no choice and neither does Jane. This is the last act she can do to prove, to demonstrate her undying love for Julian.

ANGLE—HALL

The Gammas follow Half-Pint and Jane.

HALF-PINT

You're sure it's all right with Jane?

JULIAN

Stop stalling.

SLIM DADDY

If you don't hurry up, I'll gladly pinch-hit for you.

110A **INT:** *OUTSIDE BONE ROOM—NIGHT*

The Gammas have worked themselves into a frenzy; they pound Half-Pint on the back and continue to chant. A more self-assured Half-Pint hitches up his pants. Before he goes into the bone room, Julian gives him final instructions.

JULIAN

Half-Pint, wear her out like a natural Gamma man.

Half-Pint goes in and closes the door behind him.

111 **INT:** *FRAT HOUSE—BONE ROOM—NIGHT*

Half-Pint is standing by the door, Jane is crying quietly on the bed. She sits with her head resting on her knees.

HALF-PINT

Jane, we don't have to.

JANE

Shut up and undress.

112 **EXT:** *CAMPUS—NIGHT*

Grady is walking with his arm around Vicky.

VICKY

Are you sure your roommate isn't in? Because I need my privacy.

GRADY

I got the room to myself.

He looks skyward and sends a prayer to the heavens.

113 **INT:** *GAMMA DEN—NIGHT*

Doo-Doo Breath, Double Rubber, Yoda, Mussolini, Mustafa, Sir Nose, and Slim Daddy sit outside the bone room. Their eyes are fixed on the door, trying to imagine what is going on behind it. OS we hear some sounds, maybe moans coming from the bedroom.

MUSSOLINI

Did you hear that?

DOO-DOO BREATH

I didn't hear nuthin'.

We hear the same sound again, this time more distinctly.

MUSSOLINI

There it is again. The kid must be doing OK.

114 **INT:** *BROWNER DORM HALL—NIGHT*

Jordan, Monroe, Booker T., and Edge are sitting in the hall just talking when Grady and Vicky approach. The Fellas' mouths are open, speechless—how did Grady pull someone like Vicky? Grady is proud as a peacock; he knowingly smiles at his compadres.

GRADY

How are you gentlemen this fine night?

Their mouths are still open. Grady puts the key in the door.

GRADY (contd)

Have a restful sleep.

115 **INT:** *SLICE'S ROOM—NIGHT*

Grady and Vicky enter the dark, silent room. Grady puts his massive arms around Vicky and begins to kiss her. OS we hear a noise. Vicky pulls her lips away.

VICKY

Your roommate is here. We are not alone.

GRADY

Yes we are.

VICKY

Then turn on the lights.

He hesitates, then flicks on his desk lamp and WE SEE Slice and Rachel holding each other, fast alseep. Grady turns out the light.

GRADY

I'm sorry. If we're quiet they won't even know. I won't make a sound. I'm a silent lover.

VICKY

No deal. Call me when you get it together.

Vicky leaves and Grady follows her, but forgetting the Fellas are in the hallway.

116 **INT:** *BROWNER HALL DORM—NIGHT*

Vicky storms past the Fellas, whose mouths are still open.

GRADY

I'll call in the morning.

Oops, he sees his boys.

GRADY (contd)

Thanks for walking me back to my room. I appreciate it.

BOOKER T.

That was quick.

JORDAN

She left in a huff.

BOOKER T.

I've heard of premature, but shit.

EDGE

That's right, goddamnit.

GRADY

Fuck all y'all.

The Fellas scream with laughter. Grady slams the door.

117 **INT:** *OUTSIDE BONE ROOM—NIGHT*

The Gammas are still outside the bone-room door. Unlike before, now they are pacing, fidgeting, hyper—like fathers in a hospital awaiting their firstborn.

MUSSOLINI

What's taking him?

SLIM DADDY

Damn, how long has he been in there?

YODA

I'm going in there. She might have killed the boy.

As Yoda gets up and turns the doorknob, Half-Pint is there staring him in the face. His smile is wide as a mile. Jane follows behind him as they walk out of the bone room. The Gammas surround them.

GAMMAS

Half-Pint! Half-Pint! Half-Pint!

He is completely embarrassed.

DOUBLE RUBBER

How was it?

MUSTAFA

Was it like you imagined?

DOO-DOO BREATH

Or dreamed about?

SIR NOSE

Speech! Speech!

Jane has her head down.

HALF-PINT

C'mon, guys, leave us alone. That's enough. I'm gonna walk Jane to her car.

The Gammas continue to applaud him, when—

CLOSE—JULIAN

He stares at Jane.

JULIAN'S POV

Jane looks like a wreck, the tears have streaked her makeup. This is a woman who has lost all her self-worth.

ANGLE—HALF-PINT AND JANE

Half-Pint tries to kiss her cheek, but she pulls away.

JANE

Don't flatter yourself. Half-Pint, it wasn't for you.

He looks at her. The Gammas start chanting again when in rushes Julian. He grabs her by the hand and pulls her out from the Gammas.

117A **INT:** *HALLWAY—NIGHT*

JANE

I did what you said.

JULIAN

What is that?

JANE

I did it with Half-Pint.

JULIAN

What?

JANE

You told me.

JULIAN

The hell I did. You gave it up to Half-Pint? How could you? I thought you loved me. Now you're boning my own frat brother. My own frat brother.

CLOSE—JANE

At this point Jane is gone. She loses it. She's on the express to a breakdown.

JANE

Why are you doing this to me? Why are you doing this to me? I only want to love you, that's all.

118A **EXT:** *CAMPUS—NIGHT*

Half-Pint runs through the campus.

119 **INT:** *BROWNER DORM HALL—NIGHT*

Half-Pint runs down the hall at full speed.

ANGLE—SLICE'S DOOR

Half-Pint is beating the door down.

HALF-PINT

Slice! Slice!

He continues to beat on the door; finally it's opened by a sleepy, grumpy, irritated Grady.

GRADY

Are you out of your fucking mind?

HALF-PINT

I have to see my cousin.

GRADY

It's motherfucking five o'clock in the motherfucking morning.

HALF-PINT

Get Slice.

GRADY

He's sleeping. I'm sleeping.

HALF-PINT

Wake him up then.

Grady slams the door in his face.

Half-Pint beats on the door again. This time the door is opened by a sleepy Slice.

HALF-PINT (contd)

Let me in.

SLICE

Naw, Rachel's sleeping. What do you want?

HALF-PINT

I'm over, I'm over, I'm a Gamma man, Gamma man, I told ya, I told ya.

SLICE

Congratulations, but couldn't this wait until morning?

HALF-PINT
(yelling)

G-Phi-G. G-Phi-G.

Slice is happy for him, he's never seen him act this way before, so animated, he's usually quiet as a mouse.

HALF-PINT (contd)

It takes a real man to be a Gamma man because only a Gamma man is a real man.

SLICE

Calm down, calm down. You wanna wake the whole dorm?

HALF-PINT

And guess what?

SLICE

What?

HALF-PINT

I ain't no virgin no mo'.

This is hard for Slice to believe.

SLICE

Whoa, hold on a minute. And when did this miracle occur?

HALF-PINT

Tonight. Tonight's my night. And you'll never guess who.

Slice doesn't have time to answer.

HALF-PINT (contd)

Fine-ass Jane.

SLICE

Jane Toussaint!

HALF-PINT

Jane Toussaint!

SLICE

Julian's girl?

HALF-PINT

Yeah, Big Brother Almighty's girl. He set it up. The shit was good. He hooked it up.

CLOSE—SLICE

All the joy Slice had felt for Half-Pint has quickly disappeared; it's been replaced by disgust.

SLICE

Jane Toussaint.

HALF-PINT

Yo, I fucked her good.

ANGLE—SLICE AND HALF-PINT

Slice picks his little cousin up by the neck.

SLICE

What the fuck is wrong with you? What the fuck is wrong with you? You've done it, just like the rest.

He puts him down.

HALF-PINT

I fucked her good.

SLICE

Get out of here.

HALF-PINT

That's right, I'm a Gamma man. A goddamn Gamma man. It takes a real man to be a Gamma man because only a Gamma man is a real man.

ANGLE—HALLWAY

Half-Pint flies down the hall.

120 **INT:** *SLICE'S ROOM—NIGHT*

Slice is putting on his clothes when Rachel wakes up.

RACHEL

Where are you going?

SLICE

Out.

RACHEL

Wait for me.

Slice leaves in a flash.

RACHEL

Grady, Grady, let's go, get up.

121 **EXT:** *CAMPUS—DAWN*

Slice is running through the campus. The early-morning light is making its first appearance.

CLOSE—SLICE

Slice runs directly INTO THE CAMERA, directly into a CLOSE-UP and screams.

SLICE

Wake up!

CUT TO:

CLOSE—SLICE—DIFFERENT LOCATION

He yells.

SLICE

Wake up!

CUT TO:

122 MONTAGE FINALE

This MONTAGE will be surrealistic, unlike the rest of the film. The way it will be staged and SHOT will be dreamlike. First WE CUT TO various dorm rooms across the campus. These rooms will be of the Gammas, Jigs, and Wannabees. All jump out of bed like they heard Slice's anguished cry of "Wake up!"

CUT TO:

INT: *JORDAN'S ROOM—DAWN*

Slice grabs the sleeping Jordan.

SLICE

Wake up!

CUT TO:

INT: *BOOKER T.'S ROOM—DAWN*

Slice grabs the sleeping Booker T.

SLICE

Wake up!

CUT TO:

INT: *PRESIDENT McPHERSON'S BEDROOM—DAWN*

President McPherson and Odrie bolt up from bed.

CUT TO:

INT: *CLOUD'S BEDROOM—DAWN*

Cloud wakes up.

CUT TO:

EXT: *SCHOOL BELL—DAWN*

Slice is ringing the school bell like the Hunchback of Notre Dame. It rings across the awakening campus.

CUT TO:

EXT: *SOJOURNER TRUTH HALL—DAWN*

WE SEE students emerge in bathrobes, slippers, curlers, nightgowns, etc., and walk.

CUT TO:

EXT: *BROWNER DORM—DAWN*

WE SEE the same as above. The students walk to the Administration Building. They walk very deliberately, very quietly, as in almost a trance, a sleepwalk.

CUT TO:

EXT: *FLEMISTER HALL—DAWN*

Same.

CUT TO:

CLOSE—SLICE

SLICE

Wake up! Wake up!

CUT TO:

CLOSE—SLICE

Slice runs to the Administration Building, right INTO THE CAMERA.

SLICE

Wake up! Wake up!

123 **INT:** *GAMMA HOUSE—DAWN*

Julian bolts up from his slumber; he's in bed with Gamma Ray Dina.

124 **EXT:** *ADMINISTRATION BUILDING—DAWN*

The entire student body has assembled in front of the Administration Building. No one says a word, not a peep. Slice stands on the steps, overlooking the mass of people. WE CATCH GLIMPSES of everyone—Rachel, Jane, Half-Pint, the Fellas, the Gammas, Gamma Rays. Slice is joined by President McPherson and Odrie. Slice looks out once again at the students and sees Julian.

ANGLE—JULIAN

Julian walks through the unified body, not different factions of Black people determined by class or color, hair texture, accent, education or physical features, but one unified people.

CLOSE—SLICE AND JULIAN

Julian walks right up to Slice's face, I mean right up into it. Neither is backing down, blinking an eyelid.

CLOSE—SLICE

Slice turns slowly away from Julian and faces the CAMERA, faces us, the audience.

SLICE

Please wake up.

CUT TO BLACK.

END

EPILOGUE

[X]125 **INT:** *GYM—NIGHT*

The gym is packed and the director, Spike Lee, introduces all the principal players. This is done like a player introduction to a big game. It will be also done with an up-tempo song played by the Marching Band. The student body dances and sings, it's a joyous celebration.

ROLL CREDITS

EPILOGUE

SPIKE LEE

David Picker flew into Nueva York to see our final cut of *School Daze* on October 29. After months of cutting, Barry Brown and I had finally arrived at what we felt was the best length, the best form for *School Daze*. Earlier that week, I believe I had read in *The New York Times* that David Picker had resigned from Columbia Pictures. David Puttnam had gotten the boot before that. The two Davids, Puttnam and Picker, had tried to make different movies a different way and then: kaput. Then Coca-Cola consolidated Columbia Pictures and Tri-Star. This was some serious J. P. Morgan action: DA BIG BOYS WID DE BIG MONEY. Right away I feared for *School Daze*. Dawn Steel, who ran production at Paramount, was now gonna run Columbia, with both companies being overseen by Victor Kaufman. Now, I had never met Victor Kaufman or Dawn Steel but I was aware that Dawn was the force behind the blockbusters at Paramount.

O.K., so now Dawn Steel is running things, not Puttnam or Picker, who brought me to Columbia. What is she gonna think 'bout *School Daze;* there is not a white face in it. We're talkin' uncut Negritude. No watered down, assimilated crossover shit here, buddy. What is Victor Kaufman gonna think? Neither of them may know what to think—I might be wrong. There is a market for Black films, it's proven. But I'm not sure if they're aware of this.

I don't have any plans for how I will do my next film. This is largely because the heads of the studios get fired so often. It's like musical chairs.

Look, all I want to do is make films where my creative integrity is respected and preserved. Where I'm in control—not having people fucking with me or my work.

We're almost finished mixing *School Daze,* the advertising campaign is being worked on, the February 12, 1988, release is marked, we've done the best we could do. Please go see *School Daze* at least five times. Please buy the cassette, album, or CD, and please buy the videotape when it comes out—and please baby, please baby, please write and tell me what you think.

—Spike Lee
Black to the Future
November 22, 1987

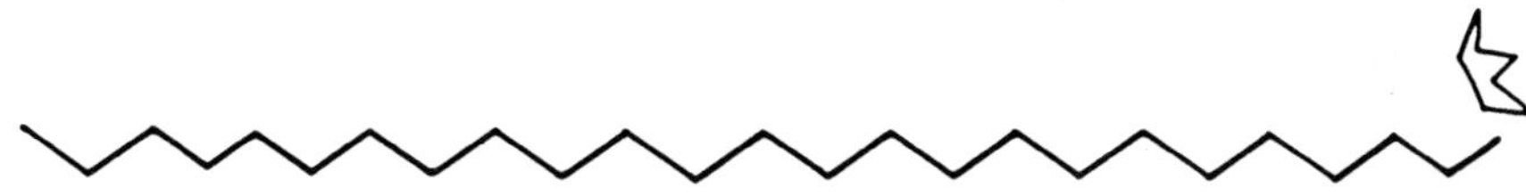

BIOGRAPHIES AND CREDITS

BIOS

Larry Banks, Gaffer ▸ Works frequently as a cameraman and lighting designer. Recent credits include: *Laser Man* (second-unit photography), *Something in Common* (director of photography), and Yurek Bogayevicz's *Anna* (lighting designer).

Grace Blake, Executive Producer ▸ Has eighteen years of experience in the industry under her belt, including work with many renowned directors such as Bob Fosse and Gordon Parks. She plans to continue producing for feature films in the future.

Barry Brown, Editor ▸ Filmmaker/editor, has edited and produced many documentaries and commercials. He received an Academy Award nomination for his documentary *The War at Home*. Former president of the independent distribution house First Run Features. He was sound designer on *She's Gotta Have It*. After *School Daze*, he'll work with director Mira Nair as editor of her Indian drama *Bombay Teaboy*.

Grace Blake and Matia Karrell.

Monty Ross and Robi Reed.

Tisha Campbell, "Jane" ▸ Won her first talent contest at age six, and originated the lead role in the long-running Off-Broadway play *Mama I Want to Sing*. Made her film debut in *Little Shop of Horrors* and currently stars in NBC's "Rags to Riches."

Ruthe Carter, Costume Designer ▸ *School Daze* was Ruthe's first time out as a costume designer for film. She frequently designs for video and television, and is currently working on a second feature film.

Addison Cook, Fourth Electric ▸ Currently developing a feature-length screenplay from his twenty-minute short, *Texas Road.*

Larry Fishburne, "Dap Dunlap" ▸ Made his feature film debut at age twelve in *Cornbread, Earl and Me,* and appeared in Coppola's *Apocalypse Now* at the age of sixteen. Recent credits include a second season of "Pee Wee's Playhouse" and the feature film *Red Heat,* directed by Walter Hill.

Randy Fletcher, First Assistant Director ▸ Recent credits include Tony Brown's *White Girl* and *Crocodile Dundee II,* and a zillion music videos.

Patrice Johnson, Costume Assistant ▸ *School Daze* marked Patrice's debut in film production. She also does free-lance publicity for music and television.

Matia Karrell, Production Manager ▸ Began her career in filmmaking as an electrician. She has worked as first assistant director with directors Richard Wang, John Sayles, and Sam Shepard. Then one day her telephone rang. She heard, "Matia?" and she said, "Yeah." And again he said, "Matia?" and she said, "Yeah. Spike, is that you?" It was and what it is.

David Lee, Photographer ▸ Did production and montage stills for *She's Gotta Have It.* His self-published book, *Snow Hill, Ala.,* documents the Black South of his ancestors in prose and images. David currently photographs for *The Village Voice.*

Joie Lee, "Lizzie Life" ▸ Made her film debut in *She's Gotta Have It.* She is currently refining her craft as an actress with classes under Alice Spivak, and she studies bass violin.

William James Edwards (Bill) Lee III, Composer ▸ Bass violist, composer, arranger, has performed with notables and lead bands since 1951. Wrote score for Spike Lee joints: *Sarah, Joe's Bed-Stuy Barbershop,* and *She's Gotta Have It.* Composer/librettist of eight folk-jazz operas.

Robi Reed, Casting Director ▸ Works as independent casting director for film, television, and video. Recent credits include: "Cosby Show" spin-off "A Different World" and Anita Baker's video "No One in the World," directed by Spike Lee.

Alva Rogers, "Doris Witherspoon" ▸ Actress/vocalist/composer, performs frequently in new-music venues in New York City. After her screen debut in *School Daze,* she was cast as the lead in independent film-maker Julie Dash's *Daughters of the Dust,* which began production in November 1987.

Monty Ross, Coproducer ▸ Has worked with Forty Acres since 1981, currently vice president of production. Writer/actor, starred in *Joe's Bed-Stuy Barbershop* and founded the Monty Ross Poetry Ensemble.

Roger Smith, "Yoda" ▸ Prior to *School Daze,* spent a season with the Guthrie Theater's repertory company in Minneapolis. Recent work in theater includes the Mabou Mines production of *It's a Man's World* and *That Serious He-Man Ball* Off Broadway at the American Place Theatre. Roger frequently collaborates with film and video artist Ben R. Caldwell.

Wynn Thomas, Production Designer ▸ Production designer on *She's Gotta Have It,* has many credits as an art director. Recent work includes: *Homeboy, Brighton Beach Memoirs, The Money Pit, Raw,* and numerous "Afterschool Specials."

CREDITS

In Memory of

Kwame Olatunji

Willi Smith

Harold Vick

Dr. Wendall P. Whalum

PLAYERS

Dap Dunlap	*Larry Fishburne*
Julian "Big Brother Almighty" Eaves	*Giancarlo Esposito*
Jane Toussaint	*Tisha Campbell*
Rachel Meadows	*Kyme*
President McPherson	*Joe Seneca*
Odrie McPherson	*Ellen Holly*
Cedar Cloud	*Art Evans*
Coach Odom	*Ossie Davis*

DA FELLAS

Grady	*Bill Nunn*
Monroe	*James Bond III*
Jordan	*Branford Marsalis*
Edge	*Kadeem Hardison*
Booker T.	*Eric A. Payne*

THE GAMMITES

Half-Pint	*Spike Lee*
Doo-Doo Breath	*Anthony Thompkins*
Double Rubber	*Guy Killum*
Mustafa	*Dominic Hoffman*
Yoda	*Roger Smith*
Sir Nose	*Kirk Taylor*
Mussolini	*Kevin Rock*
Slim Daddy	*Eric Dellums*

GAMMA PHI GAMMA

Big Brother X-Ray Vision	*Darryl M. Bell*
Big Brother Chucky	*Rusty Cundieff*
Big Brother Dr. Feelgood	*Cylk Cozart*
Big Brother Lance	*Tim Hutchinson*
Big Brother General George Patton	*Leonard Thomas*

JIGABOOS

Lizzie Life	*Joie Lee*
Doris Witherspoon	*Alva Rogers*
Delphine	*Delphine T. Mantz*
Terri	*Terri Lynette Whitlow*
Tanya	*Tanya Lynne Lee*
Jacquelyn	*Jacquelyn Bird*
Traci	*Traci Tracey*
Sharon	*Sharon Ferrol*
Laurnea	*Laurnea Wilkerson*
Stephanie	*Stephanie Clark*
Eartha	*Eartha Robinson*

GAMMA RAYS

Velda	*Angela Ali*
Kim	*Jhoe Breedlove*
Miriam	*Paula Brown*
Tasha	*Tyra Ferrell*

Dina	*Jasmine Guy*
Deidre	*Karen Owens*
Vivian	*Michelle Whitney Morrison*
Greta	*Greta Martin*
Sharon	*Sharon Owens*
Frances	*Frances Morgan*
Monique	*Monique Mannen*
Virgil Cloyd	*Gregg Burge*
Buckwheat	*Cinque Lee*

HALF-PINT'S FEMALE FRIENDS

Perry	*Kasi Lemmons*
Muriel	*Toni Ann Johnson*
Carla	*Paula Birth*
Roz	*Tracy Robinson*

GIRLS IN WINDOW

Cecilia	*A. J. Johnson*
Paula	*Cassandra Davis*
Tina	*Michelle Bailey*

LOCAL YOKELS

Counter Girl	*Tracey Lewis*
Leeds	*Samuel L. Jackson*
Moses	*Edward G. Bridges*
Eric	*Dennis Abrams*
Spoon	*Albert Cooper*
Vicky	*Kelly Woolfolk*
Student in Bathroom	*Florante P. Galvez*

MISS MISSION COLLEGE COURT

Miss Mission	*Leslie Sykes*
1st Attendant	*Dawn Jackson*
2nd Attendant	*Angela Lewis*

PHYLLIS HYMAN QUARTET

Female Vocalist	*Phyllis Hyman*
Bass	*Bill Lee*
Piano	*Consuela Lee Morehead*
Saxophone	*Harold Vick*
Drums	*Joe Chambers*

EU BAND

Guitar	*Valentino "Tino" Jackson*
Trombone	*"Go Go" Mike Taylor*
Bass and Vocals	*Gregory "Sugar Bear" Elliot*
Percussions	*Jenario "Foxy Brown" Foxx*
Keyboards and Synthesizer	*Kent Wood*
Vocals and Percussions	*Edward "Junie" Henderson*
Drums	*William "Ju Ju" House*
Keyboards	*Ivan Goff*
Trumpet	*Darryl "Tidy" Hayes*

SINGER AT CORONATION

Keith John

ALPHA PHI ALPHA

Reginald Tabor
Robert L. Cole, Jr.
Lester McCorn
William N. Ross
Keith Wright
Derrek W. Jones
Harold L. Boyd III
Rod Hodge

THANKS TO

The Marching Bands of
Morehouse College
Clark College

Morris Brown College
Southern University Drum Section
and Booker T. Washington High School
under the direction of Alfred Wyatt, Alan Ward, Richard Gordon, Jr., Roderick Smith, Thomas McKiver, Cleopas Johnson, William Sheppard, Dr. Issac Greggs, Roy Johnson, and Liz Sciabbara
Morehouse College Cheerleaders
The Brooklyn Tech Cheerleading Squad
ALPHA KAPPA ALPHA
KAPPA ALPHA PSI
OMEGA PSI PHI
DELTA SIGMA THETA
PHI BETA SIGMA
and a special thanks to the students of
Morehouse, Spelman, Clark, and Morris Brown Colleges
and Atlanta and Howard Universities

FILMMAKERS

Produced, written, and directed by	*Spike Lee*
Executive Producer	*Grace Blake*
Coproducers	*Monty Ross*
	Loretha C. Jones
Photographed by	*Ernest Dickerson*
Editor	*Barry Alexander Brown*
Original Music Score	*Bill Lee*
Production Design	*Wynn Thomas*
Costumes	*Ruthe Carter*
Choreography	*Otis Sallid*
Casting	*Robi Reed*
Sound Design	*Maurice Schell*
Production Manager	*Matia Karrell*
1st Assistant Director	*Randy Fletcher*
2nd Assistant Director	*David Taylor*
Additional 2nd Assistant Directors	*Parnes Cartwright*
	Lisa Jones
	Roderick Giles
Additional Assistant Director	*Shirlene Alicia Blake*

Production Office Coordinator	*Dale Pierce-Johnson*
Assistant Production Office Coordinator	*Alison Howard-Smith*
Production Secretary	*Tracey Willard*
Auditor	*Graig Hutchinson*
Assistant Auditor	*Eric Oden*
Location Scout	*Tyrone Harris*
Unit Manager	*Brian O'Kelly*
Script Supervisor	*Mindy Rodman*
Art Director	*Allan Trumpler*
Assistant Art Director	*John Harris*
Construction Coordinator	*Irby Langley*
Scenic Construction	*Brian Stultz*
Best Boy	*David Elliot*
Master Carpenter	*Buckey Weatherall*
Crew Chief	*Anthony "Wolf" Mays*
Construction Crew	*John Johnson*
	Rhett Johnson
	Harley Gould
	Everett Douglas
	Terry Wood
Set Decorator	*Lynn Wolverton*
Lead Person	*Alba Leone*
Set Dressers	*Richard Webster*
	Michael Shannon
	Ron Goldsmith
Property Master	*Suzi Margolin*
Assistant Props	*Christine Soloperto*
Production Assistant—Props	*Bruce Morton*
Scenics	*Mark Welch*
	Gretchen Kibbe
	Suzanne Silver
	George Balomes
Sculptures	*Tyler Smith*
	Michael Hitchcock
Production Assistant—Art Department	*Pam Stephens*
1st Assistant Camera	*Karma Stanley*
2nd Assistant Camera	*Sam Enriquez*

Steadicam Operator	*Alton Brown*
Still Photographer	*David Lee*
2nd Camera Operator	*Frank Prinzi*
2nd Camera Operator	*Leroi Patton*
1st Assistant Camera (2nd Camera)	*Norman Andrews*
Additional 1st Assistant Camera (2nd Camera)	*Mike West*
2nd Camera Assistant (2nd Unit)	*Mustafa Khan*
	Marcus Turner
Gaffer	*Larry Banks*
Best Boy	*Mark Moore*
3rd Electrician	*Carl Johnson*
4th Electrician	*John Massey*
5th Electrician	*Addison Cook*
Concert Lighting Designer	*Larry Robertson*
Pre-Rig Gaffers	*Larry Robertson*
	Marifee Cade
Generator Operator	*Dennis "Pete" Peterson*
Key Grip	*Todd McNichol*
Best Boy	*Tully McCulloch*
Dolly Grip	*Scott Leftridge*
Grips	*Bob Shuford*
	Bill Bennett
Pre-Rig Grips	*Ron Burchfield*
	Allan Bullard
	Eddie Evans
Sound Mixer	*Rolf Pardula*
Boom Operator	*Stuart Deutsch*
Hair and Makeup	*Teddy Jenkins*
Assistant Hair and Makeup	*Janay Shabbaz*
Hair Cutter	*Larry Cherry*
Costume Assistant	*Patrice Johnson*
Wardrobe Supervisor	*Jennifer Ingram*
Assistant Wardrobe	*Rebecca Schaefer*
Casting Assistant (LA)	*Mikki Powell*
Casting Assistant	*Hillary Francais*
Casting Assistant	*Lee Solomon*

Assistant Choreographer	*Dyane Harvey*
Assistant Music Supervisor	*Consuela Lee Morehead*
Music Copyist	*James "Jabbo" Ware*
Piano Tuner	*James Cheeseman*
Legal Services	*Frankfurt, Garbus, Klein & Selz*
Publicity	*Tobin & Associates*
Unit Publicist	*Willa Clinton*
Caterer	*Location Catering*
Assistant Editor	*Meredith Woods*
Apprentice Editors	*Cinque Lee*
	David Nelson
Sound Editors	*Kevin Lee, MPSE*
	Peter Odabashian
	Ira Spiegel
Looping Editor	*Harriet Fidlow Winn*
Foley Editor	*Bruce Kitzmeyer*
Music Editor	*Lou Cerborino*
Assistant Sound Editors	*Kenton Jakub*
	Leo Trombetta
	J. Kathleen Gibson
	Dan Korintus
	Brunilda Torres
	Rudy Gaskins
	Alex Steyermark
Apprentice Sound Editor	*Leander Sales*
Sound Re-Recording at	*Sound One*
Re-Recording Mixer	*Tom Fleischman*
Dolby Consultant	*Mike DiCosmo*
Transportation Coordinator	*Albert Cooper*
Fraternity Life Technical Adviser	*Zelmer "Z-Dog" Bothic*
Driver/Grip Production Assistant	*Louis "Bolaji" Bailey*
Drivers	*Arnold Shipman*
	John Monroe
	Erwin Wilson
	Victor Townsend
	Bill Butler
Production Assistants—Set	*Stephanie Jones*

	Mustafa Kahn
	Joe Rodman
Production Assistants—Office	*Jeff Cooper*
	Kevin Russell
Interns	*Tommie Burns*
	Donnell Nelson
	Miranda Dowdy
	Felicia "Fifi" Hopkins
	Alton Strange
	Sheila Tenney
	Mevelyn Shannon
	Luther Conley
	Reni Mosley
	Angela Carla Smith
	Kim Kearse
	Tony Bingham
Assistant to Spike Lee	*Pamm Jackson*
New York Office Coordinator	*Steve Jones*
Miss Mission College Court Gowns by	*Willi Smith*
Death March Gamma Ray Costumes by	*Yvette Marie Enterprises*
Sound Equipment	*AUDIO SERVICES*
Scenery Built by	*SPECIAL PROJECTS*
Floats Built by	*G. MICHAELS of North Carolina*
Completion Guarantee	*The Completion Bond Company*
Negative Matching	*Noëlle Penraat*
Main and End Titles Designed and Produced by	*BALSMEYER & EVERETT, INC.*
School Daze Designed by	*Art Sims—1124 Design and Advertising*
Color	*DuArt Laboratories*
PRINTS	*DELUXE*

PRODUCT CONSIDERATIONS

Arena Swimwear
Benetton
Adidas
Converse
The Chocolate Soup
French Connection
Marithe and Francois Girbaud
Yvette Marie Enterprises
Perry Ellis
Nike, Inc.
Ranor
Romar Apparel Group
Miriam Haskell Jewels
Street Scenes/Above The Belt
Willi Wear/Willi Smith
L.A. Gear
Ivy Images
Deerfoot by Omnisports
Giorgio de Saint Angelo
Eastern Airlines
Air Atlanta
Regency Suites
Ramada Inn

PHOTO RESEARCH

Schomburg Center for Research in Black Culture
The New York Public Library
Astor, Lenox, and Tilden Foundations

Historical Consultant/Research	*Herman "Skip" Mason, Jr.*
Photo Researcher/Consultant	*Robert Sengstacke*
	Stanley Forman

THE MUSIC

"I'm Building Me a Home"
Arranged by Dr. Uzee Brown
Performed by The Morehouse College Glee Club
Solo by Tracey Coley
Director: Dr. Wendall Whalum
Assistant Director: David Morrow

GLEE CLUB MEMBERS

Johnathan Alvarado
Patrick Amos
Devonne Baker
Sean Barnave
Roderick Belin
Cliff Booker
David Bowman
Byron Cage
Robert Connor
Eric Curtright
Todd Daniels
Edsel Davis
Illya Davis
Wesley Days
James Duke
Troy Ellis
Steward Flemister
Andre Van Fortson
Stefan Gresham
Andre Griffin
Emanuel Henighan
Samuel Howard
Michael Johnson
Mark Kellar
Scott King
Gary Maddox
Mario Majette
Warren McKenna
Maurice McRae

Larry Norton
Stacy Robinson
Benjamin Ross
Don Roy Shegog
George Sims
Marvin Smith
Anthony Toliver
Troy Underwood
Brian Warren
Korey Washington
Kevin Whalum
Earnest White
Charles Willis
Dwayne Wilson

"Straight and Nappy"
Music and Lyrics by Bill Lee
Performed by The Jigaboos and Wannabees
New Version Music (BMI)

MUSICIANS

DRUMS
Joe Chambers

Stanley Hunte Violin/Contractor for Strings

VIOLINS
Sanford Allen
Elliot Rosoff
Winterton Garvey
Sandra Billingslea
John Pintavalle
Cecelia Hobbs
Paul Peabody
Lewis Eley
Gregory Komiar
Harold Kohor
Gail Dixon

VIOLAS
Jesse Levine
Maxine Roach

Alfred Brown
Julian Barber

CELLOS

Mark Shuman
Zella Terry
Bruce Rogers
Carol Buck

BASS

Milton Hinton (Bass/Violin)

FLUTES

Frank Wess (Piccolo)
William Easley
Harold Jones
John Purcell

Harold Vick Contractor for Brass and Reeds

SAXOPHONES

Branford Marsalis (Solo)
Donald Harrison
Seldon Powell

FRENCH HORNS

Fred Griffin
Bruce Tillotson
Vincent Chauncey
John Clark

TRUMPETS

Terrence Blanchard (Solo)
Jon Faddis
Virgil Jones
Edward Preston
Cecil Bridgewater

TROMBONES

Steve Torre
Jack Jeffers
Benjamin Powell
Britt Woodman

TUBA

Howard Johnson

PIANO

Stanley Cowell

"Be Alone Tonight"
Music and Lyrics by Raymond Jones
Performed by The Rays
Tisha Campbell
Jasmine Guy
Paula Brown
Angela Ali
Zubaidah Music Inc./Warner Brothers Music

"I Can Only Be Me"
Music and Lyrics by Stevie Wonder
Performed by Keith John
Jobete Music Co., Inc./Black Bull Music Inc. (ASCAP)

"Perfect Match"
Music and Lyrics by Lenny White and
Tina Harris
Performed by TECH and The EFFX
MCHOMA/Screen Gems (BMI) and AMH Kid Music (ASCAP)

"Kick It Out Tigers"
Music and Lyrics by Consuela Lee Morehead
Performed by the Morehouse, Clark, and
Morris Brown College Marching Bands
SpringTree Music Company (BMI)

"Da Butt"
Music and Lyrics by Marcus Miller
and Mark Stevens
Performed by EU
Sunset Burgundy Inc./Tootsie Songs/MCA
Publishing, A Division of MCA Inc. (ASCAP)

"Be One"
Music and Lyrics by Bill Lee
Performed by Phyllis Hyman
New Version Music (BMI)

"We've Already Said Goodbye
(Before We Said Hello)"

Music and Lyrics by Raymond Jones
Performed by Pieces of Dream with
Portia Griffin
James Lloyd—Piano
Curtis Harmon—Drums
Cedrick Napoleon—Bass Guitar
Branford Marsalis—Tenor Saxophone
Portia Griffin—Vocals
Zubaidah Music Inc.

THE NATURAL SPIRITUAL ORCHESTRA

CONDUCTOR
Bill Lee

PIANOS
Kenny Barron
Kenny Kirkland

BASSES
Rufus Reid
Lonnie Plaxico
Michael Fleming

DRUMS AND PERCUSSION
Joe Chambers
Ray Mantia
Warren Smith
Smitty Smith
Jeff Watts
Kenny Washington

TRUMPETS
Jon Faddis (First)
Earl Gardner
Terrence Blanchard
Cecil Bridgewater
Virgil Jones
John Longo

SAXOPHONES
Harold Vick (First)
Roland Alexander

Seldon Powell
Robert Watson
Donald Harrison

FLUTES

John Purcell
Harold Jones
Patience Higgins
Bill Easley

CLARINETS

Arthur Clark
John D. Parran (Bass)
Haywood Henry
Ken Adams
Eddie Pazant

FRENCH HORNS

John Clark
Vincent Chauncey
Fred Griffin
Brooks Tiltson

TROMBONES

Steve Turre (First)
Benny Powell
Grover Mitchell
Janis Robinson

VIOLINS

Stanley Hunte
Sanford Allen
Elliot Rosoff
Winterton Garvey
John Pintavalle
R. Hendrickson
Barry Finclair
Joe Mallan
Harold Kohon
LouAnn Montesi
Paul Peabody
Lewis Eley
Regis Iandiorio

Sandra Billingslea
Cecelia Hobbs
Gregory Komar
Marion Dinheiro
Laura Smith
Patmore Lewis
Frank Wang
Jue Yao
Noel DaCosta
Gail Dixon
D. Stuckenbruck

VIOLAS

Al Brown
Tesse Levine
Juliet Haffner
Maxine Roach
Crystal Garner
H. Zaratzian
Richard Spencer
Karen Dreyfus

CELLOS

Fred Zlotkin
Marc Shuman
Bruce Rodgers
Zella Terry
Carol Buck
Eileen Fosom
Acua Dixon
Ron DeVaughn

HARP

Winifred Starks

Shot on the campuses of Morehouse,
Clark, and Morris Brown Colleges and Atlanta University
in Atlanta, Georgia, and in the great borough
of Brooklyn, New York

Many thanks to the two Davids,
Norman Bielowicz and The Georgia Film and Videotape Office

Soundtrack album, CD, and cassette available on EMI/MANHATTAN RECORDS

SCHOOL DAZE
A Spike Lee Joint
A Forty Acres and a Mule Filmworks Presentation
YA-DIG SHO-NUFF
BY ANY MEANS NECESSARY

Dolby ®
In Selected Theaters

SPIKE LEE JOINTOGRAPHY

FEATURE FILMS

She's Gotta Have It—1986
School Daze—1988

MUSIC VIDEOS

She's Gotta Have It—1986
Miles Davis—1986
Branford Marsalis—1986
Anita Baker—1987
EU - School Daze—1987

SHORT FILMS

MTV—Five one-minute spots—1986
Horn of Plenty—Saturday Night Live—1986

STUDENT FILMS (NEW YORK UNIVERSITY)

The Answer—1980
Sarah—1981
Joe's Bed-Stuy Barbershop—We Cut Heads—1982

COMMERCIALS

Air Jordan (Hang Time) Nike
Air Jordan (Cover) Nike

BOOKS

Spike Lee's Gotta Have It: Inside Guerrilla Filmmaking—1987
Uplift the Race: The Construction of School Daze—1988

Printed in the United States
69857LV00001B/13